THE WAITE GROUP'S
C++ Primer Plus®
Third Edition, Instructor's Manual

Paul Snaith

SAMS

A Division of Macmillan Computer Publishing
201 West 103rd St., Indianapolis, Indiana, 46290 USA

The Waite Group's C++ Primer Plus®, Third Edition, Instructor's Manual

Copyright © 1999 by Sams Publishing

All rights reserved. No part of this book shall be reproduced, stored in a retrieval system, or transmitted by any means, electronic, mechanical, photocopying, recording, or otherwise, without written permission from the publisher. No patent liability is assumed with respect to the use of the information contained herein. Although every precaution has been taken in the preparation of this book, the publisher and author assume no responsibility for errors or omissions. Neither is any liability assumed for damages resulting from the use of the information contained herein.

International Standard Book Number: 0-672-31591-2

Printed in the United States of America

First Printing: April, 1999

00 99   4   3   2   1

Trademarks

All terms mentioned in this book that are known to be trademarks or service marks have been appropriately capitalized. Sams Publishing cannot attest to the accuracy of this information. Use of a term in this book should not be regarded as affecting the validity of any trademark or service mark.

Primer Plus is a registered trademark of The Waite Group.

Warning and Disclaimer

Every effort has been made to make this book as complete and as accurate as possible, but no warranty or fitness is implied. The information provided is on an "as is" basis. The authors and the publisher shall have neither liability nor responsibility to any person or entity with respect to any loss or damages arising from the information contained in this book.

Executive Editor
Tracy Dunkelberger

Acquisitions Editor
Holly Allender

Development Editor
Bryan D. Morgan

Managing Editor
Jodi Jensen

Project Editor
Heather Talbot

Copy Editor
Linda Morris

Indexer
Larry Sweazy

Proofreader
Eddie Lushbaugh

Technical Editor
Paul Snaith

Interior Design
Anne Jones

Cover Design
Anne Jones

Layout Technicians
Ayanna Lacey
Heather Hiatt Miller
Amy Parker

Contents

INTRODUCTION

With the explosion of the use of C++ in programming projects on virtually every hardware and operating system environment has come the need for instruction materials for students of the language. This supplement to the third edition of Stephen Prata's *C++ Primer Plus* attempts to provide all the additional tools you need for a successful classroom learning experience in C++.

The Instructor's Manual is organized in chronological order, more or less as you would use the material in a classroom setting:

- The Statement of Purpose defines the general aim of the chapter, giving the rationale of the lessons of the chapter and the context of the material covered.

- Objectives list the specific areas of knowledge and experience that the student should be comfortable with once all the material has been digested and reviewed.

- The Lecture Outline section is a condensed outline of all the concepts covered in the corresponding chapter of the text. This outline generally follows the order of material presented in the text, but in some cases has been rearranged to flow in a way that is more useable in a classroom than in a written context. Use the material either as an actual lecture outline or as the basis of a checklist of concepts covered in a class.

- Additional Questions may be used by the student to deepen understanding of the chapter's material. Each chapter has a mix of True or False, Short Answer, longer Programming Projects, and For Further Discussion questions to help deepen understanding of the C++ language, and Activities for Learning that encourage exploration of how C++ works "under the hood." Use these exercises either as additional study aids or as the basis for testing. The mix of questions and inclusion of a particular section is determined by the material covered in that chapter. The Programming Projects have been worded so that the focus is on the concepts of the chapter, but not so as to inhibit the student's creativity in solving the problem. The questions are paged separately from the answers, making it easy to duplicate the material to distribute to students.

- The Answers to Text Programming Exercises provide solutions to the programming exercises given at the end of each chapter in the text. As with all programming solutions given in this manual, these are just a few of the many possible ways to code the solution.

- Answers to Additional Questions give responses to most of the Additional Questions posed. The only answers not provided are for the For Further Discussion and Activities for Learning.

The Programming Projects become more complex as the student starts to have more tools to work with and also as the length of the solutions grow commensurately. This way the student can get more experience with earlier tools by seeing how they work in combination with other language features. As with the text, the solutions presented are standard C++ except for the use of the std namespace. Namespaces are a new convention—you can find more information about these on page 27 of *The Waite Group's C++ Primer Plus, Third Edition*. The use of the std namespace basically means that the standard C++ components of classes, functions, and variables are placed in a namespace called std. One such item that can be placed in a namespace is the `iostream` library, you apply the following syntax to place it in the namespace:

```
#include <iostream>
using namespace std;
```

If you are using a compiler that only supports the draft C++ standard of January 1995, replace the namespace syntax with the original syntax:

```
#include <iostream.h>
```

Now the code should compile and run in any environment adhering to the draft standard as of January 1995, but perhaps with the same adaptations needed as noted periodically in the text.

CHAPTER 1

GETTING STARTED

Statement of Purpose

Chapter 1 is a general introduction to C++, covering the background of the language, its roots in C, and the basics of compiling, linking, and executing a program. The student should get a broad understanding of different approaches to programming languages and why C++ is the way it is.

Objectives

By the end of Chapter 1, the student should understand the following concepts:

- Procedural versus object-oriented programming languages
- The object-oriented extensions that C++ added to C
- The generic programming concept that C++ templates add to the language
- History and design philosophy of C and C++
- Language standardization
- Mechanics of creating a program in a given environment

Lecture Outline

Learning C++

- C++ unites two separate programming philosophies

  Procedural language tradition from C

  Object-oriented tradition of C++'s enhancements

- C++ now includes templates

  Generic programming supported by C++ templates

- Student's knowledge of C

  Helps with some of the language basics

  Hurts because C++ has a different paradigm

- Course material covers both the C core and C++ object-oriented extensions

Short history

- Recent history of computers has changed rapidly
- 1970s: C and Pascal ushered in procedural languages
- C produces compact, fast programs
- These factors led to widespread use across platforms
- The C Language

  Dennis Ritchie of Bell Labs

  Developed alongside UNIX

  Both low- and high-level features

  Portability important

- C programming philosophy

  Emphasizes algorithm side of programming

  Separate from data

  Structured programming facilitates larger projects

  Top down design: break big job into manageable tasks

- Object-oriented programming

  Shifts focus to data

  Fit language to program

  Features: class, object

  Class contains both data and algorithms

  - Reusable code
  - Information hiding

      Polymorphism

      Inheritance

   Bottom-up approach

- Generic Programming

   It is a new feature supported by modern C++ compilers

   Is a tool for performing common tasks

   It shares the OOP philosophy of reusable code

   Like C it emphasizes the algorithmic aspect of programming

   Generic functions are type independent

- C++

   Bjarne Stroustrup at Bell Labs

   Focus on usefulness rather than adherence to theory

   OOP roots in Simula67

   C++ is superset of C, having both OOP and generic templates, as well as C functionality

   Name comes from increment operator

   First implemented as a C++ to C translator

Portability and standards

- Ability to simply recompile program for different hardware
- Obstacles

   Hardware features

   Language divergence

- A published standard aids portability

   ANSI X3J16 committee

   ISO joined with ANSI

   Based on Stroustrup's ARM and ANSI C

   Standard C and C++ libraries

Creating a C++ program

- Steps vary with different platforms but all environments must contain the following features

   Text editor to write and save program

   Compile to object code

   Link to executable code

- Programs in book are generic standard C++ with the following exceptions

   Some compilers may not support namespace

   Some compilers may not support generic templates

- Can (and should) split programs into multiple files

  Source files

  Header files

  Library files

Additional Questions

True or False

1. C only works on a UNIX platform.

2. C is a procedural language.

3. C++ emphasizes the algorithmic side of programming.

4. C is a superset of C++.

5. C++ generic functions are type-independent.

6. The same compiler will work on a Pentium PC and a SUN workstation.

7. The file containing the final runtime product is called the executable code.

8. The source file is an ASCII text file.

9. The term IDE is an acronym for integrated development environment.

Short Answers

1. State the three separate programming aspects supported by C++.

2. State the fundamental purpose of the compiler.

3. Briefly describe what is meant by top-down design.

4. Briefly describe what is meant by bottom-up design.

5. State the single main philosophical difference between programming in C and C++.

6. Briefly describe the emphasis of generic programming.

7. State the two main inherent issues that make a compiled language said to be portable.

8. State the steps involved in creating a C++ program.

Activities for Learning

Compare the methods of compilation and linking used by the following systems:

1. UNIX

2. Turbo C++ 3.1

3. Borland C++ version 5

4. Microsoft Visual C++ version 5 or version 6

5. Symantec C++

Answers to Additional Questions

True or False

1. F
2. T
3. F
4. F
5. T
6. F
7. T
8. T
9. T

Short Answers

1. Procedural languages are represented by C; object-oriented languages are represented by the class enhancements that C++ adds to C; generic programming is represented by C++ templates.

2. Compilers translate a high-level language to the internal language of a particular computer.

3. Top-down design allows the program designer to break a problem down into smaller, more manageable tasks. These smaller tasks can again be broken down. The process continues until a point is reached where each module can be easily programmed in the target programming language, in our case C.

4. Bottom-up design is the process of going from a low level of organization by designing and combining objects to produce an overall solution. In the case of C++, we use and combine classes to produce a computer program that meets the overall requirements.

5. C concentrates on tasks and algorithms, C++ concentrates on concepts.

6. Generic programming emphasizes the code reuse and algorithm-style programming.

7. A programming language is said to be portable if its high-level code can reliably access the machine hardware via its operating system and be understood on the target machine after compilation. Different machines require different compilers, but essentially the same program source code can be applied to any compiler and still work on the target machine if it sticks to using the standard C++ libraries.

8. (a) Write the source code in a text editor. (b) Compile the source code to produce the object code. (c) Link the object code to produce the executable code.

SETTING OUT TO C++

Statement of Purpose

The key to effective use of C++ (or any computer or spoken language) is a solid understanding of the foundation and basic elements of the language. This chapter provides that foundation by examining the structure of a C++ program and begins an introduction to its more powerful constructs, including an introduction to object-oriented programming. For students with a background in C, the chapter also includes notes about how C++ builds on the concepts of C.

Objectives

By the end of Chapter 2, the student should understand the following concepts:

- A thorough understanding of the structure of a C++ program
- The use of the `main()` function
- The use of comments and why they are used
- Using simple input and output streams in C++ programs
- Why header files and preprocessor directives are used
- Formatting programs for easy understanding and maintenance
- Statements: what they are and why they are used
- Variables, declarations, and assignments
- Introducing a basic concept of classes and objects
- Ability to understand and predict the results of the sample programs

Lecture Outline

The structure of a C++ program

While C++ as a language has a great deal of flexibility, there are very specific and detailed requirements with which a program must comply. This section introduces the student to the basics of those requirements.

Sample Program: myfirst.cpp—display "Come up and C++ me some time"

- Introduction to C++ output streams
- Functions and how they are structured
- The use of the `main()` function
- Returning a value from a function
- Using arguments in calling a function
- Comments and their importance in structured programming

C++ preprocessor and its use

The preprocessor gives greater flexibility to the language and provides a structured way to include the standard features of the language. This section is a brief introduction to the preprocessor so the student can begin using its features.

- Header files and how they are included
- Standard C++ header files describing typical content and use

    Old style C

    Old style C++

    New style C++

    Converted C

- `#include`

C++ output

C++ has many ways to output information, and `cout` is one of the simplest and most flexible. The student can now begin to display the results of programs.

- Using `cout` for simple output
- Variable conversion using `cout`
- `cout` and `printf()`
- The `<<` insertion operator
- `\n` newline character

C++ source code formatting

By their nature, programming languages are usually not a direct extension of native spoken language. A simple C++ program, perhaps more than most, can be obfuscated by poor structure. It is time to begin developing good formatting habits.

- Procedural languages

- ; terminated statements

- Introduction to language syntax

- C++ coding style conventions

Some basic C++ statements

Statements in C++ do the real work of the program. This section is an introduction to a variety of statements available in the language and how they are constructed.

Sample programs: fleas.cpp—"My cat has 28 fleas."

yourcat.cpp—input the number of fleas your cat has

- Use of variables in C++

- C++ language keywords

- Declaration statement to create a variable

- Assignment statement

- Operator overloading

- Input using `cin`

Functions

Functions are one type of C++ statement. Here the student learns about how to call functions, both from the standard library and user-defined.

Sample programs: sqrt.cpp—using the library function `sqrt()`

ourfunc.cpp—user-defined function

convert.cpp—convert stones to pounds

- Calling conventions, with and without arguments

- Return values

- Function prototype for every function

    Prototype: how the function relates to the outside world

    Function: black box

- Using header files for function prototypes

- Standard library functions

    No input parameters

    Single input parameter

    Several input parameters

    Problems with too many input parameters

- User-defined functions
- Function header

  Return value type

  Name of function

  Arguments to functions
- Function body in braces
- All functions are created equal

Introduction to C++ objects

With the foundation laid so far, we now introduce one of the keys of the power of C++: objects. Objects are covered in great detail starting in Chapter 9, but the student starts to understand object-oriented programming in this chapter.

- Concept of classes
- Objects—particular instance of a class
- Class libraries
- Messages to objects
- Class methods

Additional Questions

True or False

1. The C++ language is case sensitive, so `cout` and `Cout` are different.

2. Instructions placed between `//` and the end of the line are preprocessor directives.

3. Every C++ program requires an `execute()` function that must be placed first before any other functions or declarations.

4. In C++, the use of a semicolon at the end of statement lines is optional.

5. `void progress(int)` means that the `progress()` function takes one argument of type `int` and returns nothing.

6. In order to convert programs originally written in C into C++, all comments must be converted from the `/* */` format to the `//` format.

7. Using the preprocessor to include the `iostream.h` file is required to use `cout` and `cin`.

8. `cout` is a predefined object in C++ that can handle different types of output data and is usually written to the screen.

9. The C++ program
   ```
   #include <iostream>
   using namespace std;
   int main (void) {cout << "Come up and see me some time."; cout << "\n"; return 0;}
   ```

   is exactly the same as
   ```
   #include <iostream>
   ```

```
using namespace std;
int main (void)
{
    cout << "Come up and see me some time.";
    cout << "\n";
    return 0;
}
```

10. All variables must be declared before use in C++ unless a value is immediately assigned to the variable.

11. Classes are a form of data type in C++ and must be defined by the programmer.

12. Objects are a type of function used to represent tangible things to the program.

13. All user-defined functions must be prototyped before being called the first time.

14. A semicolon is required at the end of a function prototype, but must not be placed at the end of a function header.

15. All functions, both user-defined and standard library functions, must return a value unless they are declared as type `return`.

Short Answers

1. Explain what each of the following does in a C++ program: `cin`, `cout`, ";", ">>", "<<", `#include`, "//", `int`, `main()`, "\n", `return`, "{", and "}".

2. Define the following terms and tell what role they play in programming and programs:

   a) function

   b) function prototype

   c) function definition

   d) function body

   e) function interface

   f) statement

   g) terminator and separator

   h) argument list

   i) preprocessor

   j) insertion operator

   k) operator overloading

   l) whitespace

   m) declaration statement

   n) assignment statement

   o) concatenate

   p) class

   q) object instance/instance variable

   r) class libraries

   s) class method

3. How is the return value of a function used? Why would some functions have return values and some not?

4. Each of the following lines are complete C++ statements. Tell whether each of them will compile without error. If not, what changes are needed to correct the problem? If you aren't sure, write a bare-essentials program to test what you think.

   a) `include <iostream.h>;`

   b) `i = j + k`

   c) `{}`

   d) `;`

   e) `void calcAnnuity(int, float, int)`

   f) `capitalReturned = investment + (investment * interestRate);`

   g) `cout << \n;`

   h) `#include <iostream> /* Needed for cout and cin */`

   i) `// exampleFunc()`

   j) `return;`

5. What errors are there in this code snippet?

```
#include (iostream.h)
using namespace std;

int main (void)
{
    cout < "Enter the number of rooms:\n"
    cin >> rooms;
    cout << "\nA house with" < rooms < "is a mansion!"
}
```

6. What kind of information is included in header files?

7. Write a function prototype for each of these functions:

   a)
```
    void fooBar(int alpha, float beta)
{
    cout << alpha * beta;
}
```

   b)
```
    int temperatureChange(int startTemp, int endTemp)
{
    return (endTemp - startTemp);
}
```

   c)
```
    void printChars()
{
    for (int i = 32; i < 128; i++)
        cout << (char) i;
}
```

Programming Projects

1. What does this program do? Work it out without typing it in and running it.

```cpp
#include <iostream>
using namespace std;

int main(void)
{
    int x = 23;
    int y = 4;
    cout << "\n";
    cout << x + y << "    " << x * y;
    cout << "\n";
    return 0;
}
```

2. What does this program do? Work it out without typing it in and running it.

```cpp
#include <iostream>
using namespace std;

void ShowtheFunction();

int main(void)
{
    cout << "Let's start the program running...\n";
    ShowtheFunction();
    cout << "Let's finish up in main!\n";
    return 0;
}

void ShowtheFunction()
{
    cout << "Here we are in the ShowtheFunction() function.\n";
}
```

3. What will this program do?

```cpp
#include <iostream>
using namespace std;

int MultiplyInts(int x, int y);

int main(void)
{
    int a, b;
    cout << "First, we need two integers:\n";
    cin >> a;
    cin >> b;
    cout << "The product is " << MultiplyInts(a, b);
    cout << ".\n";
    return 0;
}

int MultiplyInts(int x, int y)
{
    cout << "The MultiplyInts() function multiplies\n";
    cout << "the numbers, but doesn't show them.\n";
    return (x * y);
}
```

4. Write a program to accept the entry of variables X and Y from the keyboard. Calculate the sum, difference, product, and quotient of the numbers, using the operators +, -, *, /, respectively. Label the output so that each result is clearly understood. Explore different X and Y values to see how your compiler handles different conditions, including division by zero.

5. Design and write a program that asks the user to input their year of birth and the current year. Output that information back to the screen like this: "A child was born in 1957. And now you are 42 years old!" Use a function to calculate the person's age.

6. What happens with your compiler if you compile and link a program with no `main()`?

For Further Discussion

1. What is so important about structured programming? Is it worth the extra time to indent code and write comments? Doesn't that just take up more disk space?

2. If C++ is such a complete language, why is there a need for a preprocessor? Doesn't that just make the code less readable?

3. Why should there be a standard for programming? All the compiler manufacturers are going to do their own extensions, after all.

Activities for Learning

1. Review the manuals for your C++ compiler. What standard libraries and header files are available, and when are they used?

2. What class libraries, if any, does your compiler come with?

3. Obtain a copy of a reasonably complex C++ program listing (samples probably came with your compiler). Without trying to thoroughly understand it, review it and answer the following: Find `main()`, other function prototypes and definitions, header files used, and how statements are used. What function calls are included in `main()`? What preprocessor directives are used (all statements starting with `#`)?

4. Look in your compiler's manual for the section that discusses how your compiler differs from the ANSI/ISO C++ draft standard (most manuals will at least mention the differences). How close does the compiler stay to the draft standard?

5. What programming tools, besides the compiler itself, come with your compiler? What are they used for?

Answers to Text Programming Exercises

1. Write a C++ program that displays your name and address.

```
// pe2-1.cpp
#include <iostream>
using namespace std;
int main(void)
{
    cout << "Lolita Lobmacher\n";
    cout << "4030 Net Court\n";
    cout << "Backhand, CO 82388\n";
    return 0;
}
```

2. Write a C++ program that asks for a distance in furlongs and converts it to yards (one furlong is 220 yards).

```cpp
// pe2-2.cpp
#include <iostream>
using namespace std;
int main(void)
{
    cout << "Enter a distance in furlongs: ";
    int furlongs;
    cin >> furlongs;
    int yards = 220 * furlongs;
    cout << furlongs << " furlongs = " << yards << " yards\n";
    return 0;
}
```

3. Write a C++ program that uses three user-defined functions (counting `main()` as one) that produces the following output:

```
Three blind mice
Three blind mice
See how they run
See how they run
```

One function, called twice, should produce the first two lines, and the remaining function, called twice, should produce the remaining output.

```cpp
// pe2-3.cpp
#include <iostream>
using namespace std;
void mice(void);     // prototypes
void run(void);
int main(void)
{
    mice();
    mice();
    run();
    run();
    return 0;
}
void mice(void)
{
    cout << "Three blind mice\n";
}
void run(void)
{
    cout << "See how they run\n";
}
```

4. Write a program that has `main()` call a user-defined function that takes a Celsius temperature value as an argument and returns the equivalent Fahrenheit value. The program should request the Celsius value as input from the user and display the result as shown below:

```
Please enter a Celsius value: 20
20 degrees Celsius is 68 degrees Fahrenheit.
```

For reference, here is the formula for making the conversion:

Fahrenheit = 1.8 * Celsius + 32.0

```cpp
// pe2-4.cpp
#include <iostream>
using namespace std;

float c_to_f(float ct);
int main(void)
{
```

```
        cout << "Please enter a Celsius value: ";
        int c_temp;
        cin >> c_temp;
        int f_temp;
        f_temp = c_to_f(c_temp);
        cout << c_temp << " degrees Celsius is ";
        cout << f_temp << " degrees Fahrenheit.\n";
        return 0;
    }
    float c_to_f(float ct)
    {
        return 1.8 * ct + 32;
    }
```

Answers to Additional Questions

True or False

1. T	6. F	11. T
2. F	7. T	12. F
3. F	8. T	13. T
4. F	9. T	14. T
5. T	10. F	15. F

Short Answers

1.

a) `cin` is a C++ object that receives keyboard input and converts that input into a form acceptable to a variable receiving that data.

b) `cout` is a C++ object that converts data stored in a variable into a form acceptable to the monitor.

c) C++ uses a semicolon ; as a terminator to mark the end of a statement.

d) The extraction operator >> is used in conjunction with `cin` to transfer data from the input stream to a variable.

e) The insertion operator << is used in conjunction with `cout` to transfer data from a variable to the output stream.

f) `#include` is a preprocessor directive to allow predefined libraries to be used in a program.

g) A double slash // introduces a single line comment.

h) `int` is a C++ data type meaning a whole number.

i) `main()` is a special C++ function from where all actions are orchestrated.

j) "/n" is the control character to start a new line.

k) A `return` statement terminates a function.

l) The open brace delimiter { is used to mark the start of a block of code.

m) The close brace delimiter } is used to mark the end of a block of code.

2.

a) C++ programs are built from blocks called functions.

b) The function prototype describes the function interface.

c) A function definition has two parts, the function heading and the section enclosed in paired braces called the function body.

d) The function body contains statements within the paired braces, this is the action part of the program.

e) The function interface is the heading that dictates how the function interacts with the program.

f) A statement represents a complete instruction to a computer.

g) A separator is used to mark the break between one statement and the next. C++ separates statements with a semicolon acting as a terminator.

h) The parts within the paired braces are called the argument list.

i) Preprocessor directives are processed before the main compilation takes place.

j) The insertion operator << is used to place data into the output stream.

k) In C++ most operator symbols can be overloaded to have different meanings depending upon the context.

l) A space, tab, and carriage return are collectively known as white spaces.

m) A declaration statement indicates the data type of storage and a label for the storage location.

n) An assignment statement places a value into a storage location.

o) Concatenate means "to join together."

p) A class is a user-defined data type that describes data members and member functions that manipulate that data.

q) When a class is used in a program, it is instantiated to grab computer memory, this is an object instance.

r) Class libraries contain predefined classes that can be included by the programmer in her program.

s) Class methods are functions that belong to a class.

3. In the calling function, the return value is directly substituted for the call to the function in the statement or expression. Some functions only perform actions and don't directly calculate or retrieve a value (although more often than not a status or error value will be returned).

4. a) Won't compile. Delete the ; and prefix with # for older style compilers or modify to

```
#include <iostream>
using namespace std;
```

for modern compilers.

b) Won't compile. It needs ; at the end of the statement.

c) Compiles

d) Compiles

e) Compiles

f) Compiles

g) Won't compile: needs quotes around \n

h) Depends on compiler's implementation of the ANSI/IOS standard: Won't compile under older draft standard, because file name needs extension. Will compile under newer standard.

i) Compiles

j) Compiles (whether function is void or not)

5. The Microsoft Visual C++ 5.0 compiler gives the following list of compilation errors and warnings:

```
#include (iostream.h) has two errors and should be #include <iostream>
```

The < should be << on the first **cout** line

There is a ; missing at the end of the first **cout** line.

The variable **rooms** is not declared at the start of the program.

The **cin** line requires extraction operator >>, not insertion operator <<.

Final **cout** line has two errors where < is used instead of <<, and has ; missing at its end.

There is also a warning because the main function should contain **return(0)**;

6. A header file will typically contain function prototypes, constant definitions, class definitions, and even code fragments.

7. a)

```
void fooBar(int alpha, float beta);
```

b)

```
int temperatureChange(int startTemp, int endTemp);
```

c)

```
void printChars();
```

Programming Projects

1. Prints "**27 92**"

2. The following is printed to the screen:

```
Let's start the program running...
Here we are in the ShowtheFunction() function.
Let's finish up in main!
```

3. This is the result of a session:

```
First, we need two integers:
15
10
The MultiplyInts() function multiplies
the numbers, but doesn't show them.
The product is 150.
```

4. Here is one way to do it:

```cpp
#include <iostream>
using namespace std;

int main(void)
{
    float x;
    float y;

    cout << "enter two numbers : " << '\n';
    cin >> x >> y;
    cout << "        Sum of x and y: " << x + y << "\n";
    cout << "Difference of x and y: " << x - y << "\n";
    cout << "    Product of x and y: " << x * y << "\n";
    cout << "  Quotient of x and y: " << x / y << "\n";
    return 0;
}
```

5. One way to do it is

```cpp
#include <iostream>
using namespace std;

int calcAge(int currentYear, int birthYear);

int main(void)
{
    int yearBorn;
    int    yearNow;

    cout << "Please enter the year of your birth: ";
    cin >> yearBorn;
    cout << "Please enter the current year: ";
    cin >> yearNow;
    cout << "\n\nA child was born in " << yearBorn;
    cout << ". And now you are ";
    cout << calcAge(yearNow, yearBorn);
    cout << " years old!\n";
    return 0;
}

int calcAge(int currentYear, int birthYear)
{
    return (currentYear - birthYear);
}
```

6. Here is an example program. Try compiling it and then linking (or building) it.

```cpp
#include <iostream>
using namespace std;

void Test(void)
{
    cout << "Look no Main program!!!" << '\n';
}
```

The program compiles okay. In fact, this is a common method of preparing code sections.

Linking generates two errors due to the absence of a main function. The linker error reported by Microsoft Visual C++ version 5 is as follows:

```
Linking...
LIBC.lib(crt0.obj) : error LNK2001: unresolved external symbol _main
Release/PP06.exe : fatal error LNK1120: 1 unresolved externals
Error executing link.exe.
```

CHAPTER 3

DEALING WITH DATA

Statement of Purpose

This chapter introduces the various data types available in C++. The rich variety of basic types raises the possibility of subtle implications for code, particularly when variables of different types are combined in C++ statements. The language imposes some specific rules on the use of variables, but also gives the programmer enormous flexibility. Chapter 3 provides the foundation needed for the student to build effective and correct C++ programs.

Objectives

By the end of Chapter 3, the student should understand the following concepts:

- Uses and naming of variables in C++ programs

- The two fundamental classes of variables: integers and floating-point

- The types of variables available in each class, and when each should be used

- In the absence of explicit data type instructions from the programmer, the assumptions and priorities the compiler uses

- The five basic C++ arithmetic operators and how they act with the different data types

- The effect that different hardware and compiler implementations have on data types

- The changes and extensions that C++ brought to data types from C

- Numeric constants and their place in a C++ program

- Symbolic constants: the new and improved `const` replaces `#define`

Lecture Outline

Variable naming rules

Despite the enormous flexibility that C++ allows the programmer, there are rules that must be followed in the naming of variables, so that the compiler can do its job effectively.

- Alphabetic characters, digits, and underscore

- First character not a digit

- Case insensitive

- Can't be C++ keyword

- Any length, and all characters are significant

- Names consisting of multiple words have two widely used conventions:

  Words separated by underscores, for example: first_letter

  Capitalize the first letter of each word, for example: FirstLetter

Integers

Integers are the first major class of data types in C++, and perhaps the most common. There are a number of variations to consider including memory used, ranges of values available. The `char` type is unique because it represents both a form of an integer and characters.

Sample programs	limits.cpp—print limits and sizes of integers
	exceed.cpp—Sam and Sue's deposits; overflow behavior
	chartype.cpp—inputting and echoing a `char` with `cout`
	morechar.cpp—comparing `char` and `int` types

- Integer definition: number with no fractional part

- Memory used for different types

  Varies by type of integer

  Varies with compiler implementation

  `signed` and `unsigned` integers

- `short`, `int`, and `long` integer types

  C++ standard

  `short` is at least 2 bytes

  `int` is at least as big as `short`

  `long` is at least 4 bytes and at least as big as `int`

  Dependent on implementation

  Full names

  `short int`

  `int`

  `long int`

- `char type`

    Special form of integer type

    Typically one byte, so can use for integer shorter than `short`

    ASCII and EBCDIC character sets

    Neither `signed` nor `unsigned` by default: implementation dependent

    Wide character `wchar_t`

    Unicode

    Used to represent character sets from languages other than the Western Latin–based alphabet such as Greek, Arabic, and Japanese. Has more than 38,000 symbols defined so far.

    ANSI made a basic C++ type

    Use L prefix

- `unsigned` types

    Range of values: implementation dependent

    Default is `signed`

- Deciding type of integer to use

    `int` is usually set to the most efficient size for numbers

    No negative values: use `unsigned`

    Range of possible values

    Use `short` to conserve memory even if same size as `int`

Character and integer constants

Even though it appears on the surface that a constant is a fixed value and hence cannot change, there is power and flexibility in using constants in C++. The programmer has to be familiar with the options for constants, both to use them effectively and to be aware of the subtleties arising from their use together.

Sample programs   hexoct.cpp—using hex and octal constants

                                    bondini.cpp—using escape sequences for agent code input

Refer to Appendix A

- Integer

    Number bases: notations

        Base 10, decimal

        Base 8, octal: 065

        Base 16, hexadecimal: 0x1AF

    Compiler determination of type: order of priority:

        Uses `int` unless there is a compelling reason not to

        Suffix appended to number

        Size too large for `int` and no suffix

- Character

  Options for writing **char** constants

    Character in single quotes: 'A'

    List of escape sequences in Table 3.2

sizeof operator

Since C++ does little to check validity of data, the programmer needs to know the limits that a particular compiler used on particular hardware puts on data in a program. The **sizeof** operator provides a tool to help stay within those limits.

- Use in C++ to determine the ranges and significance of data types
- climits header file and contents

Floating-point numbers

Floating-point numbers belong to the second major class of C++ numeric data types. The student should begin to appreciate the wide flexibility that C++ gives to represent data types.

Sample programs   floatnum.cpp—difference between floating-point types

                                   fltadd.cpp—floating-point precision problems

- Allow fractional parts and much larger range of values
- Representation in C++ programs

  Decimal-point notation: 1236.9501

  E notation: 1.2369501E3
- Floating-point types

  float

    Minimum of 4 bytes

  double

    Minimum of 6 bytes and at least as big as **float**

  long double

    At least as long as **double**
- Sizes and ranges in **cfloat** header file
- Significant digits of each type is implementation dependent
- Comparison to integers

  Can represent values between integers

  Much greater range of values

  Slower calculations without math coprocessor

  Can lose precision

  Division operation works differently in floats and integers

Floating-point constants

The issues with floating-point constant lie primarily in understanding how the compiler deals with constant data, so that it can be forced, if necessary, to do what the programmer intends.

- Default floating-point constant type is **double**

  Suffix for **float**: f, F

  Suffix for long **double**: l, L

Basic C++ arithmetic operators

When data meets arithmetic operators, sparks begin to fly. The student should now begin to fully understand and appreciate the interactions taking place in a C++ program and how to put them to effective use.

Sample programs   arith.cpp—demonstration of operators

          divide.cpp—compares integer and floating-point division

          modulus.cpp—convert pounds to stone using %

Refer to Appendix D for precedence and associativity

- Basic operators

  Addition: +

  Subtraction: -

  Multiplication: *

  Division: /

- Precision issues

- Operator precedence and associativity

  Precedence follows usual algebraic convention

    Multiplication, division, then

    Addition, subtraction

  Associativity presides for operators of equal precedence

    Left-to-right associativity

    Right-to-left associativity

  Precedence and associativity become important only when two operators share the same operand

- Behavior of division operator

  Operator overloading

    Integer division

    Floating-point division

- Modulus operator

Type conversions

When data of different types is put together in C++, the compiler has to sort through and decide how to combine the data so that it can evaluate the expressions. The default choices it makes may be acceptable, but maybe not.

Sample programs   assign.cpp—problem with type change on assignment

typecast.cpp—results of forcing type conversions

- Assign value of one type to variable of another type

  Assigning integer to integer of greater range is no problem

  Integer to `float` may lose precision

  Floating-point to integer

    Truncate fractional part

    Range may be too big—undefined result

- Combination of mixed types in expression

  Integral promotion—`char`, `unsigned char`, `signed char`, and `short` values to `int`

  Combining different types arithmetically—promote to highest type

- Pass arguments to functions

  Integral promotions

  `float` to `double`

- Type casts

  Manually force type conversions

  C and C++ forms

    C: (long) thorn

    C++: long (thorn)

Variable initialization

Variables must be declared and have data assigned to them in order to be useful. What does C++ require, and what happens when it doesn't happen?

- Assignment
- Declaration
- Contents of variable when unassigned

Symbolic constants

C++ makes use of the `const` qualifier to retire `#define`, in most cases, to allow the programmer better control of how the program does its task.

- Preprocessor directive: `#define`

  Relic from C

  Used by library files designed to work with C and C++

- `const` qualifier

  Use for values that won't change during operation

  Improvement over `#define`

    With `const`, can specify type

    Take advantage of scoping rules

    Use with complex types, such as arrays and structures

  Default type is `int`

Member function: `cout.put()`

Expanding our growing knowledge of C++ classes, `cout.put()` provides a different way to present information to the user of the program.

- Belongs to `ostream` class

- Manipulates class data

- Membership operator: `.`

- Improved `integer` and `char` output control over `<<`

New `bool` type

Programmers in C used an integer form for true/false data. The `bool` type provides an explicit way to use that data type, while making the function of a program clearer.

- Use for true/false, yes/no, on/off data

- Predefined literals: `false` and `true`

- Implicit conversion of numeric and pointer values

  Nonzero value converts to `true`

  Zero value converts to `false`

Additional Questions

True or False

1. C++ requires that all variables have the first letter of each word making up the name be capitalized.

2. It is a good idea not to start the name of a variable with an underscore, because libraries commonly name variables and functions with an underscore.

3. The ANSI/ISO standard for C++ specifies that `short` and `int` are 2 bytes long, and that a `long` is 4 bytes.

4. A `char` data type is used for C++ strings.

5. A symbolic integer constant has a set value. Whenever the compiler finds this symbolic constant, it replaces it with that numeric value, giving you easier control of numeric constant values throughout the program. To change the value associated with the symbolic constant definition, change all instances of the symbol constant throughout the program.

6. The size used for an `int` is typically the most efficient size for the particular hardware a compiler is written to run on.

7. Once a program is written with a 2-byte `int`, that is the size it will be in that program on any type of computer.

8. A numeric constant is stored as an `int` unless a compiler switch is changed.

9. When designing a C++ program, it is critical to make sure that variables do not overflow, since C++ does not automatically check.

10. `char` has a range of `-127` to `128` by default.

11. 5.9875E17 must be stored as a floating-point number.

12. Variable names declared as a `const` must be capitalized.

13. The statement `cout << 5 * 9 / 4 +10;` will display 21.

14. Assigning a `float` to an integer type may be a problem both because the size of the number may be too large for the integer type and because some significant digits may be lost.

15. The statement `cout << 45 / 10;` will display 4.

Short Answers

1. Explain why it is important that a programmer be aware of the size and range of data types in C++. How would this information affect the design and coding of programs?

2. Describe the following terms, and explain their use in a C++ program.

    a) `char`

    b) `short`

    c) `int`

    d) `long`

    e) `sizeof`

    f) `climits`

    g) initialization

    h) `#define`

    i) `cout.put()`

    j) member function

    k) `wchar_t`

    l) `bool`

    m) `true, false`

    n) `Lvalue`

    o) `float`

    p) E notation

    q) exponent, mantissa

    r) `double`

    s) `long double`

    t) `cfloat` (or `float.h`)

    u) `cout.setf(ios::fixed, ios::floatfield)`

3. Describe the relationship among declaration, initialization, and assignment as they relate to C++ variables.

4. When would it matter if char is signed or unsigned?

5. Does your compiler implement bool? If not, how can you represent true/false data?

6. Why is const in C++ an improvement over #define in C? Find const in your compiler documentation and review its use. Why might you still use #define in C++?

7. Locate the climits and cfloat files for your compiler. What information do they contain? How would you use that information?

8. Using the rules for precedence and associativity and the variables below, what result will each of the following produce?
```
float a=2;
float b=3;
float c=5;
int i=2;
int j=3;
```

   a) a*(b+c)

   b) a*b+c*i

   c) a*(b+c)*i

   d) b/c*a

   e) a/i/j

   f) a/b/c/i/j

   g) i/j/a

   h) a/i/j

   i) 18/4

   j) 4/3/4

   k) 4/(3/4)

   l) (4/3)/4

   m) 21%4%3

   n) (21%4)%3

   o) 21%(4%3)

9. Are the following acceptable variable names in C++? If not, why?

   a) int

   b) my toy

   c) net'op'income

   d) count*5

   e) netOpIncome

   f) 45speed

   g) Speed_of_Light

   h) LightSpeed

   i) Jack.2

j) `I.S.0`

k) `vb0ne`

l) `Jack2`

m) `Mod%3`

n) `main`

o) `profit(pi)`

p) `Get`

q) `__`

Programming Projects

1. Write a program to accept numerical input from the user in hex, octal, and decimal, and convert that input to decimal.

2. Write a program to display the following information for `float`, `double`, and `long double` on your system: number of significant digits, number of bits in mantissa, maximum exponent values, and minimum mantissa values.

3. Modify Listing 3.8, fltadd.cpp, to test whether using a `double` or a `long double` variable type will give the correct result. If not, use the results of Programming Project 2 to reduce the value of **a** by changing its exponent.

4. Write a program to test how your compiler handles the modulus operator when one or both of the operands is negative. Display all possible combinations of positive and negative operands. What happens if you use a floating-point operand?

5. Write a program to test your responses to question 8 in the Short Answers section above.

Activities for Learning

1. Run Listing 3.7, floatnum.cpp, in your compiler. What results do you get? Review your documentation for `cout.setf(ios::fixed, ios::floatfield)`. Why does the output display as it does?

2. What other header files are provided with your compiler? Review the documentation to find out when each should be used.

Answers to Text Programming Exercises

1. Write a short program that asks for your height in integer inches and then converts your height to feet and inches. Have the program use the underline character to indicate where to type the response. Also use a `const` type.

    ```
    // pe3-1.cpp

    #include <iostream>
    using namespace std;

    const int Inch_Per_Foot = 12;

    int main(void)
    {
    ```

```
// Note: some environments don't support the backspace character
    cout << "Please enter your height in inches: ___/b/b/b ";
    int ht_inch;
    cin >> ht_inch;
    int ht_feet = ht_inch / Inch_Per_Foot;
    int rm_inch = ht_inch % Inch_Per_Foot;
    cout << "Your height is " << ht_feet << " feet, ";
    cout << rm_inch << " inch(es).\n";
    return 0;
}
```

2. Write a program that asks how many miles you have driven and how many gallons of gasoline you used, and then reports how many miles per gallon your car got. Or, if you prefer, the program can request distance in kilometers, petrol in litres, and report the result European style, in litres per 100 kilometers.

```
// pe3-2.cpp

#include <iostream>
using namespace std;

int main(void)
{
    cout << "How many miles have you driven your car? ";
    float miles;
    cin >> miles;
    cout << "How many gallons of gasoline did the car use? ";
    float gallons;
    cin >> gallons;
    cout << "Your car got " << miles / gallons;
    cout << " miles per gallon.\n";
    return 0;
}
```

Answers to Additional Questions

True or False

1. F	6. T	11. T
2. T	7. F	12. F
3. F	8. F	13. F
4. F	9. T	14. T
5. T	10. F	15. T

Short Answers

1. A programmer must be aware of the maximum and minimum values that can be stored in a variable, to exceed these limits causes errors inaccuracy. Similarly the programmer must be aware of the nature of the data that can be stored in a variable of a given data type. Some data types are "type compatible" while others are not, some can be made compatible with the use of the **cast** operator. It is good programming practice to assign the correct range and data type to any declared variable.

2.

    a) Data type `char` is designed to store characters (see page 68).

    b) `short` is a modifier that forces an integer to be 16 bits.

    c) `int` stands for integer, it is a whole number. It is 16 or 32 bits depending upon the system environment.

    d) The `long` modifier is used to force an integer to be at least 32 bits.

    e) The function `sizeof` is contained in the `climits` library and is used to determine the number of bytes occupied by a data item.

    f) In the `climits` library there are functions and symbolic constants that give information about data type limits.

    g) Initialization combines assignment with the declaration of a variable.

    h) `#define` is a pre-processor directive that declares and initializes global symbolic constants.

    i) The `cout.put()` function displays a single character.

    j) A member function belongs to a class and describes a method to manipulate data within the class.

    k) `wchar_t` is a data type associated with Unicode and allows sufficient space to represent the largest extended character set used on the system.

    l) `bool` is a data type with only two possible values—`false` and `true`.

    m) `false` and `true` are literals associated with the data type `bool`. `false` has a promoted integer value of `0` and `true` has a value of `1`.

    n) `Lvalue` is an error message generated by the compiler when an attempt is made to change the value of a constant after its original definition.

    o) `float` is a data type used to handle numbers containing a decimal point.

    p) E-notation is a C++ mechanism for showing numbers in scientific notation.

    q) Exponent and mantissa are associated with e-notation. The mantissa is the number part while the exponent is the power of ten it is raised to (see page 77).

    r) `double` is a modifier that guarantees a `float` to be at least 48 bits.

    s) `Long double` is a modifier that guarantees a `float` to be at least 80, 96, or 128 depending upon the system environment.

    t) `cfloat` is a library containing symbolic constants that aid the programmer in determining system floating-point limitations.

    u) `cout.setf(ios::fixed,ios::floatfield)` forces the compiler to display floating-point numbers to a fixed number of decimal places.

3. Declaration defines the variable name and data type.

For example   `int x;`

Initialization defines the variable name and data type while giving it a valid or sensible starting point.

For example   `int x = 42;`

Assignment is used to alter the value of the data held in a variable at some point during program execution.

For example   `x = 911;`

4. This applies when a `char` is used to represent a one-byte integer value. An unsigned `char` has a range of 0...255, whereas a signed `char` has a range of –128...+127. If `char` data type is used to hold a character, it doesn't matter which version is used.

5. The data type **bool** can be represented by an enumeration as it was before it became part of the C++ language. For example

```
#include <iostream>
using namespace std;

enum Bool {FALSE,TRUE};

int main (void)
{
    Bool george = TRUE;

    if (george == TRUE)
            cout << "A true Britton\n";
    else
            cout << "He must be French\n";
    return(0);
}
```

6. In C++, a **const** allows the explicit specification of the data type, whereas **#define** does a "best guess" to pick the most appropriate type. C++ scoping rules can be applied to limit the **const** to a particular function or file, whereas **#define** is global. Compound data type such as arrays or structures can be used with **const**, whereas **#define** is limited to simple data types.

7. The key information for **cfloat** is given on page 79 of *C++ Primer Plus*. The key information for **climits** is given on page 61 of *C++ Primer Plus*.

8. See the program in the Programming Projects to test the results:

   a) 16

   b) 16

   c) 32

   d) 1.2

   e) 0.333333

   f) 0.0222222

   g) 0

   h) 0.333333

   i) 4

   j) 0

   k) compiler error

   l) 0

   m) 1

   n) 1

   o) 0

9.

   a) no: reserved keyword

   b) no: no spaces allowed

   c) no: no quotes allowed

   d) no: no asterisk allowed

e) OK

f) no: number can't start

g) OK

h) OK

i) no: no period

j) no: no period

k) OK

l) OK

m) no: no % operator

n) OK, but not advisable

o) no: no parentheses

p) OK

q) OK, but may be implementation problem

Programming Projects

1. Here is one way. Note that this solution doesn't test for overflow numbers.

```
// decconv.cpp -- converts input to decimal

#include <iostream>
using namespace std;

int main(void)
{
    long inputNum;

    cout << "Enter the number to convert, using the form 0x1FF for hex, \n";
    cout << "0165 for octal, and 194 for decimal: ";
    cin >> inputNum;
    cout << "\nYour input converts to " << inputNum << " decimal.\n";

    return 0;
}
```

2. This solution exclusively makes use of the #defines in float.h:

```
// flimits.cpp -- floating-point limits and sizes

#include <iostream>
#include <cfloat>          // defines limits for floats
using namespace std;

int main(void)
{
    cout << "Significant Digits\n";
    cout << "      float: \t" << FLT_DIG << "\n";
    cout << "     double: \t" << DBL_DIG << "\n";
    cout << "long double: \t" << LDBL_DIG << "\n\n";

    cout << "Bits in Mantissa\n";
    cout << "      float: \t" << FLT_MANT_DIG << "\n";
    cout << "     double: \t" << DBL_MANT_DIG << "\n";
    cout << "long double: \t" << LDBL_MANT_DIG << "\n\n";

    cout << "Maximum Exponent\n";
```

```
    cout << "     float: \t" << FLT_MAX_10_EXP << "\n";
    cout << "    double: \t" << DBL_MAX_10_EXP << "\n";
    cout << "long double: \t" << LDBL_MAX_10_EXP << "\n\n";

    cout << "Minimum Exponent\n";
    cout << "     float: \t" << FLT_MIN_10_EXP << "\n";
    cout << "    double: \t" << DBL_MIN_10_EXP << "\n";
    cout << "long double: \t" << LDBL_MIN_10_EXP << "\n";

    return 0;
}
```

3. This solution was run on Microsoft Visual C++ version 5.0:

```
// fltaddx.cpp -- precision problems with float

#include <iostream>
using namespace std;

int main(void)
{
    float a = 2.34E+18;
    float b = a + 1;

    cout << "a = " << a << "\n";
    cout << "b - a = " << b - a << "\n";

    double c = 2.34E+18;
    double d = c + 1;

    cout << "c = " << c << "\n";
    cout << "d - c = " << d - c << "\n";

    long double e = 2.34E+18;
    long double f = e + 1;

    cout << "e = " << e << "\n";
    cout << "f - e = " << f - e << "\n";

    return 0;
}
```

4. Using a **float** for a modulus calculation will produce a compiler error.

```
// negmod.cpp -- modulus operation with negative operand

#include <iostream>
using namespace std;

int main(void)
{
    int posOp1 = 2345;
    int posOp2 = 92;
    int negOp1 = -964;
    int negOp2 = -6;
    float fltOp = 92.45;

    cout << "\nPositive % Positive " << posOp1 << " % " << posOp2
         << ": \t" << posOp1 % posOp2;
    cout << "\nPositive % Negative " << posOp1 << " % " << negOp2
         << ": \t" << posOp1 % negOp2;
    cout << "\nNegative % Positive " << negOp1 << " % " << posOp2
         << ": \t" << negOp1 % posOp2;
    cout << "\nNegative % Negative " << negOp1 << " % " << negOp2
         << ": \t" << negOp1 % negOp2;

    return 0;
}
```

5. Note that the line with the compile error should be commented out.

```cpp
// prec.cpp - test precedence

#include <iostream>
using namespace std;

int main(void)
{
    float a=2;
    float b=3;
    float c=5;
    int i=2;
    int j=3;

    cout << "\n    a*b+c: " << a*b+c;
    cout << "\n  a*(b+c): " << a*(b+c);
    cout << "\n  a*b+c*i: " << a*b+c*i;
    cout << "\na*(b+c)*i: " << a*(b+c)*i;
    cout << "\n    b/c*a: " << b/c*a;
    cout << "\n    a/i/j: " << a/i/j;
    cout << "\na/b/c/i/j: " << a/b/c/i/j;
    cout << "\n    i/j/a: " << i/j/a;
    cout << "\n    a/i/j: " << a/i/j;
    cout << "\n     18/4: " << 18/4;
    cout << "\n    4/3/4: " << 4/3/4;
    cout << "\n  4/(3/4): " << 4/(3/4);        //compile error
    cout << "\n  (4/3)/4: " << (4/3)/4;
    cout << "\n   21%4%3: " << 21%4%3;
    cout << "\n (21%4)%3: " << (21%4)%3;
    cout << "\n 21%(4%3): " << 21%(4%3);

    return 0;
}
```

DERIVED TYPES

Statement of Purpose

Derived Types is an introduction to arrays, enumerations, unions, structures, and pointers, and their use in C++ programs. Building on the previous chapter's discussion of data types, the student learns how to create far more powerful types to use in modeling data and for later use in program control. Pointers are introduced for the first time, setting the foundation for unleashing the full power of C++.

Objectives

By the end of Chapter 4, the student should understand the following concepts:

- Arrays, enumerations, structures, unions, and pointers: how to create and initialize
- Dynamic memory and why it is used
- Basic management of dynamic memory with new and `delete`
- String input and output using basic `istream` and `ostream` classes and member functions
- Null terminated strings versus arrays of characters
- Enumeration variables and ranges of values
- Type of memory use in C++ and its scope
- Referencing members of static and dynamic structures

Lecture Outline

Static arrays

Arrays provide the C++ programmer with flexibility in working with data. While their full benefit won't be realized until loops are discussed later, this section introduces concepts of data management.

Sample program   arrayone.cpp—using arrays to explore yams

- Used for multiple values of same data type
- Creating an array

   Type of value to be stored

   Name of the array

   Number of elements (static arrays)

      Constant number

      `const` value

      Constant expression
- Derived type: based on other types
- Access to members: subscript of index
- `sizeof` returns number of bytes in array
- Initializing arrays

   Initialization form only when declaring array

   Remaining elements if initialize fewer than all elements

   Using empty brackets to let compiler count elements

Strings

Strings are an extension to the basic concept of arrays, and now the student learns how C++ handles strings and continues to build upon the ability to use arrays contained in cstring or string.h.

Sample programs   strings.cpp—storing strings with string constant and keyboard input, `strlen()`

                                         instrl.cpp—using `cin` and problem with whitespace

                                         instr2.cpp—using `cin.getline(name, ArSize)` for string input

                                         instr3.cpp—using `cin.get(name, ArSize).get()` for string input

- Special form of array
- Series of characters stored in consecutive bytes of memory
- Null terminated string versus array of `char`
- Initializing using quoted string

   String constant or string literal

   Automatically includes null terminator

   Size of array must include space for null terminator

Some implementations may require use of `static` keyword

String constant with double quotes is not the same as character constant with single quotes

- Concatenation of strings separated only by whitespace
- String input

`cin` and whitespace problem

Line-oriented input and `istream` classes

> `cin.getline()` reads to `newline` character or to specified maximum length. Isn't available in some early compilers. Microsoft Visual C++ 5.0 has a bug in `iostream` implementation but no bugs in `ostream` version.

> `cin.get()` reads to `newline` and leaves the `newline` in buffer

> `cin.get().get()` to dispose of `newline`: function overloading

Input string length and array length

Empty lines and other problems associated with `failbit`

Sample program—numstr.cpp—following number input with line input

Mixing string and numeric input. Use `(cin >> year).get();`

C++ structures

C++ structures extend beyond the homogeneity of array data types to incorporate whichever data types the programmer needs to model the object. Static structures are introduced here to prepare for dynamic memory lessons.

Sample programs   structur.cpp—create inflatable structures variables

                                      assgn_st.cpp—create and initialize inflatable structure variables

- Derived data type that contains various data items related to an object
- Array of structures to contain data about several related objects
- Creating a structure

Define a structure description

> Describes and labels data types included

> `struct` keyword

> Structure scope: locate inside or outside of function

Create a structure variable/data object

> Same as any other data type

> C required `struct` keyword; C++ doesn't

> Initialize with a comma separated list of values in block

- Referencing structure members

Membership operator

- Structure properties

Pass structure as argument to functions

Structure as return value from function

Arrays of structures

Assign one structure to another with assignment operator

Bit fields

Unions

Enumerations

Enumerations combine the best of integer arrays and constants. While restricted in their flexibility compared to other derived types, they handle certain types of data very effectively.

- `enum` as alternative to `const`

- Enumeration types and enumerated symbolic constants

- Valid values for enumeration variables—integers

- Arithmetic operators not defined

- Explicit type cast to assign `int` to enumeration variable

- Explicitly setting enumerator values

- Value ranges for enumeration

Pointers: variables turned upside down

Pointers are the flip side of ordinary variables, a kind of cross between a basic and a derived data type. Pointers begin the exploration of efficient and effective memory management in C++.

Sample programs   address.cpp—find variable address with `&` operator

                                        pointer.cpp—declaring and initializing a pointer

                                        init_ptr.cpp—declare and initialize pointer in same step

- Pointer variables treat the `location` as the named quantity and the `value` as a derived quantity

- Ordinary variables treat the `value` as a named quantity and the `location` as a derived quantity

- Compile-time versus runtime

    Static binding

    Dynamic binding

- Address operator: `&`

    Hexadecimal is default notation for addresses

- Indirect value or dereferencing operator: `*`

- Declaring and initializing pointers

    `int* ptr`: `ptr` is a type that points to a type `int`; `ptr` contains the address of a type `int`

    `int*` is a derived type name, a pointer to `int`

    Typically a pointer is the same size for all data types

    Declaring pointer does not allocate memory for data—separate and required step

- Pointers and numbers

  Pointers are not integers, so cannot assign `int` to pointer

  Use `(int*)` type cast to assign integers to pointers

`new`: allocating dynamic memory

`delete`: de-allocating dynamic memory

Dynamic memory management with `new` and `delete` begin to give the student the tools to take control of the program and put it to good use.

Sample program   use_new.cpp—new operator with different data types

- Allocating memory: `int* pn = new int;` is the same as `int higgens; int* pi = &higgens;`
- Pointer points to a data object
- Allows greater control over use of memory
- Reuse pointers to dynamic memory
- `new` returns address of memory block or `0` if no memory available

Dynamic arrays and `new`

Refining the concepts of dynamic memory, the student begins to learn its real advantages and uses. Dynamic arrays give the programmer the ability to react to conditions not known at compile time without wasting valuable memory.

Sample program   arraynew.cpp—create and use dynamic array

- Useful when don't know if need array or its size
- Static and dynamic binding redux
- Creating dynamic array with `new`

  `int* ptr = new int [10];`
- Using dynamic arrays

  `*ptr` is the value of first element of array

  Array notation for pointers: `ptr[3]`
- Near equivalence of pointers and array names

  Name of array is address of first element

Pointer arithmetic

With the basic concepts of dynamic memory now learned, the student extends those concepts and actively begins to manipulate data and its location in memory.

Sample program   addpntrs.cpp—accessing array elements with pointer addition

- Incrementing pointer variable moves to next data element, by number of bytes of size of data type pointed to

- Notation: `arrayname[i]` is same as `*(arrayname + i)`, and `ptrname[i]` is same as `*(ptrname + i)`

- `sizeof` returns size of array in bytes, size of data type for pointer

Pointers and strings

When put together, strings and pointers exhibit behaviors that must be understood for effective programming. There are dangers in their use, however!

Sample program   pntstr.cpp—three different strings passed to `cout` and `strcpy()`

- Give `cout` address of a `char`, and it prints to first null character

   String constants, name of array of `char`, and a pointer to `char` are all passed to `cout` as an address

- Beware: compilers may treat string constants as read-only, or may use one copy of the same string

Dynamic structures and `new`

Taking dynamic memory another step forward, dynamic structures are introduced in anticipation of later discussions of structure arrays.

Sample program   newstrct.cpp—dynamic structures

- Allows allocation of only as much memory as is needed

- Create structure with `inflatable* ps = new inflatable;`

- Accessing structure members

   Arrow membership operator: `->`

   Membership operator: `(*ps).price`

Freeing memory with `delete`

With the power to use memory management in C++ comes responsibility as well. Memory that is obtained from the free memory must be returned to it so that programs can coexist with others.

Sample program   delete.cpp—using `delete` operator

- `delete` returns memory to the memory pool

- Beware of freeing memory already freed

- Can't use `delete` to free memory of declared variables

- Applying `delete` to null pointer does nothing

- Delete dynamic arrays with `delete []`

- Memory can be freed in a function other than where it was allocated

Introduction to memory management in C++

Now that the student has a feel for memory management in C++, the different types of memory allocations are discussed in anticipation of more detail later.

- Automatic variables

  Ordinary variables defined in a function or block

  Memory freed at end of that block

- Static variables

  Exists throughout execution of program

  Define outside of a function or with `static` keyword

- Free store

  Dynamic memory with `new` and `delete`

  Separate from automatic and static memory

Additional Questions

True or False

1. An uninitialized regular array declaration must always explicitly declare the array size.

2. An array can contain any combinations of data types, as long as there are enough elements to hold the data.

3. The statements
   ```
   int clients[];
   clients = {"Porter & Associates", "Hiltay Health", "Smith & Sons"};
   ```
   will result in an array containing three elements.

4. The statement
   ```
   int pets[12] = {14, 26, 13, 25, 13};
   ```
   will result in an array with integers in the first five elements and zeros in the following seven elements.

5. `short blurb[] = {1, 3, 10, 15}` is good programming practice.

6. Under standard C++, a string must occupy contiguous and consecutive bytes in memory.

7. `char animal[] = {"Horse", \0}` is a valid initialization of a string array.

8. An array of `char` is a string only if a null terminator is the last character.

9. An array used to hold "We attack at dawn!" will need a minimum of 19 elements.

10. `cin` stops accepting input to the current variable when `\0` is received from the keyboard.

11. `getline()` adds a null character to the end of a string, and `get()` leaves the `newline` in the input buffer.

12. C++ requires the use of the `struct` keyword both when defining a structure and declaring a structure variable.

13. While not good programming practice, `struct inflatable{char name[20],float volume, double price};` is a proper `struct` definition.

14. Structures must be defined outside of a function and variables must be declared inside a function.

15. Variables can be defined both inside and outside a function.

16. Unless explicitly recast as numeric data types, enumerated symbolic constants can only perform addition, subtraction, multiplication, and division.

17. The following is a valid use of enumerators:

```
int result;
enum {False, True, Maybe};
result = True * Maybe;
```

18. The range of permissible values for sheepskin is **0** to **3**.

```
enum sheepskin {horse, dog, pig, elephant};
```

19. A pointer points to a particular data type but itself contains an integer form. However, it is not an integer.

20. Memory for a regular array is allocated at compile time and for a dynamic array at runtime.

21. The derived quantity for a pointer is an address and for an ordinary variable is a value.

22. When a pointer is assigned a new memory address, it can point to a **long** even if it was declared as a pointer to an **int**.

23. The following establishes roughneck as a pointer to a string constant:

```
char* roughneck = "Let's point here for fun, okay?";
```

24. The following lines of statements are functionally equivalent:

```
float* teddy = new float;
float Smokey; float *teddy = &Smokey;
```

25. `long* ptr = new int;` is invalid because the contents of `ptr` will not be big enough to hold an address.

26. If memory is exhausted, the following will return a null pointer.

```
int* stuff = new int;
```

27. To access a field within an array of structures you only need to specify the array element.

28. Assuming the following declaration

```
inflatable one [5];
inflatable two[5];
```

Is this assignment valid?

```
one = two;
```

29. Bit fields are used to access single elements in a structure.

30. A union can have several fields, but only one can hold an accessible value at any one time.

Short Answers

1. Describe explicitly what each of the following does:

   a) `char diamond [9] = {'e', 'x', 'p', 'e', 'n', 's', 'i', 'v', 'e'};`

   b) `char cat[5] = {'f', 'i', '\0', 'd', 'o'};`

c) `char sex = "M";`

2. Describe the following terms with respect to a C++ program.

   a)   derived variable types

   b)   arrays

   c)   strings

   d)   structures

   e)   pointers

   f)   `new`, `delete`

   g)   array element

   h)   array subscript, index

   i)   initialization list

   j)   NULL character

   k)   string constant

   l)   string literal

   m)   concatenation

   n)   `strlen()`

   o)   cstring

   p)   indirect value

   q)   dereferencing operator

   r)   memory address

   s)   named memory

   t)   unnamed memory

   u)   static binding

   v)   dynamic binding

   w)   dynamic array

   x)   structure description

   y)   structure variable

   z)   external declaration

   aa) memberwise assignment

   ab) enumeration

   ac) `enum`

   ad) automatic variables

   ae) free store

3. Draw a picture of memory showing what is in memory at the referenced data location. Refer to Figure 4.2 in the text for a sample of string initialization.

   a) `char people[10] = "Jane Roe";`

b) `char dog [5] = {'b', 'e', 'a', 'u', 'x'};`

4. Suppose that you are writing a database application to catalog all of the items in the room you are now sitting. Write a structure definition that would be appropriate for that use. Include a variety of data types.

5. Why would you ever define a structure with no type name?

6. Define enumerators and declare an enumerator variable for each of the following:

   a) days of the week

   b) months of the year

   c) names of your family members, assigning their ages to the constants

   d) the seven dwarfs

7. What is the range of valid values for `bigrange`?

   ```
   enum bigrange{furry = -3, soft, lever, door = 12, kite};
   ```

8. After each of the numbered statements execute, what will `ptr` contain?

   ```
   int* ptr = new int [10]
   cout << "sizeof int = " << sizeof (int) << "\n";   //prints 2
   cout << ptr;       //prints 0x37B4
   ```

   a) `ptr = ptr + 2;`

   b) `ptr = ptr + 1;`

   c) `delete ptr;`

Programming Projects

1. Write a program that will create an array of structures describing relevant statistics of the members of your favorite sports team (preferably in a sport not out on strike). Read the data about your favorite team member into the first element of the array, and then print out the information. Include an array for the member's three highest scoring totals over the last five years. At the end, include a statement of the amount of memory each array element uses.

2. Modify assgn_st.cpp to demonstrate if assigning one structure to another makes a copy of the data.

3. As discussed in the text, some compilers treat string literals as read-only constants, and some compilers use one copy of a string for all occurrences of the string in the program. Write a program that demonstrates how your compiler handles this situation.

For Further Discussion

Why is `int*` considered a derived type name? How is that consistent with other data types?

Activities for Learning

Modify the example programs in this chapter, changing them with different ways of using pointers until you feel comfortable with each type of pointer notation.

Answers to Text Programming Exercises

1. Write a C++ program that requests and displays information as shown below. Note that the program adjusts the grade downward, that is, up one letter. Assume the user requests an A, B, or C so that you don't have to worry about the gap between a D and an F.

```
What is your first name? Betty Sue
What is your last name? Yew
What letter grade do you deserve? B
What is your age? 22
Name: Yew, Betty Sue
Grade: C
Age: 22

// pe4-1.cpp

#include <iostream>
using namespace std;

const int Arsize = 20;

int main(void)
{
    char fname[Arsize];
    char lname[Arsize];
    char grade;
    int age;

    cout << "What is your first name? ";
    cin >> fname;
    cout << "What is your last name? ";
    cin >> lname;
    cout << "What letter grade do you deserve? ";
    cin >> grade;
    cout << "What is your age? ";
    cin >> age;
    cout << "Name: " << lname << ", " << fname << "\n";
    grade = grade + 1;
    cout << "Grade: " << grade << "\n";
    // note that using << grade + 1 wouldn't work correctly
    cout << "Age: " << age << "\n";
    return 0;
}
```

2. William Wingate runs a pizza-analysis service. For each pizza, he needs to record the following information:

   • the name of the pizza company, which may consist of more than one word

   • the diameter of pizza

   • the weight of the pizza

   Devise a structure that can hold this information and write a program using a structure variable of that type. The program should ask the user to enter each of the items of information listed above, and then the program should display that information. Use cin (or its methods) and cout.

```
//pe 4-2.ccp

#include <iostream>
using namespace std;

const int Slen = 70;
```

```
struct pizza {
    char name[Slen];
    float diameter;
    float weight;
};

int main(void)
{
    pizza pie;
    cout << "What is the name of the pizza company? ";
    cin.getline(pie.name, Slen);
    cout << "What is the diameter of the pizza in inches? ";
    cin >> pie.diameter;
    cout << "How much does the pizza weigh in ounces? ";
    cin >> pie.weight;
    cout << "Company: " << pie.name << "\n";
    cout << "Diameter: " << pie.diameter << " inches\n";
    cout << "Weight: " << pie.weight << " ounces\n";
    return 0;
}
```

3. Do Programming Exercise 2, but use **new** to allocate a structure instead of declaring a structure variable. Also, have the program request the pizza diameter before it requests the pizza company name.

```
//pe 4-3.ccp

#include <iostream>
using namespace std;

const int Slen = 70;

struct pizza {
    char name[Slen];
    float diameter;
    float weight;
};

int main(void)
{
    pizza *ptr = new pizza;
    cout << "What is the diameter of the pizza in inches? ";
    cin >> ptr->diameter;
    while (cin.get() != '\n')
        ; // get rid of rest of line before reading a string
    cout << "What is the name of the pizza company? ";
    cin.getline(ptr->name, Slen);
    cout << "How much does the pizza weigh in ounces? ";
    cin >> ptr->weight;
    cout << "Company: " << ptr->name << "\n";
    cout << "Diameter: " << ptr->diameter << " inches\n";
    cout << "Weight: " << ptr->weight << " ounces\n";
    return 0;
}
```

Answers to Additional Questions

True or False

1. T	11. T	21. F
2. F	12. F	22. F
3. F	13. F	23. T
4. T	14. T	24. T
5. F	15. T	25. F
6. T	16. F	26. T
7. F	17. F	27. F
8. T	18. T	28. T
9. T	19. T	29. F
10. F	20. F	30. T

Short Answers

1. a) Creates an array of `char`. Not a string because no null terminator.

   b) Places five characters in memory. The first three constitute a string.

   c) Nothing. C++ won't compile it.

2. a) A derived data type is based upon another data type known as the underlying data type. Derived data types include arrays and structures.

   b) An array is a data form that can hold several values, all of the same underlying data type.

   c) A string is a data structure containing a sequence of characters and terminated by a NULL character.

   d) A structure is a data form that can hold items of differing data types.

   e) A pointer is a variable that contains the address of a memory location where data is stored.

   f) The `new` keyword is used to obtain memory for the storage of data. The `delete` keyword is used to release memory when the data is finished with it.

   g) An array element is a single variable within the array. Remember that all elements in the array must be of the same underlying data type.

   h) Individual elements in an array are accessed by the subscript or index (they mean the same thing). The first array element is index 0, the second is index 1, the third is index 2, and so forth.

   i) An initialization list is the values within the curly brackets assigned to the array at initialization.

   That is, `int yamcosts[3] = {20,30,40};`

   j) The NULL character `\0` is used to mark the end of a string.

   k) A string constant is a list of letters enclosed in quotes

   That is, `char fish[] = "Bubbles";`

   l) A string literal is the same as a string constant.

m) Concatenation joins two strings together to form a single string.

n) `strlen()` is a function contained in the cstring library which returns the number characters excluding the NULL terminator contained in a string.

o) The cstring library contains declarations and many other string-related functions.

p) The `*` operator is called the indirect value operator. So if `mydata` is a pointer variable, then `mydata` represents an address and `*mydata` represents the data contained in the pointed to address.

q) The dereferencing operator is another name for the indirect value operator.

r) A memory address is a location within the computer where data can be stored.

s) Variables and constants are named memory allocated at compile time.

t) Pointer variables whose memory is allocated at runtime are said to be unnamed memory.

u) Allocation of memory for variables at compile time is said to be static binding.

v) Variables created at runtime are said to be dynamic binding.

w) A dynamic array is created at runtime using the `new` keyword.

x) The structure description is the definition of the structure that contains the structure name along with the data types and variables associated with the structure.

y) A structure variable is a variable whose data type is a defined structure.

z) An external declaration is outside of any function and preceding `main` which allows the declaration to be accessed by all code in the file.

aa) When one structure is assigned to another using the assignment operator, it is called memberwise assignment.

ab) An enumeration is a means of creating a sequence of symbolic constants that can be used as a user-defined data type.

ac) An enumeration is declared in C++ with the `enum` keyboard.

ad) Ordinary variables defined inside a function are called automatic variables. They come into existence automatically when the function is invoked and terminate when the function terminates.

ae) The free store is an area of computer memory that can be allocated at runtime by using the `new` keyword. It is deallocated by using the `delete` keyword.

3. Each position represents a memory location. **?** represents unknown garbage.

   a) ¦J¦a¦n¦e¦ ¦R¦o¦e¦\0¦\0 ¦

   b) ¦b¦e¦a¦u¦x¦

4. Here is one of many ways to do it:
```
struct things {
    char name[30];
    char location[30];
    char owner[30];
    int color;
    int height;
    int weight;
    float density;
};
```

5. No type name is needed when only one structure variable of that type will be used. However, it is better to name the structure to make code both more understandable and flexible for when changes are needed.

6. a) `enum days {Monday, Tuesday, Wednesday, Thursday, Friday, Saturday, Sunday}; days newsSumm;`

   b) `enum months {January, February, March, April, May, June, July, August, September, October, November, December }; months thisYear;`

   c) `enum family {Paul = 72, Jackie = 42, Don = 37, Julia = 37, Sharon = 32, Sondra = 32}; family kiely;`

   d) `enum dwarfs {Doc, Grumpy, Sleepy, Sneezy, Bashful, Dopey, Happy}; dwarfs SnowWhite;`

7. Range of -3 to 13.

8. After c), `ptr` will probably still be 0x37ba, but won't point to a valid area of memory.

   a) 0x37B8

   b) 0x37BA

   c) 0x37BA

Programming Projects

1.
```
// scores.cpp--structures and arrays

#include <iostream>
using namespace std;

struct players {
    char name[30];
    int height;
    int scores[3];
};

int main(void)
{
    players angels[20];
    cout << "Enter the name of player 1: ";
    cin.get(angels[0].name, 30).get();
    cout << "Enter the player's height: ";
    cin >> angels[0].height;
    cout << "Enter score 1: ";
    cin >> angels[0].scores[0];
    cout << "Enter score 2: ";
    cin >> angels[0].scores[1];
    cout << "Enter score 3: ";
    cin >> angels[0].scores[2];
    cout << "\nThanks! Here is the player data:\n";

    cout << angels[0].name << "\n";
    cout << angels[0].height << "\n";
    cout << angels[0].scores[0] << "\n";
    cout << angels[0].scores[1] << "\n";
    cout << angels[0].scores[2] << "\n";

    cout << "\nThe angels structure occupies ";
    cout << sizeof angels[0];
    cout << " bytes of memory.";
    return 0;
}
```

2. This should show that bouquet and choice have different memory address, so data is copied.

```cpp
// assgnst.cpp -- assigning structures duplicates data?

#include <iostream>
using namespace std;

struct inflatable
{
    char name[20];
    float volume;
    double price;
};

int main(void)
{
    inflatable bouquet =
    {
        "sunflowers",
        0.20,
        12.49
    };

    inflatable choice;
    cout << "Address of bouquet = " << &bouquet;
    cout << "\nAddress of choice = " << &choice;
    return 0;
}
```

3.

```cpp
// strLoc.cpp

#include <iostream>
using namespace std;

int main(void)
{
    char strOne[] = "Here is a string.";
    char* strLoc;
    char strTwo[] = "Here is a string.";
    char strThr[] = "Here is a string.";

    strLoc = strOne;
    cout << "\nstrOne is located at " << (int*) strLoc;
    strLoc = strTwo;
    cout << "\nstrTwo is located at " << (int*) strLoc;
    strLoc = strThr;
    cout << "\nstrThr is located at " << (int*) strLoc;

    *strLoc = "Another string.";   //This probably won't compile.
    cout << "\n\n*strLoc is now " << strLoc << " at " << (int*) strLoc;
    return 0;
```

CHAPTER 5

LOOPS AND RELATIONAL EXPRESSIONS

Statement of Purpose

Chapter 5 begins the introduction of data analysis with C++, using loops and relational expressions to control program flow. Now the student can start to take advantage of the language's features to begin writing efficient code to solve problems. The student can also begin to understand the flow of a program, taking data from start to finish, using input, data analysis, and output.

Objectives

By the end of Chapter 5, the student should understand the following concepts:

- The `for` loop: how it is built and how it is used

- The `while` loop: its structure and when to use it instead of the `for` loop

- The `do while` loop: how and why to use an exit condition

- Multidimensional arrays

- Nested loops to process multidimensional arrays

- For students of C, how C++ extends and improves these features

- Expressions and the role they play in C++ statements

- How expressions are related to statements

- The increment and decrement operators, and how the prefix and postfix forms affect the result

- Relational operators and using them to control loops

- Compound statements, or blocks, and their part in loops

- Using the comma operator to put two expressions where C++ calls for one

- Using `typedef` to keep code flexible and write portable code

- The different forms of `get()` and when to use each

- Testing for end-of-file conditions both from disk files and the keyboard

Lecture Outline

`for` loop

The `for` loop provides the introduction of C++ loops and how they can be used. The student begins to see how the structures in the language can be used to control program flow.

Sample programs	forloop.cpp—simple for loop to repeat printing of a string
	num-test.cpp—demonstrates numeric test in for loop to count down
	express.cpp—values of expressions and precedence
	formore.cpp—for loops, external declaration, and arrays to calculate factorials
	bigstep.cpp—changing the step size to count by 17
	forstr1.cpp—input string and print in reverse order

- C++ loops perform repetitive tasks
- Structure of a `for` loop: `for (initialization; loop test; loop update) statements;`

  Initialization

  > Done once in the loop

  > May include declaration of loop variable

  > Variable may be used in `for` loop statements and after loop is complete

  Loop test

  > Determines whether loop is executed

  > Generally a relational expression, but any expression is acceptable

  > Ends loop when evaluates to `0`

  Loop update

  > Evaluated at the end of each loop

  > Generally used to increase or decrease value of test variable

  > Step size can be any size

  Loop statements

  > May be one C++ statement or several within `{}`

- Expressions in `for` loops control section

  Any valid combination of values and operators

  All C++ expressions have a value

  Assignment expression is the new `lvalue`

  `Lvalues` are expressions that evaluate to a type other than `void` and that designate a variable

  Relational expressions evaluate to `0` or `1`

  Side effects: when evaluating an expression changes data in memory

  Any expression can become a statement by adding a semicolon, but not all statements become expressions by removing semicolon

  Entire `for` loop is considered a single expression

Declaration-statement expression: new C++ term

- **for** loops are entry-condition loops

  Evaluates loop test before executing any statements

  Statements may not be executed at all

- **for** loops and strings

Increment and decrement operators

Increment and decrement operators are an integral part of loops, with subtle differences in results using the prefix and postfix forms.

Sample program   plus-one.cpp—effect of prefix and postfix operators

- Increment operator: ++

  Inspiration for the name C++

- Decrement operator: - -

- Prefix and postfix versions

  Each has same effect on the operand, but a different one when the action takes place

  Prefix: increment or decrement value, and then use the new value to evaluate expression

  Postfix: use the current value, and then increment or decrement

- With pointers, value changes by size of data type pointed to

- Overuse in complex expressions is not defined

Combination assignment operators

These operators provide a conciseness to code, making for fewer keystrokes and more precision in the meaning of code.

- Addition: +=

- Subtraction: -=

- Multiplication: *=

- Division: /=

- Modulus: %=

External declarations

Variable scoping is revisited and extended, showing how the location of declarations affects the lifetime of variables.

- Variable exists for the duration of the program

- Variable can be used in all functions in the program file

Compound statements: blocks

This section expands upon the concept of a statement in C++, shows that loop constructs are single statements syntactically, and how the language allows multiple statements in loops.

Sample program   block.cpp—using block statements to sum and average values

- Notation used to include multiple statements in loop body: {}
- Indentation does not make statements part of a block
- Variables defined within a block have a lifetime only within that block

Comma operator

Much like compound statements, the comma operator allows multiple expressions in statements. It provides both power and danger for the programmer.

Sample program   forstr2.cpp—using comma operator and statement blocks to reverse letters in a word

- Allows putting multiple expressions where syntax only allows one
- In declarations, comma is a separator not an operator
- In loops, cannot **declare** multiple variables in control structure
- First expression is evaluated before second expression
- Value of a comma expression is the value of the second expression
- Lowest precedence of any operator

Relational expressions

The student can now begin to see how C++ reacts to data to make decisions about how to proceed. This section expands upon the idea that every expression has a value.

Sample program   equal.cpp—confusing equal-to and assignment operators to find quiz scores

- C++ relational operators
  Less than: <
  Less than or equal to: <=
  Equal to: ==
  Greater than: >
  Greater than or equal to: >=
  Not equal to: !=
- Valid for numeric values, including **char**
- True results in **1** and false results in **0**
- Precedence is lower than for arithmetic operators
- Danger of confusing assignment and equal-to operators

String comparisons

Now that the basic concepts of loops are understood, the special case of string handling is discussed. Again, the student sees that strings can't be handled like numbers. Special string handling functions are contained in cstring or string.h library.

Sample program   compstr.cpp—use `strcmp()` to find missing letter in string

- Relational operators don't work because string constants and array names are addresses
- `strcmp()` library function

  Returns `0` if strings are identical

  Returns negative value if first string precedes second alphabetically

  Returns positive value if first string follows second alphabetically

  System collating sequence governs result

`while` loops

Now that the students understand the concepts of loops and many of the details of their structure and use, they can expand that knowledge to fine-tune their use of loops.

Sample program   while.cpp—steps through a string, printing it "verticalized and ASCIIized"

- Essentially a `for` loop without initialization and update sections
- Another entry-condition loop: statements may not be executed
- `Body` is either a single statement or block of statements
- Loop continues until test-condition is false (`zero`)
- Something within loop body must affect test-condition

When to use `for` versus `while` loop

At this point in the student's learning, the differences are subtle, but will become more important as programs become more complex.

- All `for` loops can be rewritten as `while` loops and vice versa
- Primarily a matter of style, unless a `continue` statement is needed
- `for` is used more for counting loops
- `while` is used more often when the programmer doesn't know number of times through loop in advance

Time-delay functions

Here the student can see a practical application of loops, and learn more about portability.

Sample program   waiting.cpp—portable time-delay function

- Simply counting loops will produce different results on different hardware
- Use `clock()` function in standard ctime or time.h library with

`CLOCKS_PER_SECOND` symbolic constant

`clock_t` as alias for `clock()` return type

Type aliases

Building on the last chapter's introduction of derived data types, type aliases allow even more flexibility with code.

- Two ways to define in C++

  `#define` preprocessor directive

  `typedef` keyword

- `typedef` gives more flexibility because it can be used with complex data types

`do while` loop: exit-condition loop

Now the student can see the importance of exit-condition loops, and why there are real problems that are suited for their use.

Sample program   dowhile.cpp—`do while` loop to guess favorite number

- Statements always execute at least once
- Test-condition evaluated at end of loop

Using loops for text input

Again the special case of string handling is discussed, particularly as it applies to students with a background in C, using three different forms of `get()` for input.

Sample programs   textin1.cpp—using sentinel character to stop input, but whitespace skipped

textin2.cpp—using `cin.get(ch)` to read all characters

textin3.cpp—testing for end-of-file condition

textin4.cpp—using `cin.get()` for input, test for EOF

- Traditionally use a `while` loop for text input
- Different forms of `cin` for input

  Plain, simple `cin`: `cin >> ch;`

  A sentinel character stops input

  Basic `cin` skips all whitespace

  Buffers input so can type past sentinel

  `cin.get(ch)` solves problems: `cin.get(ch);`

  Reads all characters, whitespace or not

  Input is still buffered

  Argument declared as a reference

  Variable `ch` is modified, even though not sending address

Another form: `cin.get()` and `cout.put()`

> Works similarly to C's `getchar()` and `putchar()` functions

> Reads next character from input, and returns the character as an `int ch= cin.get();`

> `cout.put(ch)` works like `putchar()`

> Returns EOF for end-of-file: usually defined as `-1`

> Variable should be `int`, so can receive `-1`

Which form to use?

> `cin.get(ch)` form is most closely tied to the object orientation

> `cin.get()` good for converting C programs

- Function overloading

Use the same function name to accept different argument lists

Compiler selects the proper form to use with particular argument list

- End of file condition

Redirection with < in UNIX and DOS

Keyboard equivalents

> UNIX: <CTRL>-<d> at beginning of line

> DOS: <CTRL>-<Z> then <ENTER> anywhere on line

> Symantec C++ on Mac: <CTRL>-<d>

`cin.get(ch)` returns 0 if end-of-file received

End-of-file condition ends `cin` input: `cin.clear()` clears end-of-file flag

Two-dimensional arrays and nested loops

And now, many of the lessons of the last chapters come together to loop and process row and column data. The student can now really begin to use the sleek efficiency of C++.

Sample program   nested.cpp—nested loops to output yearly temperatures of several cities

- One-dimensional arrays: row of data

- Two-dimensional arrays: table of data with rows and columns

- Declaration: `int maxtemps[4][5];` results in an array of arrays

`maxtemps[0]` is first element, an array

`maxtemps[0][0]` is first element of first array, an `int`

- Initializing a two-dimensional array

Comma-separated series of one-dimensional arrays enclosed in brackets

- An array of pointers to `char` may be essentially an array of pointers to strings

- Use nested loops to process all elements of a multidimensional array

Additional Questions

True or False

1. After the following statements execute, i will be 12.

   ```
   for (int i = 0; i < 12; i += 4)
       cout << models[i];
   ```

2. In the loop in question 1, three values of model will print.

3. The test-expression in a **for** loop must be a true/false type expression involving a relational operator.

4. **For** loops are most useful in situations where you can't know before runtime the number of times the loop needs to execute.

5. All valid expressions in C++ have a value, except for those containing a comma operator, because the comma operator merely separates expressions.

6. All control variables initialized in the control structure of a **for** loop are zero when the loop's statement or block completes execution.

7. A useful technique is to use a **const** external declaration of an array size, because the size is readily available for both array declarations and **for** loops that process the array.

8. The statement

   ```
   for (int i = 0, int j = 10; i < j; i++, j++);
   ```

   is not valid because of the two declarations and will produce a compiler error.

9. The statement

   ```
   long j = 40000, i = strcmp("C++ Rules!", "C is Number 1!");
   ```

   is not valid because the comma operator cannot be used in a declaration statement, and a function call can't be used to initialize a variable anyway.

10. **k** will be **1** after this statement is executed.

    ```
    k = (j = 40000, i = strcmp("C++ Rules!", "C is Number 1!"));
    ```

11. The following expression always evaluates to true.

    ```
    ("ABC" < "abc")
    ```

12. **for** loops can virtually always be easily changed into **while** loops.

Short Answers

1. Describe the following terms, and explain their use in a C++ program.

   a. **for** loops

   b. **while** loops

   c. **do while** loops

   d. loop initialization

   e. loop test

f. loop body

g. loop update

h. increment operator

i. test-expression

j. update expression

k. relational expression

l. decrement operator

m. entry-condition loop

n. expression side effect

o. declaration-statement expression

p. prefix form

q. postfix form

r. compound statement

s. comma operator

t. relational operators

u. combination assignment operators

v. `cstring`

w. `strcmp()`

x. `NULL` statement

y. `ctime`

z. `clock()`

aa. `CLOCKS_PER_SEC`

ab. `clock_t`

ac. `typedef`

ad. exit-condition loop

ae. `istream` class

af. `cin.get(ch)`

ag. reference argument

ah. function overloading

ai. redirection

aj. end-of-file condition

ak. `getchar()`, `putchar()`

al. `ch = cin.get()`

am. EOF

an. `cityTemps[6][9]`

ao. nested loops

2. What will be the result of this program loop?

```
for (int i = 0; i < 10; i++)
    {
    int j = 0;
    cout << i * j;
    j++;
    }
```

3. What will be the result of this program? Why?

```
// incrtest.cpp

#include <iostream>
using namespace std;

int main (void)
{
    int x=1;
    int y;
    y = x + ++x;
    cout << "x + ++x = " << y;

    x = 1;
    y = ++x + x;
    cout << "\n++x + x = " << y;

    x = 1;
    y = x + x++;
    cout << "\nx + x++ = " << y;

    x = 1;
    y = x++ + x;
    cout << "\nx++ + x = " << y;

    return 0;
}
```

4. Which of these `for` loop control structures are valid?

```
a)    for (int k = 0; k == 24; k += 2)
b)    for (int i = 0, int j = 4; i > 21, j < 2; i ++)
c)    for (i = 10, i != 25, i += 2)
```

5. Write a `for` loop's control structure for each of the following:

   a. Initialize a counter variable to **0**, and increment it until it is **14**.

   b. Initialize i to **20** and j to **0**. Increment j and decrement i until they are equal.

   c. Print out every third character in reverse order of a string array containing "C++ is fun to use to solve problems!"

   d. Print out all integers from **0** through **1000** that are multiples of **100**.

6. Rewrite each of the `for` loops in question 5 to make them `while` loops.

7. Given the variable declarations, which of the following are valid C++ expressions, and what are their values?

```
int i = 0
int j = 144
float pi = 3.1
float flt = 1.3E5
a)    123 * flt
b)    i == j
c)    i < j + pi > flt
d)    14 + (i = 14) + (j > 20)
e)    i = j
```

8. If `i` is an integer and is 5 coming into each of these expressions, what is the value of each expression?

```
a)    i++
b)    ++i
c)    i += 14
d)    i /= 10
e)    i *= 10
f)    i -= 6
g)    (i = 5) + i
h)    (i == 5) + i
```

9. What will happen when the following code is executed? Why?

```
int i = 0;
while (i < 25)
    cout << "Loop number " << i << "\n";
    i++;
cout << i << " loops altogether.";
```

Programming Projects

1. Revisit your grade school math class, and write a program that will output a multiplication table for the values 1 through 12. Store the results in a two-dimensional array and use nested loops for the calculations and output.

2. Write a personal information manager (PIM) for yourself. Create a structure to hold information about people you know, including, at a minimum, their name, address, city, state, ZIP, phone number, and year of birth. Using an array of these structures, input at least two people and output the information to the screen.

3. Modify the program in exercise 2 to allocate memory using `new`.

4. Write a program to input two strings from the keyboard, and then return how many characters are the same from the beginning of each string. Write the program once using a `for` loop, and then modify it to use a `while` loop.

5. Write yourself a personal finance manager (PFM). Create an array of structures to hold the name, annual budget amount, and type of budget (income or expense). Use a two-dimensional array to hold the monthly amounts actually spent for each budget category, and another one-dimensional array to hold the month names. In both the budget structure and the array of monthly data, use positive numbers for income and negative numbers for expenses. Sum the annual budget amounts from the array of structures and divide by 12 for the total monthly budget. Output data in this form:

```
Month           Budget  Actual
January         2166    2065
February        2166    1865
March           2166    2213
April           2166    2093
May             2166    1914
June            2166    2352
July            2166    2121
August          2166    2191
September       2166    1955
October         2166    2029
November        2166    1823
December        2166    2370

Total budget for year:  26000
Total spent for year:   24991
```

6. Write a delay function that runs for 10 seconds, and prints "1 seconds have passed.", "2 seconds have passed.", and so on as each second passes. Hint: after each printing of the string, use `endl` instead of `\n` so that each line prints immediately and doesn't wait for the completion of the program.

For Further Discussion

1. Discuss specific cases in which you would use the three different types of loops.

2. Is it possible to write a loop without any body statements? Why would you want to do that?

3. Is it possible to write a loop that never ends? When might you deliberately use an unending loop?

Activities for Learning

1. Investigate your compiler's implementation of `cout.put()`. What prototypes are provided for the use of different arguments?

2. Review the documentation for your compiler for `for`, `while`, and `do while` loops. Are there any special limits on the use of loops? What extra features does your compiler have?

3. Run the example programs in this chapter. Experiment with changes to get a feel for how the different C++ constructs are used. Modify them to make them more general and more useful to you.

Answers to Text Programming Exercises

1. Write a program that requests the user to enter two integers. The program should then calculate and report the sum of all the integers between and including the two integers. At this point, assume that the smaller integer is entered first. For instance, if the user enters 2 and 9, the program would report that the sum of all the integers from 2 through 9 is 44.

```cpp
// pe5-1.cpp

#include <iostream>
using namespace std;

int main(void)
{
    int start;
    cout << "Enter the starting integer: ";
    cin >> start;

    int end;
    cout << "Enter the ending integer: ";
    cin >> end;

    int sum = 0;

    for (int i = start; i <= end; i++)
        sum += i;

    cout << "The sum of the digits " << start
            << " through " << end << " is "
            << sum << ".\n";
    return 0;
}
```

2. Write a program that asks you to type in numbers. After each entry, the number reports the cumulative sum of the entries to date. The program terminates when you enter a zero.

```
// pe5-2.cpp

#include <iostream>
using namespace std;

int main(void)
{
    double sum = 0.0;
    double in;
    cout << "Enter a number (0 to terminate) : ";
    cin >> in;
    while (in != 0) {
        sum += in;
        cout << "Running total = " << sum << "\n";
        cout << "Enter next number (0 to terminate) : ";
        cin >> in;
    }
    cout << "Bye!\n";
    return 0;
}
```

3. Design a structure called **car** that holds the following information about an automobile: its make (as a string in a character array) and the year it was built (as an integer). Write a program that asks the user how many cars to catalog. The program should then use **new** to create a dynamic array of that many **car** structures. Next, it should prompt the user to input the make and year information for each structure. Note that this requires some care, for it alternates reading strings with numeric data. (See Chapter 4, "Derived Types," for more information.) Finally, it should display the contents of each structure. A sample run should look something like the following:

```
How many cars do you wish to catalog? 2
Car #1:
Please enter the make: Hudson Hornet
Please enter the year made: 1952
Car #2:
Please enter the make: Kaiser
Please enter the year made: 1951
Here is your collection:
1952 Hudson Hornet
1951 Kaiser
```

```
// pe5-3.cpp

#include <iostream>
using namespace std;

struct car { char name[20]; int year;};

int main(void)
{
    int n;
    cout << "How many cars do you wish to catalog?: ";

    cin >> n;

    while(cin.get() != '\n')    // get rid of rest of line
        ;

    car * pc = new car [n];

    for (int i = 0; i < n; i++)
    {
```

continues

```
            cout << "Car #" << (i + 1) << ":\n";
            cout << "Please enter the make: ";
            cin.getline(pc[i].name,20);
            cout << "Please enter the year made: ";
            cin >> pc[i].year;
            while(cin.get() != '\n')    // get rid of rest of line
                ;
        }
        cout << "Here is your collection:\n";
        for (i = 0; i < n; i++)
            cout << pc[i].year << " " << pc[i].name << "\n";

        return 0;
    }
```

Answers to Additional Questions

True or False

1. T

2. T

3. F

4. F

5. F

6. F

7. T

8. T

9. F

10. T

11. F (comparing addresses)

12. T

Short Answers

1. a. The `for` loop repeats a sequence of statements a fixed number of times. See page 156.

   b. The `while` loop continues as long as a condition holds true. The conditional test is done at the start of the loop. See page 180.

   c. The `do while` loop is virtually identical to the `while` loop, but the conditional test is done at the end. See page 186.

   d. Setting the loop control variable to an initial value is loop initialization.

   e. When the loop control variable is tested to determine a `false` or `true` condition, it is known as a loop test.

   f. The statements to be executed are contained in the loop body.

   g. Any variables updated within the loop are known as loop updates.

   h. The increment operator `++` is used to increase he value of its operand by 1.

i. The test expression evaluates to `true` or `false` and determines whether the loop body gets executed.

j. The `update` expression is used to increase or decrease the value of the variable keeping track of the number of loop cycles.

k. A list of relational expressions is given on page 174 in Table 5.2.

l. The decrement operator `--` is used to decrease the value of its operand by 1.

m. An entry condition loop has the conditional test at the start of the loop. These are the `for` and `while` loops.

n. When the act of evaluating an expression changes the value of data in memory, we say the evaluation has a side effect.

o. The declaration statement expression is described on page 162 under the title "Bending the rules."

p. In prefix form, `++x` (or `--x`) the increment (or decrement) comes before the operand.

q. In postfix form, `x++` (or `x--`) the increment (or decrement) comes after the operand.

r. Several statements grouped together by paired braces constitute a single compound action and is referred to as a compound statement.

s. The comma operator combines two expressions into one. For example, `j++,I--`.

t. A list of relational operators is given on page 174 in Table 5.2.

u. A list of combinational assignment operators is given on page 169 in Table 5.1.

v. `cstring` (formally `string.h`) is a library containing string handling routines.

w. `strcmp` is a function in the `cstring` library that compares the alphabetic relationship between two strings. See page 179.

x. The `NULL` terminator is used to mark the end of a string.

y. `ctime` (formally `time.h`) is a library containing functions and symbolic constants to deal with time.

z. The `clock()` function contained in the `ctime` library returns the system time elapsed since the program started execution.

aa. `CLOCKS_PER_SECOND` is contained in the `ctime` library and is a symbolic constant that equals the number of system time units per second.

ab. `clock_t` is a data type contained in the `ctime` library and is used to aid the storage of data returned by `clock()`.

ac. `typedef` is used to create an alias for data types. For example, `typedef char byte;`.

ad. An `exit` condition loop has the conditional test at the end of the loop. This is the `do while` loop.

ae. The `istream` class is associated with input streams.

af. `cin.get(ch)` is described on page 189.

ag. A reference argument is a memory location and allows a function to change the data held at the specified address.

ah. Function overloading allows several functions to have the same name as long as their argument list is different.

ai. An operating system that supports redirection enables you to substitute a file for a keyboard input.

aj. The end-of-file condition is used to terminate a redirection input stream.

ak. `getchar()` and `putchar()` are C functions to read and write characters to the IO stream.

al. `ch=cin.get()` reads in an integer value and assigns it to `ch`.

am. `EOF` is a symbolic constant that marks the end of file.

an. `cityTemp[6][9]` is a reference to a two-dimensional array specifying the seventh row tenth column of data. (Don't forget the offset starts at `0`.)

ao. A nested loop is one loop within another loop. See page 198.

2. `0000000000` - `j` is reinitialized to `0` at the start of each loop.

3.
```
x + ++x = 4
++x + x = 4
x + x++ = 3
x++ + x = 3
```

4. a. Valid

   b. Not valid—multiple declarations. `j` not changed, but it might be in the loop

   c. Not valid—commas instead of semicolons, and it will never end unless the loop changes `i`

5.
```
a)    for (int i = 0; i <= 14; i++);
b)    int i, j; for (i = 20, j = 0; j != i; i--, j++);
c)    for (int i = strlen(anArray) - 1; i >= 0; i -= 3)
d)    for (int i = 0; i <= 1000; i += 100)
```

6.
```
a)  int i;
    while (i <= 14)
        i++;
b)  int i = 20, j = 0;
    while (j != i)
    {   i--;
        j++;
    }
c)  int i = strlen(anArray) - 1;
    while (i >= 0)
        i -=3;
d)  int i = 0;
    while (i <= 1000)
        i += 100;
```

7. All are valid expressions.
```
a)    1.599e+007
b)    0
c)    0
d)    29
e)    144
```

8.
```
a)    5
b)    6
c)    19
d)    0
e)    50
f)    -1
g)    10
h)    6
```

9. "Loop number 0" will be printed ad infinitum because only the first indented statement is executed without {} in the `while` loop.

Programming Projects

1. This solution combines the calculations and output in one nested loop, but two can be used.

```cpp
// mult_tbl.cpp

#include <iostream>
using namespace std;

int main (void)
{
    int mult[12][12];
    int i, j;

    for (i = 1; i <= 12; i++)
    {
        for (j = 1; j <= 12; j++)
        {
            mult[i-1][j-1] = i * j;
            cout << mult[i-1][j-1] << "\t";
        }
        cout << "\n";
    }

    return 0;
}
```

2.

```cpp
// pim.cpp

#include <iostream>
using namespace std;

const int ArSize = 30;

struct people {
    char name[ArSize];
    char address[ArSize];
    char city[ArSize];
    char state[ArSize];
    char zip[ArSize];
    char phone[ArSize];
    int birth;
};

int main (void)
{
    people mail[3];
    for (int i = 0; i < 2; i++)
    {
        cout << "Enter the name: ";
        cin.getline(mail[i].name, ArSize);
        cout << "Enter address: ";
        cin.getline(mail[i].address, ArSize);
        cout << "Enter city: ";
        cin.getline(mail[i].city, ArSize);
        cout << "Enter state: ";
        cin.getline(mail[i].state, ArSize);
        cout << "Enter zip: ";
        cin.getline(mail[i].zip, ArSize);
        cout << "Enter phone: ";
        cin.getline(mail[i].phone, ArSize);
        cout << "Enter year of birth: ";
```

continues

```
        cin >> mail[i].birth;
        cin.get();
    }
    cout << "\n";
    for (i = 0; i < 2; i++)
    {
        cout << "Person #" << i+1 << " in list: ";
        cout << mail[i].name << " lives in " << mail[i].city;
        cout << ", " << mail[i].state << ",";
        cout << "\n  at " << mail[i].address << ".";
        cout << "\n  The zip is " << mail[i].zip << ",";
        cout << "\n  the year of birth is " << mail[i].birth;
        cout << ".\n\n";
    }
    return 0;
}
```

3. Replace this line

```
people mail[3];
```

with this line

```
people * mail = new people [3];
```

4. This solution combines both variations into one program:

```
// strcomp.cpp

#include <iostream>
#include <cstring>
using namespace std;

const int ArSize = 30;

int main (void)
{
    char str1[ArSize];
    char str2[ArSize];

    cout << "Enter string one: ";
    cin.getline(str1, ArSize);
    cout << "Enter string two: ";
    cin.getline(str2, ArSize);

    for (int i = 0; i < ArSize, str1[i] == str2[i]; i++);
    cout << "\nfor loop: ";
    cout << i << " characters of the string are the same.";

    i = 0;
    while (i < ArSize, str1[i] == str2[i])
        i++;
    cout << "\nwhile loop: ";
    cout << i << " characters of the string are the same.";

    return 0;
}
```

5. One of many possibilities:

```
// pfm.cpp - personal finance manager

#include <iostream>
using namespace std;

const int ArSize = 20;
```

```cpp
const int Months = 12;
const int Entries = 5;

struct budget {
    char name[ArSize];
    long budgetAmt;        //annual total
    char type[ArSize];   //income or expense
};

int main (void)
{
    long totalBudget = 0;
    long avgBudget = 0;
    budget myBudget[Entries] =
    {    {"Paycheck", 40000, "Income"},
         {"Food", -2500, "Expense"},
         {"Mortgage", -5000, "Expense"},
         {"Software", -5000, "Expense"},
         {"Charity", -1500, "Expense"}
    };

    int monthSpent[Entries][Months] =
    {
        {3200,3200,3200,3200,3200,3200,3200,3200,3200,3200,3200,3200},
        {-208,-175,-196,-242,-201,-210,-187,-195,-215,-203,-220,-185},
        {-415,-415,-415,-415,-415,-415,-415,-415,-415,-415,-415,-415},
        {-402,-560,-226,-275,-495,-123,-362,-289,-475,-423,-622,-125},
        {-110,-185,-150,-175,-175,-100,-115,-110,-140,-130,-120,-105}
    };

    char * monthName[Months] =
    {
        "January    ",
        "February   ",
        "March      ",
        "April      ",
        "May        ",
        "June       ",
        "July       ",
        "August     ",
        "September  ",
        "October    ",
        "November   ",
        "December   "
    };

    // determine average monthly budget amounts
    for (int i = 0; i < Entries; i++)
    {
        totalBudget += myBudget[i].budgetAmt;
    }
    avgBudget = totalBudget/12;    // get average monthly budget

    // calculate total spent for year and print
    cout << "Month\t\tBudget\tActual\n";
    long totalYear = 0;
    for (i = 0; i < Months; i++)
    {
        long monthSum = 0;
        cout << monthName[i] << "\t " << avgBudget;
        for (int j = 0; j < Entries; j++)
            monthSum += monthSpent[j][i];

        cout << "\t " << monthSum << "\n";
        totalYear += monthSum;
```

continues

```
        }
        cout << "\nTotal budget for year:\t";
        cout << totalBudget;
        cout << "\nTotal spent for year:\t";
        cout << totalYear;

        return 0;
    }
```

6. Yes, it can be done without an **if** statement. This should probably get the student extra credit!

```
// wait.cpp -- count the time passing


#include <iostream>
#include <ctime>
using namespace std;

int main(void)
{
        int startTime, timeNow;

        startTime = int(clock() / CLOCKS_PER_SEC);
        timeNow = int(clock() / CLOCKS_PER_SEC);

        for (int i = 1; i <= 10; i++)
        {
            while (timeNow - startTime < i)
                timeNow = int(clock() / CLOCKS_PER_SEC);

            cout << i << " seconds have passed." << endl;
        }
        return 0;
}
```

CHAPTER 6

BRANCHING STATEMENTS AND LOGICAL OPERATORS

Statement of Purpose

Branching statements and logical operators take a large jump in the sophistication and usefulness of C++ programs. Using the language's decision capabilities begins to open up possibilities of evaluating input data, making decisions, and the beginnings of error recovery. Input and output are expanded by using the functions available in the cctype header file (ctype.h in the older style).

Objectives

By the end of this chapter, the student should understand the following concepts:

- The `if`, `if else`, and nested `if else` structures for decision making
- The `switch` statement and when it is better than `if else`
- Using logical operators to test more complex conditions
- The cctype library of character functions and using them in loops and decision structures
- The conditional operator and when to use it instead of `if else`
- Fine-tuning loop and `switch` behavior with `break` and `continue`
- Using loops to input numerical data

Lecture Outline

The `if` statement

The programs that the student has been able to work with up to now have necessarily been limited by the lack of an `if` statement. Now programs can be written to react to conditions and take appropriate actions.

Sample programs: if.cpp—using `if` to count spaces and characters

ifelse.cpp—using `if else` to scramble string

ifelseif.cpp—guessing a number with `if else`

- Used to choose whether to take a particular action

- True condition causes the statement to execute

- Entire `if` statement is single statement

- `if else` extends decisions to other alternatives

  Entire `if` statement is still one statement

  Several `else ifs` can be used for several alternatives

  Function as nested `if` structures

- Formatting `if` statements

  Indenting is not recognized by compiler

  Multiple statements enclosed in {}

  Mistakes here may cause compiler error or runtime error

Logical expressions in C++

Using logical expressions enables complex decisions, where the decision is not black and white, but all the colors of the rainbow.

Sample programs: or.cpp—gives user choices with ¦¦ operator

and.cpp—ending input with **&&** operator

more_and.cpp—contest qualification based on age

not.cpp—assuring integer entry using **NOT**

- Logical operators

  Logical **OR:** ¦¦

    Either condition true makes expression true

    Acts as sequence point

  Logical **AND: &&**

    Both conditions must be true for true result

    Acts as a sequence point

    Useful for specifying ranges of selections

- Logical **NOT**: **!**

  Changes nonzero expression to **0**, and a zero expression to **1**

  Frequently can express relationship more clearly without **!**

  Useful withfunctions that return true/false values

- Sequence points

  Left side evaluated first

  If left side results in a particular result for the whole expression, no other terms are evaluated

- Operator precedence

OR and **AND** have lower precedence than relational operators

AND has a higher precedence than **OR**

Be careful with ranges: `if(17 < age < 35)` is a valid expression, but is always true

NOT has a higher precedence than relational and arithmetic operators

Use parentheses to override default precedence

`cctype` library of character functions

C++ has inherited a whole library of functions that make coding easier for common tasks, and handles portability issues for the programmer.

Sample program: ctypes.cpp—count categories of text input

- Inherited from C
- Simplifies some logical tests and aids portability
- ANSI C functions in `cctype`

  `isalnum()`: true if argument is alphanumeric

  `isalpha()`: true if argument is alphabetic

  `iscntrl()`: true if argument is a control character

  `isdigit()`: true if argument is a decimal digit

  `isgraph()`: true if argument is any printing character, other than a space

  `islower()`: true if argument is a lowercase letter

  `isprint()`: true if argument is any printing character, including a space

  `ispunct()`: true if argument is a punctuation character

  `isspace()`: true if argument is a standard whitespace character

  `isupper()`: true if argument is an uppercase letter

  `isxdigit()`: true if argument is a hexadecimal digit character

  `tolower()`: makes argument all lowercase

  `toupper()`: make argument all uppercase

The conditional operator: `?:`

The conditional operator converts an `if else` structure into an expression with a value and is used like any other C++ expression.

Sample program: condit.cpp—find larger of two numbers

- Form: expression1 ? expression2 : expression3

  If expression1 is true, then value is expression2, otherwise value is expression3

  Expression has a value of expression2 or expression3

- Only C++ operator requiring 3 operands

- Can be used as alternative to `if else` statement: `if else` does not have a value that can be assigned

- Easy to obfuscate code, intentionally or otherwise

The `switch` statement

The `switch` statement makes complicated `if else` statements more readable and efficient.

Sample programs: switch.cpp—implement a feel good menu

                           enum.cpp—enumerated switch labels for color code selection

- Acts as a routing device, telling program which statement to execute next

- The `switch` expression must evaluate to an integer

- Each `case` label must be an integer constant expression

- If no match, jumps to `default` line, if any

- A `break` is required if processing should not continue with next `case` statement

- Enumerators are ideally suited for use as `switch` constants

`switch` versus `if else`

When should a `switch` be used instead of an `if else` statement?

- Frequently interchangeable

- `switch` not appropriate for selections in ranges

- `switch` labels must be integers but `if else` can be almost anything

- If labels are all integer constants, `switch` is usually more efficient

`break` and `continue` statements

The student now can begin to take active control of the looping and decision making in a C++ program, making a logical change in course when the data necessitates it.

Sample program: jump.cpp—count spaces in string

- **break** controls execution in `switch` and `loop` statements

  Jumps to statement following `switch` or `loop` statement

  Statements after `break` are not executed

- **continue** controls execution in `loop` statements

  Jumps to beginning of loop, starting another execution

  Statements in loop following continue are not executed in that execution of the loop

  `for` loop: update expression is executed, the test expression is then evaluated

  `while` loop: test expression is evaluated

- Another jump is `goto`—stay away from it!

Reading numbers in loops

Using C++ loops to input numbers is a common chore that is made far simpler with the newly learned tools of this chapter.

Sample program: cinfish.cpp—recording the day's catch

cingolf.cpp—recovering from nonnumeric input for golf scores

- When reading data into numbers with `cin` and something other than a digit is input

  Value of input variable is unchanged

  Incorrect input is left in queue

  Error flag is set in the `cin` object

  Call to the `cin` method returns **0**

- This behavior enables using nonnumeric input to end loop

- Error flag must be reset using `clear()` before reading more input

Additional Questions

True or False

1. Unlike loops, C++ considers the `if else` construct as separate statements, each with a distinct value.

2. Under the rules of precedence for operators in C++, the two expressions below are not the same.
    ```
    x == y || a == b
    x == (y || a) == b
    ```

3. The proper mathematical pronunciation of ! is "*bang*," not "*phffft pptz*" as is commonly thought.

4. The following expression evaluates to true if bear is between **3** and **14** inclusive, and false otherwise.
    ```
    (3 <= bear <= 14)
    ```

5. The `break` and `continue` statements are used only in `for` and `while` loops.

6. The `if else` and `switch` statements can be used completely interchangeably.

7. In C++, the conditional test `if ((x < 10) && (x >= 0))` proves true for all single-figure numbers.

Short Answers

1. Describe the following terms, and explain their use in a C++ program.

   a) `switch` statement

   b) `if`, `if else` statements

   c) logical expression

   d) Logical `AND`

   e) Logical `OR`

   f) Logical `NOT`

   g) `isalnum()`

   h) `isalpha()`

   i) `iscntrl()`

   j) `isdigit()`

   k) `isgraph()`

   l) `islower()`

   m) `isprint()`

   n) `ispunct()`

   o) `isspace()`

   p) `isupper()`

   q) `isxdigit()`

   r) `tolower()`

   s) `toupper()`

   t) conditional operator

   u) case, default

   v) break

   w) continue

2. What does this section of code do? Rewrite the code so that it is clearer, using indentation and braces.

```
int n1;
int n2;
cout << "Enter a value for n1 : ";
cin >> n1;
cout << "Enter a value for n2 : ";
cin >> n2;
if (n1 > n2)
cout << "Procedure 1" << endl;
else
if (n1 < n2)
cout << "Procedure 2" << endl;
else
cout << "Procedure 3" << endl;
```

3. Under the rules of precedence for operators in C++, if `i` is 6 going into this expression, what will `i` be after the expression is evaluated?

   `i > 14 && ++i == 6`

4. Do these expressions evaluate to true or false?

   a) `5 >= 3 && 30/6 == 5`

   b) `(5 >= 3) && (30/6 == 5)`

   c) `!(5 >= 3) && (30/6 == 5)`

   d) `5 >= 3 ¦¦ 30/6 == 5`

   e) `(5 >= 3) ¦¦ (30/6 == 5)`

   f) `!(5 >= 3) ¦¦ (30/6 == 5)`

   g) `!!10`

   h) `!!0`

5. What is the value of each of these expressions if x is 7 and y is 12?

   a) `x < y ? x— y : y— x`

   b) `x > 0 ? y / x : 0`

   c) `x == y ? x : 25`

   d) `!x ? 13 : 10`

   e) `x <= 10 && y >= 13 ? x * y : 0`

   f) `x ¦¦ !y ? 0 : -125`

6. What will the following code do?

```
int activity = isgraph'''') ? 3 : 4;
switch(activity)
{
    case 0: budget();
    case 1: cashflow();
    case 2: production();
    case 3: inventory();
    case 4: labor();
    case 5: material();
    case 6: burden();
    case 7: vacation();
}
```

7. For each of the following, would an `if else` or a `switch` be more appropriate?

   a) Choosing a month of the year and printing a calendar

   b) Selecting ranges of class scores in percentages to determine final grades

   c) Selecting menu items, using letters as mnemonics for the different choices

   d) A learning game in which the user enters the atomic weight (integers) of any element in the periodic table and receives detailed information about the element

   e) Entering dollars and cents to determine the amount of a discount

Programming Projects

1. Using enumerators for the days of the week, write a program using a `switch` statement that prints the name of the day of the week and a message when an integer from 1 to 7 is input.

2. Write a simple calculator program that performs addition, subtraction, multiplication, division, modulus, and the absolute value of the difference of two integer operands. Input the operands from the user, and then present a menu of calculation choices. Allow the input of more operands, and provide a way for the user to end the program.

3. A Fibonacci series is a series of numbers each of which, after the first two, are the sum of the two preceding numbers. Write a program to determine the nth number in the series, in the range from 3 through 1000. Test the input to make sure that it is numerical and that it is in the correct range.

4. Newton provided the key to one way to find the square root of a positive number (square roots of a negative number are nasty). The solution uses a technique of starting with an initial value (guess), then using that value to produce a better guess until you get near enough to the answer.

   This solution for the square root of y uses the equation

   `x1 = (x0 + y/x0)/2`

   to refine the approximations, where `x1` is new estimate and `x0` is the previous estimate.

Write a function to find the square root of any number greater than **0**. Input a number from the keyboard, making sure to trap nonnumeric input and that the value is **> 0**. Use **x0 = y/4.0** and **x1 = x0/4.0** for the initial values. Use doubles for all variables, and iterate through the equation above until the difference between **x0** and **x1** is **0.0001**. Display **x0** and **x1** for each iteration. Use the conditional operator to compare the value of **x0** to **x1** so that the difference is a positive number.

5. Write a program that provides a general solution of a quadratic equation:

   $$ax^2 + bx + c = 0$$

   Include tests to make sure that valid input is received. The general solution of a quadratic equation is in the form

   $$x_{1,2} = (-b \pm \sqrt{b^2 - 4ac}) / (2a)$$

   Test for an indeterminate solution (**a**, **b**, and **c** are all **0**), no solution (**a** and **b** are 0), and a single solution (**a** is **0**), and complex roots ($b^2 < 4ac$) involving the square root of negative numbers). Limit **a**, **b**, and **c** to integers, and make sure that you have received numeric input. Use the square root function you wrote above.

For Further Discussion

1. In loops, what kinds of characters are appropriate for sentinel characters to signal the end of data? How do the possible choices depend on the data itself? In menu loops, when is it better to use characters rather than numbers?

2. Why is using **goto** considered such bad programming practice? When might it be advantageous to use a **goto**? Is there always a way to program without a **goto** statement?

3. Unlike the **if else** statement, the **switch** statement is not designed to handle ranges, it only works with constants. Technically the data types that it works with are known as **ordinal** data types. Investigate the meaning of **ordinal** and find out the **ordinal** data types available in C++.

Activities for Learning

1. Examine the copy of cctype (or ctype.h) provided with your compiler. What functions and definitions does it contain? Identify all of the functions listed in the cctype section of this chapter. Are all of the listed functions available? What other character functions does your compiler include?

2. Run the example programs in this chapter. Experiment with changes to get a feel for how the different C++ constructs are used. Modify them to make them more general and more useful to you.

Answers to Text Programming Exercises

1. Write a program that reads keyboard input to end-of-file and that echoes the input except for digits, converting each uppercase character to lowercase, and vice versa. (Don't forget the cctype library.)

```
// pe6-1.cpp
#include <iostream>
#include <cctype>
using namespace std;
int main(void)
{
    char ch;
```

```
    while (cin.get(ch))
    {
        if (isupper(ch))
            ch = tolower(ch);
        else if (islower(ch))
            ch = toupper(ch);
        if (!isdigit(ch))
            cout << ch;
    }
    return 0;
}
```

2. Write a program that reads up to 10 donation values into an array of **double**. The program should terminate input on nonnumeric input. It should report the average of the numbers and also report how many number in the array are larger than the average.

```cpp
// pe6-2.cpp -- non-numeric input terminates loop

#include <iostream>
using namespace std;

const int Max = 10;

int main(void)
{
    double donations[Max];

    cout <<  "Please enter the donations.\n\n";
    cout <<  "You may enter up to " << Max
            << " donations <q to terminate>.\n\n";
    cout << "donation #1: ";
    int i = 0;
    while (i < Max && cin >> donations[i])
    {
        if (++i < Max)
            cout << "donation #" << (i+1) << ": ";
    }
    double total = 0.0;
    for (int j = 0; j < i; j++)
        total += donations[j];
    if (i == 0)
            cout << "No donations\n\n";
    else
    {
            double average = total / i;
            cout << "$" << average << " = average of "
                        << i << " donations\n";
            int above = 0;
            for (j = 0; j < i; j++)
            {
                    if (donations[j] > average)
                        ++above;
            }
        cout << above <<  " contributions above average\n";
    }
    return 0;
```

3. Write a precursor to a menu-driven program. The program should display a menu offering four choices, each labeled with a letter. If the user responds with a letter other than one of the four valid choices, the program should prompt the user to enter a valid response until the user complies. The program should then use a switch to select a simple action based on the user's selection. A program run could look something like this:

```
Please enter one of the following choices:
c) carnivore          p) pianist
t) tree               g) game
f
```

continues

```
Please enter a c, p, t, or g: q
Please enter a c, p, t, or g: t
A maple is a tree.

// pe6-3.cpp

#include <iostream>
using namespace std;

int main(void)
{
    cout << "Please enter one of the following choices:\n\n";
    cout << "c) carnivore       p) pianist\n\n"
         << "t) tree            g) game\n\n";
    char ch;
    cin >> ch;
    while (ch != 'c' && ch != 'p' && ch != 't' && ch != 'g')
    {
        cout << "Please enter a c, p, t, or g: ";
        cin >> ch;
    }
    switch (ch)
    {
        case 'c' :  cout << "A cat is a carnivore.\n\n";
                    break;
        case 'p' :  cout << "Radu Lupu is a pianist.\n\n";
                    break;
        case 't' :  cout << "A maple is a tree.\n\n";
                    break;
        case 'g' :  cout << "Golf is a game.\n\n";
                    break;
        default  :  cout <<  "The program shouldn't get here!\n\n";
    }
    return 0;
}
```

4. When you join the Benevolent Order of Programmers, you can be known at BOP meeting by your real name, your job title, or by your secret BOP name. Write a program that can list members by real name, by job title, by secret name, or by a member's preference. Base the program on the following structure:

```
// Benevolent Order of Programmers name structure
struct bop {
    char fullname[strsize]; // wordly name
    char title[strsize];    // job title
    char bopname[strsize];  // secret BOP name
    int preference;         // 0 = fullname, 1 = title, 2 = bopname
};
```

In the program, create a small array of such structures and initialize it to suitable values. Have the program run a loop that lets the user select from different alternatives:

a. display by name

b. display by title

c. display by bopname

d. display by preference

q. quit

A sample run may look something like the following:

```
Benevolent Order of Programmers Report
a. display by name      b. display by title
c. display by bopname   d. display by preference
q. quit
```

```
Enter your choice: a
Wimp Macho
Raki Rhodes
Celia Laiter
Hoppy Hipman
Pat Hand
Next choice: d
Wimp Macho
Junior Programmer
MIPS
Analyst Trainee
LOOPY
Next choice: q
Bye!


// pe6-4.cpp

#include <iostream>
using namespace std;

const int strsize = 40;
const int bopsize = 5;

// Benevolent Order of Programmers name structure
struct bop {
        char fullname[strsize];        // wordly name
        char title[strsize];      // job title
        char bopname[strsize];  // secret BOP name
        int preference;                        // 0 = fullname,
                                               1 = title, 2 = bopname
    };

void showa(bop ar[], int n);
void showb(bop ar[], int n);
void showc(bop ar[], int n);
void showd(bop ar[], int n);

int main(void)
{
    bop team[bopsize] = {
        {"Sam Mitchiee", "Senior Programmer", "UNIXMANN", 0},
            {"Roni Knowess", "Senior Programmer", "MIPSS", 1},
        {"Celia Puhteee",  "Junior Analystt", "IDEE", 2},
        {"Jon Dichedd", "Junior Analystt", "SCSI", 1},
        {"Pat Handd", "Junior Programmerr", "LOOPY" ,2 } };

    cout << "Benevolent Order of Programmers Report\n\n";
    cout << "a. display by name      b. display by title\n\n"
         << "c. display by bopname  d. display by preference\n\n"
         << "q. quit\n\n";
    cout << "Enter your choice: ";
    char choice;
    cin >> choice;
    while (choice != 'q')
    {
        switch(choice)
        {
            case 'a'    : showa(team, bopsize); break;
            case 'b'    : showb(team, bopsize); break;
            case 'c'    : showc(team, bopsize); break;
            case 'd'    : showd(team, bopsize); break;
            default     : cout << "Enter only a, b, c, d, or q.\n";
        }
        cout <<  """Next choice: """;
```

continues

```cpp
        cin >> choice;
    }
    cout << "Bye!\n\n";
    return 0;
}

void showa(bop ar[], int n)
{
    for(int i = 0; i < n; i++)
        cout << ar[i].fullname << "\n\n";
}

void showb(bop ar[], int n)
{
    for(int i = 0; i < n; i++)
        cout << ar[i].title << "\n\n";
}

void showc(bop ar[], int n)
{
    for(int i = 0; i < n; i++)
        cout << ar[i].bopname << "\n\n";
}

void showd(bop ar[], int n)
{
    for(int i = 0; i < n; i++)
        if (ar[i].preference == 0)
            cout << ar[i].fullname << "\n\n";
        else if (ar[i].preference == 1)
            cout << ar[i].title << "\n\n";
        else if (ar[i].preference == 2)
            cout << ar[i].bopname << "\n\n";
        else
            cout << "oops\n\n";
}
```

Answers to Additional Questions

True or False

1 F

2. T

3. Your choice

4. F—always false

5. F

6. F

7. F—there are 9 negative single-figure numbers.

Short Answers

1.

a) The `switch` statement is used to select a single statement or block for execution. The switching index must be a constant value (see page 223).

b) The `if`, `if else` is used to select a single statement or block for execution. The choice is made by a comparison which evaluates to a boolean expression (see page 207).

c) Logical expressions are used to test the truth of two or more operands (see page 211).

d) The logical `AND` returns true only if all operands are true. Symbol `&&` (see page 213).

e) The logical `OR` returns true if one or more of the operands is true. Symbol `¦¦` (see page 211).

f) The logical `NOT` reverses the truth of an expression. Symbol `!` (see page 217).

g) through s) These answers are given in Table 6.3 on page 221.

t) The conditional operator can be used instead of `if else`. It has the following syntax : `expression1 ? expression2 : expression3`. If `expression1` is true, the outcome is `expression2`; if false, the outcome is `expression3`.

u) The case default (which is optional) is a catch-all clause if all choices in switch case fails.

v) The break statement is used to jump out of the current block. It is used in switch case to miss out the rest of the statements once a valid case has been found. (See page 229.)

w) The continue statement causes execution to move on to the next programming statement. (See page 229.)

2. The user enters two numbers, the program evaluates their relationship and executes alternative procedures depending upon the outcome.

```cpp
#include <iostream>
using namespace std;

main()
{
    int n1;
    int n2;

    cout << "Enter a value for n1 : ";
    cin >> n1;
    cout << "Enter a value for n2 : ";
    cin >> n2;

    if (n1 > n2)
    {
            cout << "Procedure 1" << endl;
    }
    else
    {
            if (n1 < n2)
            {
                    cout << "Procedure 2" << endl;
            }
            else
            {
                    cout << "Procedure 3" << endl;
            }
    }
    return(0);
}
```

3. `i` will still be 6 because the right part of the expression isn't executed.

4.

    a) T

    b) T

    c) F

    d) T

    e) T

    f) T

    g) T

    h) F

5.

    a) 5

    b) 1

    c) 25

    d) 10

    e) 0

    f) 0

6. `activity` becomes 4, so `labor()`, `material()`, `burden()`, and `vacation()` are run because there are no `break` statements.

7.   a) `switch`, probably using enumerators

    b) `if else` because ranges of data and may not be integers

    c) `switch` with `char` input

    d) `switch`

    e) `if else` because not integers and probably need ranges

Programming Projects

1.

```
// swit.cpp - days of week switch

#include <iostream>
using namespace std;
int main(void)
{
    int dayWant;
    enum days {Monday = 1, Tuesday, Wednesday, Thursday, Friday,
        Saturday, Sunday};

    cout << "Enter the number of the day of the week you want: ";
    cin >> dayWant;

    switch (dayWant)
    {
        case 1: cout << "Today is Monday. Get to work!";
                break;
        case 2: cout << "Today is Tuesday. Do reports.";
                break;
        case 3: cout << "Today is Wednesday. No lunch today.";
                break;
```

```
            case 4: cout << "Today is Thursday. You're late!";
                        break;
            case 5: cout << "Today is Friday. Finish those reports by Monday.";
                        break;
            case 6: cout << "Today is Saturday. Kids to soccer and ballet.";
                        break;
            case 7: cout << "Today is Sunday. House work...";
                        break;
            default: cout << "Try again - number from 1 to 7.";
        }
        return 0;
    }
```

2.

```
    // calc.cpp -- simple calculator

    #include <iostream>
    using namespace std;
    void showmenu(void);
    int op1, op2;
    int main(void)
    {
        showmenu();
        int choice;

        cin >> choice;
        while (choice != 7)
        {
            switch(choice)
            {
                case 1: cout << "Add: Result is " << op1 + op2 << "\n";
                            break;
                case 2: cout << "Subtract: Result is " << op1 - op2 << "\n";
                            break;
                case 3: cout << "Multiply: Result is " << op1 * op2 << "\n";
                            break;
                case 4: cout << "Divide: Result is " << op1 / op2 << "\n";
                            break;
                case 5: cout << "Modulus: Result is " << op1 % op2 << "\n";
                            break;
                case 6: cout << "Absolute value of difference is ";
                            cout << (op1-op2 >= 0 ? op1-op2 : op2-op1) << "\n";
                            break;
                default:cout << "That's not a choice.\n";
            }
            showmenu();
            cin >> choice;
        }
        cout << "Bye!\n";
        return 0;
    }

    void showmenu(void)
    {
        cout << "Enter first operand: ";
        cin >> op1;
        cout << "Enter second operand: ";
        cin >> op2;
        cout << "Please enter 1, 2, 3, 4, 5, or 6:\n"
        "1) addition\n"
        "2) subtraction\n"
        "3) multiplication\n"
        "4) division\n"
        "5) modulus\n"
```

continues

```
        "6) absolute value of difference\n"
        "7) quit\n";
    }
```

3.

```
// fibonach.cpp - determine the nth number in a Fibonacci series

#include <iostream>
using namespace std;
int main(void)
{
    int nth;

    cout << "Enter an integer from 3 to 1000: ";
    while (!(cin >> nth))
    {
        cin.clear();
        while (cin.get() != '\n')
            continue;
        cout << "Please! Enter a number: ";
    }

    // make sure input is in range
    if (nth < 3 || nth > 1000)
        cout << "Sorry. Number isn't in the right range.";
    else
    {
        unsigned long fibValue = 1;    // value of second term
        unsigned long preValue = 1, curValue = 1;

        for (int i = 3; i <= nth; i++)
        {
            fibValue = preValue + curValue;
            preValue = curValue;
            curValue = fibValue;
        }

        cout << "\nThe value of number " << nth;
        cout << " in the series is " << fibValue << ".\n";
    }
    return 0;
}
```

4.

```
// root1.cpp - figure the square root of a number

#include <iostream>
using namespace std;
double root(double op);

int main(void)
{
    double factor;
    cout << "Enter a value > 1: ";

    while (!(cin >> factor))
    {
        cin.clear();
        while (cin.get() != '\n')
            continue;
        cout << "Please enter a number: ";
    }

    if (factor <= 0)
        cout << "Sorry. Number must be greater than zero.";
```

```
    else
        cout << "\nSquare root is " << root(factor);

    return 0;
}

double root(double op)
{
    double x0 = op/4.0;
    double x1 = x0/4.0;
    double temp;

    while (( x0 > x1 ? x0 - x1 : x1 - x0 ) > 0.000001)
    {
        cout << x0 << "\t" << x1 << "\n";
        temp = x1;
        x1 = (x0 + op/x0) / 2;
        x0 = temp;
    }
    return x1;
}
```

5.

```
// quad.cpp - figure the solutions to a quadratic equation
#include <iostream>
#include <cmath>
using namespace std;
int main(void)
{
    int abc[3];
    int a, b, c;
    double x1, x2;

    // get the values of a, b, and c
    for (char i = 'a'; i < 'd'; i++)
    {
        cout << "Enter value for " << i << ": ";
        while (!(cin >> abc[i-'a']))
        {
            cin.clear();
            while (cin.get() != '\n')
                continue;
            cout << "Please enter a number: ";
        }
    }

    a = abc[0];
    b = abc[1];
    c = abc[2];

    cout << "\nSolving the equation " << a;
    cout << "x(2) + " << b;
    cout << "x + " << c << " = 0";
    cout << "\n";

    // check for special cases and find the roots
    if (a == 0)
    {
        if (b == 0)
        {
            if(c == 0)
            {
                cout << "a,b,c are all zero: ";
```

continues

```
                    cout << "cannot determine solution.";
                }
                else
                    cout << "No solution exists.";
            }
            else
            {
                x1 = -c / b;
                cout << "Linear solution: " << x1;
            }
        }
        else if (b*b < 4*a*c)
            cout << "Complex roots. Lets wait!";
        else if (b*b == 4*a*c)
        {
            x1 = -b / (2*a);
            cout << "Roots are equal: " << x1;
        }
        else
        {
            x1 = (-b + sqrt(b*b - 4*a*c))/(2*a);
            x2 = (-b - sqrt(b*b - 4*a*c))/(2*a);
            cout << " First root x1 = " << x1 << "\n";
            cout << "Second root x2 = " << x2;
        }

        return 0;    //whew!
}
```

FUNCTIONS—C++'S PROGRAMMING MODULES

Statement of Purpose

The functions we have used throughout the book so far have had very simple uses, frequently without arguments. Now it is time to begin a close examination of C++ functions, how they are used, and the benefits they bring to the language, including recursive functions. Another level of understanding of structures and pointers is attained, where the power and flexibility of C++ can begin to be used.

Objectives

By the end of Chapter 7, the student should understand the following concepts:

- Usage of functions to this point in the C++ education

- Defining, prototyping, and calling functions: why and how, with some traditions too

- The interrelationships of the type, parameter list, and address of a function

- When to pass variables by value and reference, and why it makes a difference

- Passing and processing arrays with functions: yes, you can return an array from a function

- A special case of arrays and functions: text strings

- Preventing a function from summarily changing data it is sent

- Recursive functions and a clear idea of how they work

- Using structures with functions and a deeper understanding of variables in general

- A basic concept of using pointers to functions and why they are useful

- The next step of C++'s use of reference to objects in memory

Lecture Outline

Using functions in C++

An overview of the use of functions that we've seen so far is required before we go on to refine and extend that knowledge.

Sample programs: calling.cpp—call a simple country function

                                               protos.cpp—prototypes and compute volume of a cube

- Library functions do everything but call the function for you
- Three parts to using functions

    Define the function

    Prototype the function

    Call the function

Define the function

The fundamental utility of functions is that they do something with data we feed it. In defining the function we specify the data that will be received, what actions to take, and what to return to the calling function.

- Structure of function definition
- **void** functions

    No **return** statement

    Declared with **void** keyword
- Functions with a value

    return statement passes a value to the calling function

    Data type of value returned must match the called function's type

    Functions cannot return an array, unless part of a structure

    Called function puts **return** value in a memory location where the calling function can have access to it

    Called function terminates upon executing first **return** statement it encounters

Prototype the function

To make programming as efficient as possible, we can let the compiler catch a lot of the problems that might be overlooked. Using a function prototype tells the compiler most of what it needs to do its job.

- Specifies type of value returned, and number and types of arguments
- Describes function interface to compiler
- Enables the compiler to perform a higher level of error checking while being more efficient
- Without prototypes

    Delay compiling a function until all called functions are compiles

    Called functions may be in different files

- The programmer can avoid prototypes if the called function's definition is placed before the calling function. This is known as define before use, but is not always possible.

- Syntax

    Simplest way is to copy function header and end with a semicolon

    Argument names are not required as long as types are listed

    Using meaningful argument names increases clarity of purpose of function

    In C++, empty parentheses are the same as using `void`

    Empty parentheses in C means you are declining to state what the arguments are

    Equivalent to C empty parentheses in C++ is to use ellipses

    May be required for compatibility issues

- Benefits to programmer: compiler can

    Correctly handle return value

    Check for correct number of arguments

    Checks for correct types of arguments, and can convert if possible and makes sense

    May still be a problem if compiler needs to convert a large value to smaller

- Prototyping frequently called static type checking

Call the function

Once the function is defined and debugged to the best of the ability of the compiler, we put the function to use.

Sample programs: twoarg.cpp—call a function to print characters

                                   lotto.cpp—calling functions to calculate lotto odds

- Arguments normally passed by value

    Copy of value is made for use by called function

    Insulates data in calling function from accidental changes

    Variables receiving data are called formal arguments or parameters

    Values passed to the called function are called actual arguments

- Local variables

    All variables declared in the function are local to that function

    Memory set aside only as long as function is executing

    Preserves data integrity

    Variables in different functions can have same name without conflict

    Declare within braces containing function definition

- Multiple arguments are separated by commas

    Type must be declared for each argument

- Using function call as argument to function

    First called function returns value to calling function

    Does not pass the function itself

Functions and arrays

Calling and using arrays in functions are special extensions of the discussion so far. Functions are a natural to process the repetitiveness of arrays.

Sample programs: arrfun1.cpp—array argument to add up cookies

                                     arrfun2.cpp—cookie array argument showing same addresses but different sizes

                                     arrfun3.cpp—using **const** to prevent modifications and manage real estate

- Then use that array variable name just like any array

- Equivalent forms of array and pointer syntax

  `arr[i] == *(ar + i)`

  `&arr[i] == ar + i`

- Usually need to pass array size as well, since C++ doesn't know number of elements in use

- Arrays and pointers

  Declaration alternatives to pass an array to a function

      `int ArName[]`

      `int * ArName`

  This is only case where the forms are synonymous

  An array name is the address of first element

  Array argument is passed by value, but the value is an address

      Result: arrays are passed by reference

      Consistent with C++'s pass-by-value approach

      Passing address rather than value save time and memory of making a copy

      Allows called function to modify elements in array

  sizeof array in calling function is total size of array but **sizeof** array in called function is size of address

  No need to use entire array in called function

- Design issues and preparation for OOP

  Size array data type to fit likely data

  If know number of elements, use static arrays

  Consider the operations that you'll execute with the data

  Bottom-up versus top-down programming

- Preventing modification of array data in called functions

  const keyword when declaring formal arguments

  Doesn't affect modifications of array in calling function or other functions

  Compiler will flag any attempt to change array

- Pointers and **const**

Make pointer point to constant data: `const int * pt = &age;`

> Then can't use `pt` to change value

> Result: `*pt` cannot be modified, but `age` can be

> `pt` can be changed to point a different `const` variable

> Can't have regular pointer point to `const` variable; otherwise, could change value

> For array of constant data, must pass with `const` in formal argument

> Use `const` whenever able to protect data integrity

Make a `const` pointer point to regular data: `int const * finger = &sloth;`

> `finger` can be used to change `sloth`

> `finger` cannot be changed to point to anything else

Make a `const` pointer point to `const` data: `const double * const stick = &trouble;`

> Unable to change either the pointer or the value pointed at

Functions and strings

Given a C++ string's unique structure, there are some special considerations in using them with functions, but they simplify things as well.

Sample programs: strgfun.cpp—count characters with string array passed to function

                                strgback.cpp—returning a string to print characters

- String representations in C++: all three are pointers-to-`char`

  Array of `char`

  String literal/quoted string constant

  Pointer-to-`char` set to string address

- Actually passing the address of a string to a function

  Use `char *` as formal parameter

  String has null terminator, so no need to pass length

  Process arrays in function using `while (*str)`

  Equivalent forms

      ```
      int fcn(char * str)
      int fct(char str[])
      ```

- Returning a string from a function

  Can't return an array from a function

  Can return the address of a string array

Functions and structures

Now we can see how a complex C++ data type is used almost exactly like any basic data type.

Sample programs: travel.cpp—compute travel time by passing and returning structures

strctfun.cpp—convert rectangular to polar coordinates

strctptr.cpp—new polar coordinates function using pointers to structures

- Pass by value

  Behave like regular single-valued variables even though hold multiple data items like arrays

  Pass by value

  Return from function normally

  Disadvantage of passing by value: Large structure takes time and memory to make new copy

  Pass address to function to pass by reference

- Passing structure addresses—by reference

  Avoids overhead of making a copy of structure

  Differences from passing by value

  > Pass address of structure using **&**

  > Declare formal parameter as pointer to structure type: `polar *`

  > Use indirect membership operator (**&**) instead of membership operator (.)

  Can pass **const** structure with data and another empty structure without **const** to receive data

Controlling a `while` loop with `cin`

Using a `while` loop with a special characteristic of `cin` can simplify loops.

- `cin` is an object of the `istream` class

- Extraction operator (`>>`) returns an object of the `istream` class

- Special case when input doesn't meet operator's expectation

  Operator returns **0**

  Accepts all numeric input when input to numeric variable

  Pass `cin.clear()` to allow further input

Recursive functions

While the benefits of functions calling themselves may not be immediately intuitively apparent, recursive functions can solve certain types of problems very effectively.

Sample programs: recur.cpp—count down using recursion

ruler.cpp—subdivide task of printing ruler

- Function calls itself

- `main()` cannot call itself

- Function must include some type of termination to break chain of calls

  Typically make call part of `if` statement

  While `if` stays true, only statements before the recursive call get executed

  When `if` becomes false, start executing statements following `if`

  Control returns to previous version of function that called current version

  On way out, function statements execute in reverse order of entry order

- Each version of function creates its own set of variables

- Ideal for tasks that break down problem into smaller problems

  Divide and conquer strategy

Pointers to functions

Extending the concepts of pointers another step forward, we examine the added flexibility made possible by using a pointer to a function rather than a regular function call.

Sample program: fun_ptr.cpp—coding estimate

- Functions have addresses just like data items

  Memory address where function's machine code is stored

  Can pass address to other functions

  Allows control over what function is called when

- Using address of function

  Address is function name without parentheses: `process(think);`

  Different from calling function with return value of function: `thought(think);`

- Declare a pointer to a function

  Specify the type of function

  > Its return value

  > Signature: argument list

  Write prototype for regular function and then replace function name with `(*ptrname)`

  > Parentheses required because of precedence

  > Pointer variable must match function pointed to both in signature and return type

  Simply use name of function without parentheses to pass the address

- Use the pointer to invoke function

  Use `(*ptrname)` as though it were a function name

  Can also use in form `ptrname(arguments)`

  First form reminds that it is a pointer

Programming tips and ideas

A handy way to avoid potential computational overflow problems for large numbers is given in Listing 7.4, `lotto.cpp`, and described in the preceding text. Basically it describes a strategy of alternating division with multiply to keep the size of the number to a minimum.

- Try to break up potentially large values of intermediate calculations into smaller values by rearranging calculations

Additional Questions

True or False

1. Every function, including `main()`, must have at least one `return` statement.

2. A function's single allowed `return` statement must be the last statement at the end of the function.

3. An array variable cannot be returned from a function by value.

4. In order for a function to return a value, the calling and called functions must have a mutually accessible memory location to store and retrieve the value, and it must be sized to hold specific data.

5. Every C++ function must have a prototype prior to the function's first call in the file.

6. It is considered good programming practice to avoid prototypes by placing the definition of a function before its first call because the compiler will run faster.

7. If the compiler finds that a call to a function is being passed a `double` when the function's prototype and definition specify a `long double` for that argument, it issues a fatal error.

8. A value passed by value cannot be changed by the called function, but a value passed by reference can be.

9. Given the odds of the Lotto in most states, putting money down is a losing proposition.

10. The notations `int *Ar` and `int arr[]` are identical and either may be substituted for the other in any part of a C++ program.

11. Given proper declarations, `Ar[i]` is equivalent to `*(arr + i)` and `&Ar[i]` is equivalent to `ar + i`, and one version of each pair can be substituted for the other in any part of a C++ program.

12. Either passing a variable by value or by using `const` will prevent the called function from modifying the data.

13. Bottom-up programming involves creating supporting functions and data structures before assembling them into a program.

14. A pointer can point to constant data, and a constant pointer can point to regular data, but a constant pointer can't point to constant data.

15. Even though a function cannot return an array, it can return the address of an array, even if it is a string array.

16. If an array is part of a structure returned from a function, that portion of the structure will contain null values because arrays can't be returned from a function.

17. One good reason to pass a pointer to a structure rather than the structure itself is because of the processing time it takes to make a copy of the structure.

18. In essence, the extraction operator is implemented as a class function in C++.

19. Recursion is often called a divide and conquer strategy because it breaks a problem down into smaller parts.

20. The following statement is a proper way to invoke the function that `ptrf` is pointing to if that function returns nothing and takes an `int` argument.

```
*ptrf(5);
```

21. The following is a proper way to invoke a function if `ppp` is a pointer to a function that returns a `double` and takes a `double` argument.

```
double temp = ppp(1.23E3);
```

Short Answers

1. Describe the following terms, and explain their use in a C++ program.

   a. `return` statement

   b. `void` functions

   c. static type checking

   d. pass by value

   e. pass by reference

   f. formal argument

   g. function parameter

   h. actual argument

   i. local variable

   j. `const` modifier

   k. bottom-up programming

   l. top-down programming

   m. recursion

2. Which of the following are valid C++ prototypes?

   a. `int myFunc(int measure);`

   b. `double measure();`

   c. `int space, int time wealth(double income);`

   d. `void tuba(void)`

   e. `long * enemy(long temp, double, int, char * str, char score, int);`

3. Describe the items that a compiler can check with C++'s use of prototypes.

4. Describe the benefits to the programmer of prototyping functions.

5. For each set of statements, is the argument passed by value or reference?

   a. `temp = doit("Charles R. Smith, Inc.");`

   b. `int scores[5] = {75, 82, 68, 100, 45};`

      `performance = avgScore(scores);`

   c. `int score = 97;`

      `grade = letterGrade(score);`

   d. `long stockNum = 93828;`

      `int temp = order(&stockNum);`

6. Given this program, for each variable used, identify whether its use is local or global in each function.

```cpp
// grade.cpp - determine final grades

#include <iostream>
using namespace std;

int letterGrade(int score);

char grade;

int main(void)
{
    int score = 89;
    char grade;

    grade = letterGrade(score);
    cout << "With a score of " << score;
    cout << ", the final grade is " << grade;

    return 1;
}

int letterGrade(int score)
{
    if (score > 0 && score <= 100)
    {
        if (score < 50)
            grade = 'F';
        else if (score < 65)
            grade = 'D';
        else if (score < 75)
            grade = 'C';
        else if (score < 87)
            grade = 'B';
        else
            grade = 'A';
    }
    else
    {
        cout << "Error in data input!";
        grade = 'X';
    }
    return grade;
}
```

7. Will the compiler flag any errors because of the variables in this program? What will the output be?

```cpp
// scope.cpp

#include <iostream>
using namespace std;

int measure(int);

int main(void)
{
    int step = 5;
    int increment = 1;
    int result;

    result = measure(step);
    cout << step << " " << increment << " " << result;

    return 0;
}
```

```
int measure(int op)
{
    if (op < 3)
        op = 25;
    else if (op > 3)
        op = 0;

    int increment = 12;
    return increment * op;
}
```

8. In the `for` loop of the `odds()` function in Listing 7.4, why is **n** not tested in the test expression as well as **p**, even though both **n** and **p** are initialized and decremented?

9. Why must a called function be provided the total number of elements in the array rather than just calculating it on its own?

10. In each of the following, what type of data will the called function receive?
```
char label[] = "This is an array of type int.";
char * pl = "This is a function of type long double.";
a)  int temp = muon(label);
b)  int temp = muon(pl);
c)  int temp = muon("Label of structure:");
```

11. If 5 is input for `temp`, what does `cin` return? What if `%` is entered by the user?
```
int temp;
cin << temp;
```

12. What happens when this program is compiled and run?
```
int main(void)
{
    int temp = 5;
    while (temp > 0)
        temp = main();

    return 0;
}
```

13. Write the appropriate statements to declare a pointer that will point at each of these functions, and then initialize the pointer, and then invoke the function.

   a. `int getdata(double need);`

   b. `void calcValue(double op1, double op2, int ind);`

   c. `void printRept(void);`

   d. `char * numCtrl(char *);`

Programming Projects

1. Write a program that calls a `void` function that takes a float argument and cuts the argument in half so that the calling program can print it. Use only one `float` variable in `main()`, and only the single argument in the called function.

2. Write a function that receives as a parameter a string array, returns a count of all the lowercase letters in the original string, and encrypts the string by increasing the ASCII value of the character by four. Use this string:
```
The smurfs are planning an attack at dawn. Warn the village.
```

The resulting encrypted string should be

```
Xli$wqyvjw$evi$tperrmrk$er$exxego$ex$he{r2$[evr$xli$zmppeki2
```

Print the original string, the number of lowercase letters, and the encrypted string.

3. You are the marketing director of Wooly Warmth, a clothing and outdoor equipment manufacturer. You have the following products in your catalog:

Item	Price	In Stock
Woolsy Sweater	$49.55	5
Sheer Bodice	$27.95	0
Inuit Parka	$95.25	8
Safari Hat	$53.35	7
African Map	$10.65	9

Write a program that will print out an inventory report. Use a structure array for the above data, pass the array to the function showCatalog(), and from that function call sumValue() that totals the value of inventory and prints that value as the last line of the report. (Total value of inventory is the sum of all prices multiplied by the number in stock.) To notify the inventory manager of stock problems, print three asterisks next to any items that are completely out of inventory.

4. Recall from the last chapter that a Fibonacci series is a series of numbers each of which, after the first two, is the sum of the two preceding numbers. Write a program to determine the nth number in the series, in the range from 1 through 30, using a recursive function. Test the input to make sure that it is numerical and that it is in the correct range.

5. Write another calculator program that performs addition, subtraction, multiplication, division, modulus, and the absolute value of the difference of two integer operands (like in Chapter 6), but also add functions to calculate the percentage that the first operand is of the second and the average of the two operands. Input the operands from the user, and then present a menu of calculation choices. Allow the input of more operands, and provide a way for the user to end the program. Write the program using pointers to functions to perform the different calculations and print the results. Use float results where appropriate, and use cin with two numeric inputs as demonstrated in this chapter. Test for appropriate error conditions in the operands. Include an error function that prints an error message for any illegal arithmetic operations showing a short description of the problem before prompting for the next input. Cast the input operands to types appropriate for the type of calculation.

For Further Discussion

1. Discuss how using local variables helps to prevent data corruption and allows the same variable name to be used in many functions in the same program.

2. What good reasons are there to use variable names in function prototypes? Why might you omit them? (Laziness isn't a valid answer!)

3. Why will sizeof in a calling function return the total array size in bytes, but in a called function to which the array is passed will only return an address size?

4. When passing data to functions, why is it a good idea to use const wherever possible?

5. In Listing 7.9, strgback.cpp, memory is allocated for an array in the buildstr function. If the scope of variables declared in a function only have the lifetime of that function, why is that array usable in main()?

Activities for Learning

1. Write a short program to find out if your compiler will issue a warning when a **long double** is passed to a function specifying an **int**. What does the compiler documentation say?

2. Run the example programs in this chapter. Experiment with changes to get a feel for how the different C++ constructs are used. Modify them to make them more general and more useful to you.

3. As an example of passing pointers to functions in a function call, check out your compiler's implementation of **qsort()**, which takes as one parameter a pointer to a function to control the sort order of the data set. If it is included with your compiler, examine the source code for **qsort()**.

Answers to Text Programming Exercises

1. Write a program that repeatedly asks you to enter pairs of numbers until at least one of the pair is zero. For each pair, the program should use a function to calculate the harmonic mean of the numbers. The function should return the answer to **main()**, which reports the result. The harmonic mean of the numbers is the inverse of the average of the inverses and can be calculated as follows:

```
    harmonic mean =  2.0 * x * y / (x + y)
//pe7-1.cpp -- harmonic mean

#include <iostream>
using namespace std;

double h_mean(double x, double y);

int main(void)
{
    double x,y;

    cout << "Enter two numbers (a 0 terminates): ";
    while (cin >> x >> y && x * y != 0)
        cout << "harmonic mean of " << x << " and "
            << y << " = " << h_mean(x,y) << "\n";
/* or do the reading and testing in two parts:
    while (cin >> x && x != 0)
    {
        cin >> y;
        if (y == 0)
            break;
            ...
*/
    cout << "Bye\n";
    return 0;
}

double h_mean(double x, double y)
{
    return 2.0 * x * y / (x + y);
}
```

2. Write a program that asks you to enter up to 10 golf scores. You should provide a means for the user to terminate input prior to entering 10 scores. The program should display all the scores on one line and report the average score. Handle input, display, and the average calculation with three separate functions.

```cpp
// pe7-2.cpp

#include <iostream>
using namespace std;

int getgolf(int ar[], int n);
void showgolf(const int ar[], int n);
double ave(const int ar[] , int n);

const int Scores = 10;

int main(void)
{
    int golfscores[Scores];

    int games = getgolf(golfscores, Scores);
    showgolf(golfscores, games);
    if (games > 0)
        cout << ave(golfscores, games) << " = average\n";
    else
        cout << "No scores!\n";

    return 0;
}

int getgolf(int ar[], int n)
{
    cout << "Enter up to " << n << " scores <q to quit>:\n";
    for (int i = 0; i < n; i++)
    {
        if (!(cin >> ar[i]))
        {
            cin.clear(); // in case more input needed later
            while (cin.get() != '\n')
                continue;
            break;
        }
    }
    return i;
}

void showgolf(const int ar[], int n)
{
    for (int i = 0; i < n; i++)
        cout << ar[i] << " ";
    cout << "\n";
}

double ave(const int ar[] , int n)
{
    double tot = 0.0;
    for (int i = 0; i < n; i++)
        tot += ar[i];
    return tot / n;
}
```

3. Here is a structure template:

```
struct box
{
    char maker[40];
    float height;
    float width;
    float length;
    float volume;
};
```

a. Write a function that passes a **box** structure by value and that displays the value of each member.

b. Write a function that passes the address of a **box** structure and that sets the **volume** member to the product of the other three dimensions.

c. Write a simple program using these two functions.

```
// pe7-3.cpp

#include <iostream>
using namespace std;

struct box {
    char maker[40];
    float height;
    float width;
    float length;
    float volume;
};

void showbox(box b);
void setbox(box * pb);

int main(void)
{
    box carton = {"Bingo Boxer", 2, 3, 5}; // no volume provided
    setbox(&carton);
    showbox(carton);
    return 0;
}

void showbox(box b)
{
    cout << "Box maker: " << b.maker
         << "\nheight: " << b.height
         << "\nwidth: " << b.width
         << "\nlength: " << b.length
         << "\nvolume: " << b.volume << "\n";
}

void setbox(box * pb)
{
    pb->volume = pb->height * pb->width * pb->length;
}
```

4. Define a recursive function that takes an integer argument and returns the factorial of that argument. Recall that 3 factorial, written **3!**, equals **3 × 2!**, and so on, with **0!** defined as **1**. In general, **n! = n * (n - 1)!**. Test it in a program that uses a loop to allow the user to enter various values for which the program reports the factorial.

```
// pe7-4.cpp

#include <iostream>
using namespace std;

double rfact(int n);

int main(void)
{
    int num;
    cout << "Enter an integer (< 0 to quit): ";
    while(cin >> num && num >= 0)
    {
        cout << num << " factorial = " << rfact(num) << "\n";
        cout << "Enter next value (<0 to quit): ";
    }
    cout << "Bye!\n";
    return 0;
}

double rfact(int n)
{
    if (n <= 1)
        return 1;
    else
        return n * rfact(n-1);
}
```

5. This exercise provides practice in writing functions dealing with arrays and structures. Below is a program skeleton. Complete it by providing the described functions.

```
#include <iostream>
using namespace std;

const int SLEN = 30;

struct student {
    char fullname[SLEN];
    char hobby[SLEN];
    int ooplevel;
};
// getinfo() has two arguments: a pointer to the first element of
// an array of student structures and an int representing the
// number of elements of the array. The function solicits and
// stores data about students. It terminates input upon filling
// the array or upon encountering a blank line for the student
// name. The function returns the actual number of array elements
// filled.
int getinfo(student pa[], int n);

// display1() takes a student structure as an argument
// and displays its contents
void display1(student st);

// display2() takes the address of student structure as an
// argument and displays the structure's contents
void display2(const student * ps);

// display3() takes the address of the first element of an array
// of student structures and the number of array elements as
// arguments and displays the contents of the structures
void display3( const student pa[], int n);

int main(void)
{
```

```
        cout << "Enter class size: ";
        int class_size;
        cin >> class_size;
        while (cin.get() != '\n')
            continue;

        student * ptr_stu = new student [class_size];
        int entered = getinfo(ptr_stu, class_size);
        for (int i = 0; i < entered; i++)
        {
            display1(ptr_stu[i]);
            display2(&ptr_stu[i]);
        }
        display3(ptr_stu, entered);
        cout << "Done\n";
        return 0;
}

// pe7-5.cpp

#include <iostream>
using namespace std;

const int SLEN = 30;

struct student {
    char fullname[SLEN];
    char hobby[SLEN];
    int ooplevel;
};
// getinfo() has two arguments: a pointer to the first
// element of an array of student structures and an int
// representing the number of elements of the array. The
// function solicits and stores data about students. It
// terminates input upon filling the array or upon
// encountering a blank line for the student name. The
// function returns the actual number of array elements
// filled.
int getinfo(student pa[], int n);

// display1() takes a student structure as an argument
// and displays its contents
void display1(student st);

// display2() takes the address of student structure as an
// argument and displays the structure's contents
void display2(const student * ps);

// display3() takes (1) the address of the first element of
// an array of student structures and (2) the number of
// array elements as arguments and displays the contents
// of the structures
void display3( const student pa[], int n);

int main(void)
{
    cout << "Enter class size: ";
    int class_size;
    cin >> class_size;
    while (cin.get() != '\n')
        continue;

    student * ptr_stu = new student[class_size];
    int entered = getinfo(ptr_stu, class_size);
```

```
            for (int i = 0; i < entered; i++)
            {
                display1(ptr_stu[i]);
                display2(&ptr_stu[i]);
            }
            display3(ptr_stu, entered);
            cout << "Done\n";
            return 0;
        }

        int getinfo(student pa[], int n)
        {
            for (int i = 0; i < n; i++)
            {
                cout << "Enter student name: ";
                cin.getline(pa[i].fullname, SLEN);
                if (pa[i].fullname[0] == '\0')
                    break;
                cout << "Enter student hobby: ";
                cin.getline(pa[i].hobby, SLEN);
                cout << "Enter student oop level: ";
                cin >> pa[i].ooplevel;
                while (cin.get() != '\n')
                    continue;
            }
            return i;
        }

        void display1(student st)
        {
            cout << st.fullname << ": " << st.hobby << ": "
                << st.ooplevel << "\n";
        }

        void display2(const student * ps)
        {
            cout << ps->fullname << ": " << ps->hobby << ": "
                << ps->ooplevel << "\n";
        }

        void display3( const student pa[], int n)
        {
            for (int i = 0; i < n; i++)
                cout << pa[i].fullname << ": " << pa[i].hobby << ": "
                    << pa[i].ooplevel << "\n";
        }
```

6. Design a function `calculate()` that takes two type `double` values, and a pointer to a function that takes two `double` arguments and returns a `double`. The `calculate()` function should also be type `double`, and it should return the value that the pointed-to function calculates using the `double` arguments to `calculate()`. For example, suppose we have this definition for the `add()` function:

```
double add(double x, double y)
{
    return x + y;
}
```

Then the function call in

```
double q = calculate(2.5, 10.4, add);
```

would cause `calculate()` to pass the value `2.5` and `10.4` to the `add()` function and then to return the `add()` return value (`12.9`).

Use these functions and at least one additional function in the add() mold in a program. The program should use a loop allowing the user to enter pairs of numbers. For each pair, use calculate() to invoke add() and at least one other function. If you are feeling adventurous, try creating an array of pointers to add()-style functions and use a loop to successively apply calculate() to a series of functions by using these pointers. Hint: here's how to declare such an array:

```
double (*pf[3])(double, double);
```

You can initialize such an array using the usual array initialization syntax and using function names as addresses.

```
//pe7-6.cpp

#include <iostream>
using namespace std;

double calculate(double x, double y, double (*pf)(double, double));
double add(double x, double y);
double sub(double x, double y);
double mean(double x, double y);

int main(void)
{
    double (*pf[3])(double,double) = {add, sub, mean};
    char * op[3] = {"sum", "difference", "mean"};
    double a, b;
    cout << "Enter pairs of numbers (q to quit): ";
    int i;
    while (cin >> a >> b)
    {
        // using function names
        cout << calculate(a, b, add) << " = sum\n";
        cout << calculate(a, b, mean) << " = mean\n";
        // using pointers
        for (i = 0; i < 3; i++)
            cout << calculate(a, b, pf[i]) << " = "
                << op[i] << "\n";
    }
    cout << "Done!\n";
    return 0;
}

double calculate(double x, double y, double (*pf)(double, double))
{
    return (*pf)(x, y);
}

double add(double x, double y)
{
    return x + y;
}

double sub(double x, double y)
{
    return x - y;
}

double mean(double x, double y)
{
    return (x + y) / 2.0;
}
```

Answers to Additional Questions

True or False

1. F	8. T	15. T
2. F	9. T	16. F
3. T	10. F	17. T
4. T	11. T	18. T
5. F	12. T	19. T
6. F	13. T	20. F
7. F—recasts it	14. F	21. T

Short Answers

1.

   a. The `return` statement is used by the called function to hand back a value of the appropriate data type to the calling function.

   b. A `void` function has no `return` value and does not require a `return` statement.

   c. Static type checking takes place at compile time and uses the function prototypes to catch data type mismatches. Such mismatches are difficult to spot at runtime.

   d. Pass by value is a term used when a value in the calling function is copied into a called function formal argument. It is the copy that is used or manipulated, not the original value.

   e. Pass by reference gives the address of the variable (or function) to the called function. The called function can thus use or manipulate the original value.

   f. A variable in a function header used to receive a value from the calling function is known as a formal parameter.

   g. A function parameter is another name for a formal argument.

   h. The value passed to the called function from the calling function is known as the actual argument.

   i. Local variables are declared in the function header or within its body. They are private to that function and can be accessed only by that function.

   j. The `const` modifier allows data to be used by a function but not modified by a function.

   k. Taking small "building blocks" of program code and piecing them together to produce a working program is known as bottom up programming.

   l. Top down design programming starts from the overall concept and breaks it down into manageable-sized tasks that can be coded.

   m. Recursion is a programming technique where a function can call itself. To be recursive, it must call itself and it must have a terminating condition. A full description is given on page 280.

2. a. Valid

    b. Valid—C++ assumes void

    c. Invalid—no multiple return types

    d. Invalid—no semicolon

    e. Valid

3. The prototype describes the function to the compiler, that is:

    a. The return data type.

    b. The number of arguments.

    c. The data type of the arguments.

4. The advantages are that the compiler can catch errors associated with return data type, number of arguments, and data type of arguments. Without this facility, errors would be allowed to move into runtime, and at this stage they can be very difficult to spot.

5. a. Reference

    b. Reference

    c. Value

    d. Reference

6. grade: Global everywhere but `main()`. Local in `main()`.

    score: Local in both functions.

7. Compiles without problem. Output: 5 1 0

8. `p` specifies the number of picks to process. It isn't necessary for both variables to be in any particular section just because the other is.

9. The called function has no way of determining the array size because all it is passed is the address of the first element.

10. In all cases, the function receives the address of a string.

11. For `5`, `cin` returns an object of the `istream` class. For `%`, it returns `0`.

12. If it compiles, it should produce a runtime error, since `main()` can't call itself in C++.

13. Substitute `(*ptrf)` for function name in each case.

    a.
```
int (*ptrf)(double need);

ptrf = getdata;

int temp = (*ptrf)(1.35E22);
```

    b.
```
void (*ptrf)(double op1, double op2, int ind);

ptrf = calcValue;

(*ptrf)(1.23E-8, 3.25E3, 7);
```

    c.
```
void (*ptrf)(void);

ptrf = printRept;

(*ptrf)();
```

    d.
```
char * (*ptrf)(char *);

ptrf = numCtrl;

char * strtmp = (*ptrf)("Procedure A-25");
```

Programming Projects

1.

```cpp
#include <iostream>
using namespace std;

void inHalf(float *);

int main(void)
{
    float aNum;
    cout << "Enter a float: ";
    cin >> aNum;

    cout << "One half of " << aNum;
    inHalf(&aNum);
    cout << " is " << aNum;
    return 0;
}

void inHalf(float * num)
{
    *num = *num / float(2.0);
}
```

2.

```cpp
// strproc.cpp - count lowercase and encrypt string

#include <iostream>
#include <cctype>
using namespace std;

int strProc(char *);

int main(void)
{
    int lowerCount;
    char str[] = "The smurfs are planning an attack at dawn.
                                Warn the village.";
    cout << str << "\n";

    lowerCount = strProc(str);
    cout << "String had " << lowerCoun << " lowercase letters.\n";
    cout << str << "\n";
    return 0;
}

int strProc(char * str)
{
    int lcount = 0;
    while(*str)
    {
        if (islower(*str))
            lcount++;
        *str = *str + 4;
        str++;
    }
    return lcount;
}
```

3.
```cpp
// strucupd.cpp

#include <iostream>
using namespace std;

const int strSize = 30;

struct catalog {
    char name[strSize];
    float price;
    int onhand;
};

float sumValue(const catalog * products, int arrNum);
void showCatalog(const catalog * prodStruc, int arrNum);

int main(void)
{
    const int arrSize = 5;
    catalog products[arrSize] = {
        {"Woolsy Sweater", 49.55, 5},
        {"Sheer Bodice", 27.95, 0},
        {"Inuit Parka", 95.25, 8},
        {"Safari Hat", 53.35, 7},
        {"African Map", 10.65, 9}
    };

    showCatalog(products, arrSize);
    return 0;
}

float sumValue(const catalog * products, int arrNum)
{
    float totalValue = 0;
    for (int i = 0; i < arrNum; i++)
        totalValue += products[i].price * products[i].onhand;
    return totalValue;
}

void showCatalog(const catalog * prodStruc, int arrNum)
{
    for (int i = 0; i < arrNum; i++)
    {
        cout << prodStruc[i].name << "\t$";
        cout << prodStruc[i].price << "\t";
        cout << prodStruc[i].onhand;
        if (prodStruc[i].onhand == 0)
            cout << " ***";
        cout << "\n";
    }
    cout << "\nTotal value of inventory: $" << sumValue(prodStruc, arrNum);
}
```

4.
```cpp
// fibona1.cpp - determine the nth number in a Fibonacci series
//               using a recursive function

#include <iostream>
using namespace std;

unsigned long fib(int nth);

int main(void)
{
```

```
        int nth;
        cout << "Enter an integer from 1 to 30: ";
        while (!(cin >> nth))
        {
            cin.clear();
            while (cin.get() != '\n')
                continue;
            cout << "Please! Enter a number: ";
        }

        // make sure input is in range
        if (nth < 1 || nth > 30)
            cout << "Sorry. Number isn't in the right range.";
        else
        {
            unsigned long fibValue;
            fibValue = fib(nth);

            cout << "\nThe value of number " << nth;
            cout << " in the series is " << fibValue << ".\n";
        }
        return 0;
}

unsigned long fib (int nth)
{
    if (nth < 3 )
    {
        return (1);
    }
    else
    {
        return( fib(nth-2) + fib(nth-1));
    }
}
```

5.

```
// calc_pf.cpp -- simple calculator using pointers to functions

#include <iostream>
using namespace std;

void showmenu(void);
void add();
void subtract();
void multiply();
void divide();
void modulus();
void absdiff();
void percent();
void average();
void errorEvent(char * msg);

int op1, op2;

int main(void)
{
    showmenu();
    int choice;

    void (*pf)();
    while (cin >> choice)
    {
```

```cpp
        cout << "Enter op1 and op2: ";
        while (cin >> op1 >> op2)
        {
            switch(choice)
            {
                case 1: pf = add; break;
                case 2: pf = subtract; break;
                case 3: pf = multiply; break;
                case 4: pf = divide; break;
                case 5: pf = modulus; break;
                case 6: pf = absdiff; break;
                case 7: pf = percent; break;
                case 8: pf = average; break;
                default: cout << "That's not a choice.\n";
            }
            cout << "\n";
            (*pf)();
            cout << "\n";
            break;
        }
        cin.clear();        // in case non-numerical entry
        showmenu();
    }
    cout << "Bye!\n";
    return 0;
}

void showmenu(void)
{
    cout << "Menu of choices:\n"
    "1) addition\n"
    "2) subtraction\n"
    "3) multiplication\n"
    "4) division\n"
    "5) modulus\n"
    "6) absolute value of difference\n"
    "7) Op 1 percent of Op 2\n"
    "8) average\n"
    "q) quit\n";
    cout << "Please enter choice 1 through 8 or q: ";
}

void add()
{
    cout << "Add: Result is " << op1 + op2 << "\n";
}
void subtract()
{
    cout << "Subtract: Result is " << op1 - op2 << "\n";
}
void multiply()
{
    cout << "Multiply: Result is " << op1 * op2 << "\n";
}
void divide()
{
    if (op2 != 0)
        cout << "Divide: Result is " << (float(op1) / float(op2)) << "\n";
    else
        errorEvent("Op 2 is zero, so can't divide.");
}
void modulus()
{
```

```
    if (op2 != 0)
            cout << "Modulus: Result is " << op1 % op2 << "\n";
        else
            errorEvent("Op 2 is zero, so can't calculate modulus.");

}
void absdiff()
{
    cout << "Absolute value of difference is ";
    cout << (op1 - op2 >= 0 ? op1 - op2 : op2 - op1) << "\n";
}
void percent()
{
    if (op2 != 0)
        cout << "Op 1 is " << (((float(op1)/float(op2))*100.0)) << "% of Op 2.\n";
    else
        errorEvent("Op 2 is zero, so can't divide for percentage.");
}
void average()
{
    cout << "Average: Result is " << (float(op1+op2)/2,0);
}
void errorEvent(char * msg)
{
    cout << "** " << msg << " ** \n";
}
```

CHAPTER 8

ADVENTURES IN FUNCTIONS

Statement of Purpose

C++ dramatically expands upon C's function capabilities. Most of the improvements were added to increase the reliability of C++ programs through both reducing coding errors and introducing OOP concepts. With the discussion of multi-file programs and storage classes, the student begins to understand the structure of an entire C++ program.

Objectives

By the end of Chapter 8, the student should understand the following concepts:

- Inline functions and when they are appropriate

- Why the compiler may reject the request for inline function

- Reference variables, the other side of pointers

- Giving a function the capability to modify data by using reference variables

- Using default arguments to cover the "normal" situation

- Function overloading/polymorphism: customizing function to the data

- Templates to partially automate function overloading to save work and reduce errors

- Template specializations to cover particular function signatures

- Breaking a program into separate files and assembling an entire C++ program

- Storage classes and how they allow finer control of variables in a program

- Scope and linkage rules

Lecture Outline

Inline functions

Now that students have a grasp of the fundamentals of functions, they can begin to fine-tune their use with inline functions

Sample program: inline.cpp—squaring a number

- Designed to speed up code execution by reducing number of function calls

  A program jumps around memory while executing

    Loops and branching

    Function calls

  Functions are stored as memory addresses

  Each function call has overhead that takes time

    Storing return address

    Putting variables on the stack

    Storing return value

- Compiler puts inline function's code into the calling procedure

  Eliminates jump to function location

  Costs memory if function is called multiple times

- Best when function is short and called many times

- Using inline functions

  Preface function header with `inline`

  Put function definition and prototype above all functions that call it

- Compiler may or may not place inline

  Too large

  Calls itself

  `inline` not implemented in compiler

- Acts just like a normal function

- Improvement over C's macros because eliminates the side effects

Reference variables

Reference variables give control over the modification of data by called functions, while making code clearer and easier to understand. Their use requires an understanding of how C++ uses variables and how the compiler makes decisions about them.

Sample programs: firstref.cpp—counting rodents & rats

                                     secref.cpp—trying to change a reference with rats & bunnies

                                     swaps.cpp—comparing references and pointers to swap values

cubes.cpp—danger of letting function alter data

strtref.cpp—structure references with Rick "Fortran" Looper

- New C++ derived type
- Name that acts as a name, or alternate name, for a previously defined variable
- Main use is as a formal argument to a function, so function has access to actual data

  Alternative to pointers for large structures

  Essential for classes
- Creating reference variable

  Declare using form `int & rodents = rats;`

  The ampersand is not the address operator

  Reference variable points to same address as other variable

  Still able to use a pointer to variable as well

  Must initialize when declaring it

    Assigning a value later changes the value of the original variable

  Cannot change reference—acts like a `const`
- Using as function parameters

  Makes the variable name in the function an alias for variable in calling program

  Gives called function direct access to the data

  Arguments in calling and called functions look the same as those passed by value

  Look at function prototype and definition to find whether passed by value or reference

    By value: no operators

    Pointer: dereferencing operator `*`

    By reference: reference operator `&`
- To prevent called function from altering referenced value, use `const`
- Must pass a variable that can be referenced to the function
- Temporary variables

  Generated by compiler if actual argument doesn't match a reference argument

    Correct type but isn't an `lvalue`

    Wrong type but can be easily converted

  `Lvalue` is data type that can be referenced

    Variable

    Array variable

    Array element

    Structure member

    Reference

    Dereference pointer

  Non-`lvalues` include

Literal constants

Expressions with multiple terms

Temporary variables last for the duration of the called function

Permitted only if argument is a `const` reference

If function can modify values, they are lost at end of function

Reasons to declare reference arguments with `const`

Protects data from inadvertent modifications

Allows function to process both `const` and non-`const` actual arguments

Allows compiler to use temporary variables as necessary

- References with structures

Structures were the main reason for introduction of references

Use in same manner as with basic data types

- Allows use of a function as an argument to another function that calls for a reference

Useful for class design for overloading operators

- Reference return type

Makes it possible to assign a value to a function invocation

Acts as an alias for the referred-to variable

Also useful for operator redefinition

Data object must continue to exist after called function ends

Have function return reference or pointer that was passed as an argument, or

Use `new` to create new storage

Best if storage created with `new` is created and deleted in the same function

- Reasons to use reference arguments

Allow alteration of data in called function

Speed up program to pass reference rather than large data object

These are the same reasons to use pointer arguments

- Guidelines if function uses passed data without modifying it:

If small, pass by value

If array, must use pointer, but use with `const`

If large, use `const` pointer or `const` reference to save time and memory

If class object, use `const` reference (sometimes required)

- Guidelines if function modifies passed data:

If built-in data type, use pointer

If array, must use pointer

If structure, use reference or pointer

If class object, use reference

Default arguments

C++ introduced default arguments that allow function calls using only the arguments that change from call to call, eliminating the need to constantly enter redundant data.

Sample program: left.cpp—extract left n characters from string

- New with C++
- Value is used automatically if argument omitted from function call

  Passing a value for the default argument overrides the default

- Good for situation where argument value is normally one value, but occasionally need to override
- Define in function prototype

  Initialize the argument in the prototype

  Must use defaults from right to left

  Can't skip default arguments in function call

  Function header does not show the default

Function polymorphism/overloading

C Function overloading is a key feature of OOP and is fully implemented by C++. Multiple definitions with a single function name enable the student to take the same actions with different data. This feature is not available in C, which is not an OOP language.

Sample program: leftover.cpp—`left()` function with overloading

- Allows use of multiple functions with same name

  Usually the functions do the same thing, but with different argument lists

      Function signature

      Differ in number or type of arguments or both

  Compiler uses context of function to decide which form to use

- Important to use correct argument types when calling function

  C++ will try to use standard type conversion to force match

  If multiple versions match: compiler error

  Signatures that only appear different can't coexist

      Reference to a type and type itself considered same signature

  Compiler considers `const` and non-`const` different

- Return type of function doesn't determine which version used
- Must have function prototype and definition for each version
- Use of function overloading

  Careful to not overuse

  Different versions should perform basically same task

Default arguments may achieve same end, using less memory and keeping simple

Use when there are different types of arguments

Function templates

Templates take function overloading one step further, using the compiler to choose which multiple function definitions are created for particular data.

Sample programs: funtemp.cpp—swap function for different types

twotemps.cpp—swap function with overloaded templates

twoswap.cpp—swap with specialization

- Generic function description for overloading functions
- Compiler generates function for each signature
- Saves programming time and reduces errors
- Definition

  Specify arbitrary type in statement before prototype: `template <class Any>`

  Word `<class>` can be replaced by `<typename>` in modern compilers

  Use type name `Any` as type of arguments

  Can specify specific data types for some arguments
- Template does not create functions; tells compiler how to define functions
- Templates don't make code shorter
- Overloading templates

  Use when algorithm varies with data type

  Need distinct function signatures
- Can convert `const` to non-`const` by casting away `const`

  May change with final standard specification
- Explicit specializations

  Compiler automatically uses specialized function definition if signature matches exactly

  First Generation Approach

    Use regular function prototype specifying all argument types

    Can lead to unexpected results, such as different definition in header file with same name

  Second Generation Approach `void swap<int>(int, &a, int & b);`

    Include `<type>` in both prototype and function definition header

  Third Generation Approach `template<> void swap<int>(int, &a, int & b);`

    Prototype and definition proceeded by `template<>`
- Selection of function by compiler

  Phase 1: Assemble a list of candidate functions. These are functions and function templates with the same name as the called function.

Phase 2: From the candidate functions, assemble a list of viable functions. These are functions with the correct number of arguments and in which there is an implicit conversion sequence.

Refer to Table 8.1: Trivial conversions allowed for an exact match.

Phase 3: Determine whether there is a best viable function. If so, use it. Otherwise, error.

Separate compilation

Breaking a programming project into multiple files aids with code management and saves programming time by compiling only the parts of a program that have changed.

Sample program: coordin.h—coordinates conversion with three files

- C++ encourages separating component functions into separate files

  Compile only changed files

  Easier to manage large programs

  Compiler environments provide code management tools

  Eliminates duplicates of structure and prototype definitions

- Divide into three parts

  Header file with structure declarations and prototypes

  Common components contained in header file

  Source code file with structure-related functions

  Source code file with code that calls those functions

- Specify `#include` with quotations so compiler first looks in program's directory for header files

- Project file includes source only

  Headers managed with `#include` directives

Storage classes

This section is a review of what the student has learned so far about C++ storage classes, preparing for the extensions coming next.

Sample program: auto.cpp—scope demonstrations with Texas and year

- Review of data storage schemes and how long preserved in memory

  Automatic variables declared inside a function definition

     Memory freed at termination of function

  Static variables defined outside of a function or using `static`

     Persist for entire program

  Dynamic storage allocated using `new`

     Persist until deleted or program ends

Scope and linkage

What parts of a program can "see" particular variables? How does C++ handle cases where variables with the same name can potentially be in scope at the same time?

Sample programs: external.cpp—different types of variables for global warming

                                twofile.cpp—external and static external with tom, dick, and harry

- Scope describes how widely visible a name is in a program

    Local or Block scope: only within block where it is defined

    Global or File scope: throughout file after it is defined

    Class scope: within the class it is defined

    Namespace scope: within the declarative region where it is used

    C++ functions have file, class, or namespace scope, except for class member functions

- Linkage determines which names are usable where

    Internal linkage: usable only in current file

    External linkage: usable in other files to refer to same variable or data

    Internal linkage

        Using **static** modifier with external makes local to file containing it

    External linkage

        Only one file can contain external definition for variable

        Other files using variable must use **extern**

Automatic variables

Automatic variables are the workhorses of functions, and their correct use makes for the best functions that are simple and effective.

- Function parameters and variables defined inside a block
- Local scope: determines which of any duplicate names are used in the function
- New definition hides any other duplicate names currently in scope
- **auto** keyword indicates automatic variables explicitly, but not required

    Perhaps use to indicate intentional reuse of a global variable's name

- Stack usage with automatic variables

    Memory used by variables grows and shrinks during program execution

    Stack is a block of memory allocated for automatic variables

    Default stack size depends on implementation, but usually can change

    Program uses pointers to keep track of top and bottom of stack

        Top pointer points to next available memory location

        Puts function's variables on stack when starting execution and repositions top pointer

        At end of function, relocates top pointer to position right before function call

    Last-in, first-out design

register variables

The use of `register` variables can speed execution significantly.

- Requests that compiler put that variable in a CPU register
- Registers are accessed faster
- Preface type with `register` when declare variable
- Compiler may not comply if `register` isn't available or if it doesn't fit
- Most modern compilers already use `register` variables efficiently

Static storage class

Static variables give the programmer a say in the scope of variables, allowing selected data to be hidden from other parts of the program.

Sample program: static.cpp—sum of string lengths using `static`

- Duration is for entire program
- Not stored on stack: memory needed doesn't change during execution
- `static` variables, arrays, and structures set to `0` if not initialized
- External: available to all files in program

    Defined outside of a function

    Use in any function that follows declaration

    Also called global variables

    Automatic variables hide externals

    `extern` keyword can redeclare previously defined external variable to document use of global

    Can initialize variable only if allocating memory

- `static`: in single function

    Exists even when function not executing

    Preserves value between function calls

    Program initializes at startup

- External static: all functions in a single file
- Uses of word `static` in C++ program

    Variable persists for duration of program

    How widely variable is known: scope and linkage

- Use scope resolution operator `::` to access hidden variables
- Avoid globals to protect data
- Use `const` with global variables to protect data

Storage class qualifiers

The storage class qualifiers give greater control over variables and the program's interactions with its environment.

- Qualifiers provide additional information about storage
- `volatile`

  Value in that memory location may be altered by another program

  Allows compiler to optimize code as a whole

- `mutable`

  Allows alteration of a structure member even if structure variable is `const`

- `const`

  `const` external variable has internal linkage by default

  Includes `static` keyword implicitly

  Makes it easier to include `const` variables in header files

  > Prevents error having declarations in multiple files

  Use `extern` keyword in all files using constant to override

  Must initialize the variable

  `const` declared in a block have block scope

Function storage classes

Functions are similar to variables in some ways and have their own storage classes.

- All functions automatically have `static` storage class
- By default, all functions are external linkage

  Can use `extern`, but is optional

- Use `static` to give function file scope

  Apply both to prototype and definition

  Then able to use the same function name in another file without conflict

  Avoid conflicting prototype in header file

- `inline` functions have internal linkage by default
- Where C++ finds functions

  If `static`, look only in that file

  Otherwise, looks in all program files

  > Error if finds multiple definitions

  Then searches libraries

  So naming a function the same as a library function overrides the library version

Dynamic allocation storage classes

Dynamic memory has its own rules in C++, bestowing greater power but also more responsibility on the programmer.

- Storage classes don't apply to dynamic memory

- Controlled by `new` and `delete` operators, not by scope and linkage

    `new` and `delete` can be in separate functions

    Dynamic memory isn't LIFO like regular variables

- Storage classes do apply to pointers to dynamic memory

    If goes out of scope, can't reference or `delete` the block of memory

    Usually freed when program ends

Namespaces

Names in C++ can refer to variables, structures, enumerations, classes, class members, and structure members. When names are drawn from more than one library source, there is a potential for conflict. Such conflicts are known as namespace problems, and modern C++ compilers provide namespace facilities to minimize these problems.

- Traditional C++ namespaces

- Declarative Region is the region in which a declaration is made.

- Global declaration

- Local declaration

- Potential Scope: begins at the point of declaration and extends to the end of its declarative region.

- Actual Scope: is the region where reference can occur

- Hidden variables: global variables will be hidden by a local variable of the same name within a declarative region

- New namespace features

- C++ now adds the capability to create namespaces

- New kind of declarative region in which to declare names

- Can be located at a global or local level or nested inside other namespaces

- New keyword `using`

- `using declaration` adds a particular name from a given namespace to a declarative region

- `using directives` makes all names from a given namespace available to a declarative region

Additional Questions

True or False

1. An `inline` function permits multiple function definitions for different function signatures.

2. The `reference` variable is new with C++ and is a derived data type.

3. When using a `reference` variable in a function, accepted practice is to declare it in the calling function and initialize it in the called function.

4. Since pointers are very similar to references, a value can be assigned to a function that returns a pointer.

5. If a function returns a reference or pointer to a data object, the object can neither be deleted nor used when the reference or pointer ceases to exist.

6. For a function with a default argument and a regular argument, it is not necessary to include a value in the function call for the second argument, but at least one argument must be passed.

7. For function signatures to be considered the same, the argument types and names must match, and the functions' data type must be the same.

8. To specify a particular data type in a function template, include that data type instead of the class name in that position in the argument list.

9. Function templates can be overloaded, much as regular functions can.

10. After a constant variable has been declared, there is no way to modify the value.

11. A specialization in a C++ program is a function with the same name as a template, but with a signature with specified data types.

12. Breaking up a program in a single file is simply a matter of copying functions to different files and recompiling.

13. Variables that pass to a function as parameters and those declared within the function block are both automatically `auto` variables.

14. Using the `auto` keyword in a function changes the scope of the variable.

15. Using a `register` variable can speed up program execution, but the compiler may not actually store the value in a register.

16. If a `static` variable is not initialized, C++ initializes it to `0` during the first execution of the function.

17. The `extern` keyword can only be used with variables that are defined in another file.

18. In C++, a variable can be initialized in a declaration only if the declaration actually allocated memory for the variable.

19. Use of the `volatile` keyword allows the compiler to allocate more storage for `register` variables.

20. An external `const` definition is equivalent to a `static` external definition.

21. The two function prototypes below are exactly the same.
    ```
    extern int sweep(double precise);
    int sweep(double precise);
    ```

22. Namespaces are used to make all library contents global.

23. The `using Jill::pal;` directive adds the variable `pal` to the declarative region in which it occurs.

24. An unnamed namespace offers an alternative to static external variables.

Short Answers

1. Describe the following terms, and explain their use in a C++ program.

    a. `inline` functions

    b. `#define` statement

    c. `reference` variables

    d. default argument

    e. function polymorphism

    f. function overloading

    g. function signature

    h. function template

    i. `"proga.h"` versus `<ctype.h>` form

    j. scope

    k. linkage

    l. external scope

    m. internal scope

    n. namespace scope

    o. `automatic variable`

    p. stack

    q. `Register variable`

    r. const

    s. volatile

    t. `mutable`

    u. storage class qualifier

2. Explain when it is appropriate to specify an `inline` function. What is the compiler guaranteed to do?

3. Modify the following program so that it uses `printAst()` as an `inline` function.

```
#include <iostream.h>
void printAst(const int times);
int main(void)
{
int rep;
cout << "Enter the number of asterisks to print: ";
cin >> rep;
printAst(rep);
return 0;
}
void printAst(const int times)
{
for (int i = 0; i < times; i++)
cout << "*";
}
```

4. What specifically does this code do? What are the values of all the variables after it executes?

```
Int grade = 12;
int forest = 125;
int & trees = grade;
trees = forest;
```

5. For each of the following, what type of variables does street receive?

    a. void street(`int & main`)

    b. double street(`long main, short second`)

    c. void street(`int * main, const char grid, char * location`)

    d. char street(`double main, char * founder, int repair = 3`)

6. Refer to the `printAst()` function in question 3 above and the declarations below. For each function call, will the function use a temporary or regular variable?

    ```
    Long result = 22;
    int scores[5] = {99, 85, 87, 92, 56};
    int * pi = result;
    char grade = 0x46;
    ```

    a. `printAst(result);`

    b. `printAst(scores[0]);`

    c. `printAst(*pi);`

    d. `printAst(grade);`

    e. `printAst(result + scores[2]);`

    f. `printAst(grade + *pi);`

    g. `printAst(sumAr(scores)); //sumAr returns an int value`

    h. `printAst(14);`

    i. `printAst(scores[4]);`

7. Why is it best to use a `reference` argument as a reference to `const` data?

8. Using the function `printAst()` in question 3 above, is this call valid?

    `PrintAst(rep) = rep+4;`

9. If a program must run in tight memory, is it better to pass a large structure argument to a function by value, by reference, or as a pointer, assuming that any of the three would work and be allowed? Why? How about if the program needed maximum execution speed?

10. In general, how should an argument be passed to a function in the following cases? Give all of the reasonable alternatives.

    a. A constant structure containing a member for the name and part number for each part in a luxury car

    b. A structure in which five of the six integer members will be updated by the function

    c. A class object is passed that will not be changed

    d. A `long` that will not be modified by the function

    e. A class object that will be changed

    f. A constant array

    g. An `int` that is put in the call to the function as `&beets`

    h. An array in which elements `25` and `123` will be swapped

11. Write an appropriate function prototype and definition for each of the following. Fill in any details needed to make it a complete prototype or definition.

    a. Has an `int` argument with a default of `10`, two `double` arguments, and a pointer to `char`

    b. Two `char` arguments which default to `a` and `A` respectively, and a reference to a double

    c. A pointer to a constant `short`, a `long` with a default of `1,425`, and a pointer to a function that returns a structure of type `beans`

12. Is this a valid set of overloaded functions? For each line, state whether it will work relative to other lines and why.

    a. `char category(const char *, int);`

    b. `char category(char * avenue, int & storage);`

  c. `char category(char, double pattern);`

  d. `char category(char * avenue, int & storage, long pizza);`

  e. `long category(char * avenue, int & storage);`

  f. `char category(const char * classType, int horses);`

13. Break Listing 8.4 into a header file for the prototypes, source code file for swap functions, and a source code file for main0. Compile it to make sure that it works and that the results are the same as shown in the text.

14. For the following program, make a list of each variable name used and describe its storage class, scope, and linkage.

```
//visible.cpp ñ variable scopes
int eat(long c);
int sqrit(int c);
int cubeit(int apple);
char type = 'Z';
int main(void)
{
int a = 12;
static int b = 25;
int c;
long apple = 100000;

c = eat(apple);
{ // block 1
int c;
c = sqrit(b);
}
{ // block 2
c = cubeit(a);
}
return 0;
}
int eat(long c)
{
int apple = 2;
long b;
b = (c * apple);
return int(b % 3L);
}
int sqrit(int c)
{
int a = 2;
return c * c * a;
}
int cubeit(int apple)
{
return apple * apple * apple;
}
```

15. For visible.cpp in question 14, describe what happens to the stack when the program executes.

16. Explain how the potential scope and actual scope of a variable may be different.

Programming Projects

1. Write a program using function overloading that will print any of the following: string literal, string array, all or part of array of `char`, or a `long`. Use the following to print:

```
String literal: Now printing a string literal.
    String array: Now printing a string array.
    Entire array of char: Array of chars.
    First ten elements of same array of char: Array of c
    A long: 125365
```

Define each of the overloaded functions separately. For each item printed, prefix the output with a `PrintX:`, where X is a unique number for each function. The output should look like this, but with numbers for the Xs:

```
PrintX: Now printing a string literal.
PrintX: Now printing a string array.
PrintX: Array of chars.
PrintX: Array of c
PrintX: Printing a long: 125365L
```

2. Modify the program in question 1 to use templates instead of individually defined functions.

For Further Discussion

1. Why is using global variables considered to be a bad programming practice unless required? In what situations might you use global variables?

2. Given the following program fragment:

```cpp
#include <iostream>
#include <cstring>
using namespace std;

namespace Lord
{
    char hero[20];
    char author[20];
    int pages;
}

namespace Hobbit
{
    char hero[20];
    char author[20];
    int pages;
}

main()
{
    // Add your code here

    return (0);
}
```

Add code to the main program that will initialize the names of the heroes of each book using the scope resolution operator to qualify the names. The hero of *The Hobbit* is Bilbo Baggins; the hero of *Lord Of the Rings* is Frodo Baggins.

Activities for Learning

Run the example programs in this chapter. Experiment with changes to get a feel for how the different C++ constructs are used. Modify them to make them more general and more useful to you.

Answers to Text Programming Exercises

1. Write a function that normally takes one argument, the address of a string, and prints that string once. However, if a second, type **int** argument is provided and is nonzero, the function prints the string a number of times equal to the number of times that function has been called to that point. (Yes, this is a silly function, but

it makes you use some of the techniques discussed in this chapter.) Use the function in a simple program that demonstrates how the function works.

```cpp
// pe8-1.cpp
#include <iostream>
using namespace std;
void silly(const char * s, int n = 0);
int main(void)
{
    char * p1 = "Why me?\n";

    silly(p1);
    for (int i = 0; i < 3; i++)
    {
        cout << i << " = i\n";
        silly(p1, i);
    }
    cout << "Done\n";
    return 0;
}
void silly(const char * s, int n)
{
    static int uses = 0;

    int lim = ++uses;
    if (n == 0)
        lim = 1;
    for (int i = 0; i < lim; i++)
        cout << s;
}
```

2. Below is a program skeleton. Complete it by providing the described functions and prototypes. Note that there should be two **show()** functions, each using default arguments. Use **const** arguments when appropriate. Note that **set()** should use **new** to allocate sufficient space to hold the designated string. The techniques used here are similar to those used in designing and implementing classes.

```cpp
#include <iostream>
#include <cstring>      // for strlen(), strcpy()
using namespace std;

struct stringy {
    char * str;         // points to a string
    int ct;         // length of string (not counting '\0')
    };

// prototypes for set(), show(), and show() go here
int main(void)
{
    stringy beany;
    char testing[] = "Reality isn't what it used to be.";

    set(beany, testing);    // first argument is a reference,
            // allocates space to hold copy of testing,
            // sets str member of beany to point to the
            // new block, copies testing to new block,
            // and sets ct member of beany
    show(beany);         // prints member string once
    show(beany, 2);     // prints member string twice
    testing[0] = 'D';
    testing[1] = 'u';
    show(testing);     // prints testing string once
    show(testing, 3);     // prints testing string thrice
    show("Done!");
    return 0;
}
```

Here is the complete program:

```
#include <iostream >
#include <string>    // for strlen(), strcpy()
using namespace std;

struct stringy {
    char * str;        // points to a string
    int ct;            // length of string (not counting '\0')
    };

void show(const char *str, int cnt =  1);
void show(const stringy & bny, int cnt = 1);
void set(stringy & bny, const char * str);

int main(void)
{
    stringy beany;
    char testing[] = "Reality isn't what it used to be.";

    set(beany, testing);    // first argument is a reference,
            // allocates space to hold copy of testing,
            // sets str member of beany to point to the
            // new block, copies testing to new block,
            // and sets ct member of beany
    show(beany);         // prints member string once
    show(beany, 2);    // prints member string twice
    testing[0] = 'D';
    testing[1] = 'u';
    show(testing);    // prints testing string once
    show(testing, 3);    // prints testing string thrice
    show("Done!");
    return 0;
}

void show(const char *str, int cnt)
{
    while(cnt-- > 0)
    {
            cout << str;
    }
}

void show(const stringy & bny, int cnt)
{
    while(cnt-- > 0)
    {
            cout << bny.str;
    }
}

void set(stringy & bny, const char * str)
{
    bny.ct = strlen(str);
    bny.str = new char[bny.ct+1];
    strcpy(bny.str, str);
}
```

3. Here is header file:

```
// golf.h - for pe8-3.cpp

const int Len = 40;
struct golf
{
```

```
    char fullname[Len];
    int handicap;
};

// function solicits name and handicap from user
// returns 1 if name is entered, 0 if name is empty string
int setgolf(golf & g);

// function sets golf structure to provided name, handicap
void setgolf(golf & g, const char * name, int hc);

// function resets handicap to new value
void handicap(golf & g, int hc);

// function displays contents of golf structure
void showgolf(const golf & g);
```

Put together a multifile program based on this header. One file, named golf.cpp, should provide suitable function definitions to match the prototypes in the header file. A second file should contain main() and should demonstrate all the features of the prototyped functions. For example, a loop should solicit input for an array of golf structures and terminate when the array is full or when the user enters an empty string for golfer's name. The program should use only the prototyped functions to access the golf structures.

```
// pe8-golf.h - for pe8-3.cpp

const int Len = 40;
struct golf
{
    char fullname[Len];
    int handicap;
};

//   function solicits name and handicap from user
//   returns 1 if name is entered, 0 if name is empty string
int setgolf(golf & g);

// function sets golf structure to provided name, handicap
void setgolf(golf & g, const char * name, int hc);

// function resets handicap to new value
void handicap(golf & g, int hc);

// function displays contents of golf structure
void showgolf(const golf & g);

// pe8-golf.cpp - for pe8-3.cpp
#include <iostream>
using namespace std;
#include "pe8-golf.h"
#include <string.h>

//   function solicits name and handicap from user
// returns 1 if name is entered, 0 if name is empty string
int setgolf(golf & g)
{
    cout << "Please enter golfer's full name: ";
    cin.getline(g.fullname, Len);
    if (g.fullname[0] == '\0')
        return 0;                    // premature termination
    cout << "Please enter handicap for " << g.fullname << ": ";
    while (!(cin >> g.handicap))
    {
        cin.clear();
        cout << "Please enter an integer: ";
    }
```

continues

```
        while (cin.get() != '\n')
            continue;
        return 1;
    }

// function sets golf structure to provided name, handicap
void setgolf(golf & g, const char * name, int hc)
{
    strcpy(g.fullname, name);
    g.handicap = hc;
}

// function resets handicap to new value
void handicap(golf & g, int hc)
{
    g.handicap = hc;
}

// function displays contents of golf structure
void showgolf(const golf & g)
{
    cout << "Golfer:   " << g.fullname << "\n";
    cout << "Handicap: " << g.handicap << "\n\n";
}
// pe8-3.cpp
#include <iostream>
using namespace std;
#include "pe8-golf.h"
// link with pe8-golf.cpp
const int Mems = 5;
int main(void)
{
    golf team[Mems];

    cout << "Enter up to " << Mems << " golf team members:\n";
    for (int i = 0; i < Mems; i++)
        if (setgolf(team[i]) == 0)
            break;
    for (int j = 0; j < i; j++)
        showgolf(team[j]);
    setgolf(team[0], "Fred Norman", 5);
    showgolf(team[0]);
    handicap(team[0], 3);
    showgolf(team[0]);

    return 0;
}
```

Answers to Additional Questions

True or False

1. F	7. F	13. T	19. F
2. T—recast to basic type	8. T	14. F	20. T
3. F	9. T	15. T	21. T
4. F	10. F	16. T	22. F
5. T	11. T	17. T	23. T
6. T	12. F	18. T	24. T

Short Answers

1.

a) An `inline` function in C++ is coded in exactly the same manner as a normal C++ definition except it is prefixed by the keyword `inline`. When compiled, the machine code is "embedded" into the final exe every time the function is called. This saves on the time overhead of normal C++ function calls.

b) The `#define` statement is used to provide a macro that can be placed into the final code at each occurrence.

c) A reference is a name that acts as an alternative name for a previously defined variable. It provides an alternative to pointers.

d) A default argument is a value that is used automatically if the corresponding actual argument is omitted from the function call.

e) Function polymorphism allows multiple functions to have the same name but different numbers and types of input parameters.

f) Function overloading is another name for function polymorphism.

g) The function signature is its name and list of parameters.

h) Function templates are generic function descriptions, which do not define the function in terms of any particular data type. The actual data type is defined later by the programmer.

i) A library header file enclosed in quotes is stored in the working directory. A library header file enclosed in angle brackets is stored in the directory specified in the C++ `include` path.

j) Scope describes how widely visible a name is in a file.

k) Linkage describes how a name can be shared in different units.

l) A name with external linkage can be shared across files.

m) A name with internal linkage can only be shared by functions within a single file.

n) Variables declared in a namespace have namespace scope.

o) An automatic variable is local to a function and is automatically created as the function is called. It terminates automatically as the function is terminated.

p) The stack is used to store automatic variables. It grows and shrinks depending on the number of automatic variables in existence.

q) A register variable tells the compiler to use a CPU register instead of the stack to handle a particular variable.

r) The `const` modifier is used to tell the compiler that a variable once initialized should not be modified by the program.

s) The `volatile` keyword indicates that the value in a memory location can be altered.

t) The qualifier `mutable` is used to indicate that a member of a structure can be altered even if it is declared as `const`.

u) Storage class qualifiers provide additional information about storage. The most common is `const`.

2. Use an `inline` function when it is short (preferably can fit on one line) and is called many times. The compiler can opt to not make the function `inline`.

3. Simply add the `inline` keyword before the function prototype and definition, move the definition to before `main()`, and make the function a single line:

```
#include <iostream>
using namespace std;

inline void printAst(int times);
inline void printAst(int times)
{for (int i = 0; i < times; i++)    cout << "*";}

int main(void)
{
    int rep;
    cout << "Enter the number of asterisks to print: ";
    cin >> rep;
    printAst(rep);
    return 0;
}
```

4. Declares and initializes grade to **12** and forest to **125**, and then sets trees as a reference variable to grade. The value in grade and trees is then set to **125**, the value of forest. At completion, all variables are **125**.

5. Street receives these variables:

   a. `int` reference variable

   b. a regular `long` and regular `short`

   c. an int `pointer`, a constant `char`, a pointer to `char`

   d. a regular `double`, a pointer to `char`, a regular `int` with a default of 3

6. a. times is temporary

   b. times is scores[0]

   c. times is pi which is result

   d. times is temporary

   e. times is temporary

   f. times is temporary

   g. times is temporary

   h. times is temporary

   i. times is scores[4]

7. a. Prevents programming errors that alter data

   b. Function can process both `const` and non-`const` data

   c. Function can generate appropriate temporary variables

8. No—`printAst()` doesn't return a reference.

9. Either a reference or a pointer because the structure is not copied, requiring more memory to hold the copy. Also either a reference or pointer for fast execution, because the program doesn't need to take the time to copy the structure.

10. a. `const` pointer or `const` reference

    b. reference or pointer

    c. `const` reference

    d. by value

    e. by reference

f. `const` pointer

g. pointer

h. pointer

11. All default variables must be the rightmost arguments.

   a. `void theFunc(char *, double, double, int temp = 10);`

   `void theFunc(char * report, double rpt1, double rpt2, int temp)`

   b. `void theFunc(double &, char first = 'a', char second = 'A');`

   `void theFunc(double & stuff, char first, char second)`

   c. `void theFunc(beans * pf, constant * short, long count = 1425L);`

   `void theFunc(beans * pf, constant * short pants, long count)`

12. No, set is not valid.

   a. Invalid—duplicate of f. Line f merely adds variable names to the prototype.

   b. Invalid—duplicate of e. Line e has a different return, which is irrelevant.

   c. Valid—unique signature.

   d. Valid—only prototype with three arguments, so signature is unique.

   e. Invalid—duplicate of b.

   f. Invalid—duplicate of a.

13. swap1.cpp:
```
#include <iostream>
using namespace std;
#include "swaph.h"
int main(void)
{
    int wallet1 = 300;
    int wallet2 = 350;

    cout << "wallet1 = $" << wallet1;
    cout << " wallet2 = $" << wallet2 << "\n";

    cout << "Using references to swap contents:\n";
    swapr(wallet1, wallet2);   // pass variables
    cout << "wallet1 = $" << wallet1;
    cout << " wallet2 = $" << wallet2 << "\n";

    cout << "Using pointers to swap contents:\n";
    swapp(&wallet1, &wallet2); // pass addresses of variables
    cout << "wallet1 = $" << wallet1;
    cout << " wallet2 = $" << wallet2 << "\n";

    cout << "Trying to use passing by value:\n";
    swapv(wallet1, wallet2);   // pass values of variables
    cout << "wallet1 = $" << wallet1;
    cout << " wallet2 = $" << wallet2 << "\n";
    return 0;
}
swap2.cpp
#include "swaph.h"
void swapr(int & a, int & b)    // use references
{
    int temp;
```

continues

```
        temp = a;        // use a, b for values of variables
        a = b;
        b = temp;
    }

    void swapp(int * p, int * q)     // use pointers
    {
        int temp;

        temp = *p;       // use *p, *q for values of variables
        *p = *q;
        *q = temp;
    }

    void swapv(int a, int b)         // try using values
    {
        int temp;

        temp = a;        // use a, b for values of variables
        a = b;
        b = temp;
    }
    swaph.h
    void swapr(int & a, int & b);    // a, b are aliases for ints
    void swapp(int * p, int * q);    // p, q are addresses of ints
    void swapv(int a, int b);        // a, b are new variables
```

14. type: external, file scope, external linkage

```
    a in main(): automatic, function block scope, internal linkage
    a in sqrit(): automatic, function block scope, internal linkage
    b in main(): static, function block scope, internal linkage
    b in eat(): automatic, function block scope, internal linkage
    c in function block of main(): automatic, function block scope
    except for in block 1, internal linkage
    c in block 1 of main(): automatic, block scope, internal linkage
    c in eat(): automatic, function block scope, internal linkage
    c in sqrit(): automatic, function block scope, internal linkage
    apple in main(): automatic, function block scope, internal linkage
    apple in eat(): automatic, function block scope, internal linkage
    apple in cubeit(): automatic, function block scope, internal linkage
```

15. When main() starts, variables a, c, and apple are put on the stack.

```
    When eat() is called, c, apple, and b are put on the stack, and removed when the eat()
    ends.
    When block 1 begins, c is put on the stack.
    When sqrit() is called, c and a are put on the stack and removed when sqrit() ends.
    When block 1 finishes, c is popped off the stack.
    When cubeit() is called, apple is put on the stack and removed when completed.
    When main() ends, variables a, c, and apple are removed from the stack.
```

16. The potential scope of a variable is from the point from which it is declared to the end of that declarative region. However, if a local variable of the same name is declared, for instance, within a function in that declarative region, the local variable takes precedence and the first variable is hidden and thus cannot be referenced.

Programming Projects

1. Without templates:

```
    // printer.cpp - print a variety of types
    #include <iostream>
    using namespace std;
```

```
void print(char * conStr);
void print(char * chrStr, int prtNum);
void print(long lngNum);
int main(void)
{
    char charArr[] =
        {'A','r','r','a','y',' ','o','f',' ','c','h','a','r','s','.'};
    char strArr[] = "Now printing a string array.";
    long longNum = 125365;

    print("Now printing a string literal.");
    print(strArr);
    print(charArr, 15);
    print(charArr, 10);
    print(longNum);

    return 0;
}
void print(char * conStr)
{
    cout << "Print1: " << conStr << "\n";
}
void print(char * chrStr, int prtNum)
{
    cout << "Print2: ";
    for (int i = 0; i < prtNum; i++)
        cout << chrStr[i];
    cout << "\n";
}
void print(long lngNum)
{
    cout << "Print3: Printing a long: " << lngNum << "L\n";
}
```

2. Using the old form:

```
// printert.cpp - print a variety of types
#include <iostream.h>
template <class Any>
void print(Any obj);
void print(char * chrStr, int prtNum);

int main(void)
{
    char charArr[] =
        {'A','r','r','a','y',' ','o','f',' ','c','h','a','r','s','.'};
    char strArr[] = "Now printing a string array.";
    long longNum = 125365;

    print("Now printing a string literal.");
    print(strArr);
    print(charArr, 15);
    print(charArr, 10);
    print(longNum);

    return 0;
}

template <class Any>
void print(Any obj)
{
    cout << "Print1: " << obj << "\n";
}
```

continues

```
void print(char * chrStr, int prtNum)
{
    cout << "Print2: ";
    for (int i = 0; i < prtNum; i++)
        cout << chrStr[i];
    cout << "\n";
}
```

For Further Discussion Answer

2. This magic code should do the trick.

```
#include <iostream>
#include <cstring>
using namespace std;

namespace Lord
{
    char hero[20];
    char author[20];
    int pages;
}

namespace Hobbit
{
    char hero[20];
    char author[20];
    int pages;
}

main()
{
    strcpy(Lord::hero,"Frodo Baggins");
    strcpy(Hobbit::hero,"Bilbo Baggins");
    cout << Lord::hero << '\n';
    cout << Hobbit::hero << '\n';
    return (0);
}
```

OBJECTS AND CLASSES

Statement of Purpose

This chapter introduces C++ classes and is the first of several chapters to discuss these object-oriented programming concepts. This is new territory even for C programmers, and takes advantage of OOP's concepts of abstraction, encapsulation, and data hiding, plus others that are covered in later chapters. This chapter takes a close look at the structural implementation of classes in C++ by developing a simple, but concrete, example of a stock class.

Objectives

By the end of Chapter 9, the student should understand the following concepts:

- Object-oriented programming concepts of abstraction, encapsulation, and data hiding

- How these OOP concepts benefit the programmer and user

- C++ classes: the mechanics of declaring and defining them

- const member functions and the protection of data, hidden or not

- Public and private class members, both data and functions

- Class scope to understand the visibility of class members

- Creating objects and how their methods are used

- Class constructors and destructors for creating and releasing class objects

- Self identity and the this pointer to class objects

- Using arrays of objects to represent and work with collections of objects

- Abstract data types to represent more general objects

Lecture Outline

Procedural and object-oriented programming

C++ encompasses both procedural and object-oriented programming. There is a fundamental difference between the two, and understanding the difference is crucial to good C++ programs.

- Procedural: think first about how program works
- OOP: think about representing data first

    The object as the user perceives it

    Operations describing user's interaction with data

Abstraction and classes

Abstraction translates the physical object to a class object that can be used to solve problems. The student here learns the basics of using classes to model part of the world.

Sample programs: stocks.h—class declaration for stocks

stocks.cpp (1)—implementation of methods

stocks.cpp (2)—redux with full definitions

- Abstraction: representing information in terms of user interface
- Type: form of data is closely tied to the operations that can be performed on it

    Determines memory needed

    Determines methods that can be performed using data object
- Class: vehicle for translating abstraction to a user-defined type

    Packages together data and methods
- Class specification consist of

    Declaration: describes data and public interface (methods)

    Method definitions: implementation of methods
- Structure of class specification

    `class` keyword

    Class data members

    Class methods: prototypes or defined in place

    Access control

    > `private`: directly accessible only by this class's methods (default)

    > `public`: accessible by program

    > Data items normally are private

    > Interface's member functions are public
- Data hiding: insulation of data from direct access by program

    No need to know how data is represented

- Encapsulation: separate public interface (abstraction) from implementation

  Data hiding is encapsulation

  Separating class function definitions from declaration

  Allows changes to implementation with no change to interface

- Implementing class member functions

  They look much like regular function definitions except

  > The scope resolution operator (::) to identify class membership

  > They can access private data and functions

  Other methods of the class don't need to use scope resolution operator

  Qualified name: class-name::method()

- `Inline` methods

  Automatic for definitions in class declaration

  Use `inline` when defining method in implementation section

  Internal linkage unless in header file with declaration

  Rewrite rule: `inline` definition rewritten after class declaration

- Use membership operator (`.`) to call method for particular object

  Uses data members of that object

  Class's methods are shared by all objects of that type

- Use class object like regular variables

  `Create`

  > By declaring a class variable

  > Using `new` to allocate memory

  Pass as arguments

  Return from functions

  Assign one object to another

Constructors and destructors

Well-designed classes make programming an application simple and more reliable. The creation and destruction of objects is handled by the object itself, once implemented.

Sample programs: stock1.h—new and improved stocks

stock1.cpp—new class methods

usestok1.cpp—`main()` test function for stocks

- Standard class member functions implicitly or explicitly defined

- Data parts of class are private so can't initialize directly

- Class constructor

  Method to initialize object when created

Name is `Classname()`

No declared type: don't use `void`

Takes arguments as defined in prototype

    Can take default arguments

Prototype is placed in public section of declaration

Object initialization forms

    Explicitly: `Classname varname = Classname(arguments);`

    Implicitly: `Classname varname(arguments);`

    Single argument: `Classname varname = argvalue;`

    Dynamic: `Classname *varname = new Classname(arguments)`

Once defined, C++ uses constructor every time object is created

Can use to assign values to existing object

- Default constructor

Allows creation of object without explicit initialization

Takes no arguments

Either define with default arguments or no arguments at all

Usually initialize all class members

Don't use parentheses when calling default constructor

- Implicit default constructor

Provided by compiler if none specified

Do nothing function

If any type of constructor is defined, compiler doesn't provide implicit default

- Class Destructor

Releases memory and cleans up after object

Name is `~Classname()`

No return value and no type

No arguments

Can be do nothing function

Called when

    Static class object: program terminates

    Automatic: upon exit from block of definition

    `new`: when use `delete` to free memory

    Temporary objects: when finished using

Assignment of one object to another copies contents of each data member

const member functions

Hiding data from the outside world is part of the goal, but member functions can still get carried away and modify data when they shouldn't. const member functions help to keep data safe.

- Prevents modification of const object data

- Declare method with const after parentheses of both declaration and definition

- Compiler will object if an attempt is made to modify data in the program.

- Creates const member functions

- Use wherever possible

this pointer

The this pointer solves an object's identity crisis when a member function needs to reference itself.

Sample programs: stock2.h—comparing total value of stocks

                                           stock2.cpp—implementation for new stocks

- Solves problem of referring to current object when referencing multiple objects of the class

- Pointer that points to object used to invoke function

- All class members have this pointer automatically

- If function has const after parentheses, can't use this to modify data

- const pointer, so can't point to anything else

- *this is alias for the object

Arrays of objects

Rarely is an object one-of-a-kind; usually groups of objects must be used. An array of objects enables the programmer to work with multiple objects.

Sample program: usestok2.cpp—array of stock objects

- Declare same as regular array

- Methods can be used in same way on each array element

- Class must have a default constructor

- Explicitly call constructor to initialize each element when declared

Class scope

Now that we have a class and objects of the class, just who and what can get at the data and functions to put them to use?

- Applies to data and member function names defined in a class

- Items are known within class but not outside

- Can use same name in different classes

- Can't access even public member functions directly from outside class

  Use scope resolution operator, including for member function definitions

  Direct membership operator (.)

  Indirect membership operator (::)

- Symbolic constants of class scope

  Can't use because memory isn't allocated when class declared

  Use enum as a substitute

Abstract data type

Classes needn't be models of concrete objects, they can be more abstract and thus more flexible.

Sample programs: stack.h—simple stack using ADT

stack.cpp—stack member functions

stacker.cpp—testing function for stack

- Use to represent general concepts or objects
- Use #define type for member data type
- Older compilers do not recognize the bool data type, so user-defined enumeration is required

  ```
  //booly.h—boolean definitions
  // C++ bool type defined in modern compilers
  #ifndef BOOLY_H_
  #define BOOLY_H_
  enum Bool {false, true}; // false = 0, true = 1
  #endif
  ```

  Include this header file in the stack.h code, which uses the boolean data type.

Programming extensions

New C++ functions and concepts are introduced throughout the chapter.

- cerr: ostream object unaffected by redirection
- exit(): terminates program from any function

  stdlib.h provides prototype

- strncpy() copies up to specified number of characters
- Prevent duplicate declarations from header files

  Use #ifndef and #define around declarations

- Use initialization rather than assignment to set object values for efficiency

Additional Questions

True or False

1. A fundamental concept of OOP is to think about the data before you begin to plan what to do with it.

2. While data and code are closely linked in procedural programming languages, C++ and OOP take it much further.

3. A class declaration describes the private data members of a class, and a class definition describes the public member functions.

4. If an `inline` function is included in the class declaration, the compiler removes it from the declaration and rewrites it after the declaration in the file, before compiling it.

5. A C++ class binds together data and functions to provide a unified object.

6. A program cannot ever access the private data members of a class, directly or indirectly.

7. The scope resolution operator (`::`) is only required when out of scope.

8. Each new class object created in a program allocates memory for the data, but not for the member functions.

9. "Sending a message" in some OOP implementations is the same as calling a class member function with at least one argument in C++.

10. It is always a requirement to use the scope resolution operator when defining class member functions.

11. Class constructor and destructor functions can either be placed in a `public` or `private` section of the class declaration.

12. A default constructor can be defined either with default arguments for all arguments or with no arguments at all.

13. A class always has a constructor defined for it whether the programmer includes one or not.

14. The default type of both constructors and destructors is a pointer to the object.

15. When reassigning the `this` pointer in code, it must always point to an object of the same class.

16. The following is a valid declaration of an array of `Shipment` objects:
    ```
    Shipment LosAngeles[4] = {
        {"Taiwan", 40000, "electronics"},
        {"Panama", 120000, "produce"},
        {"Chile", 45000, "textiles"},
        {"Japan", 15000, "DRAMs"}
    };
    ```

17. Using the scope resolution operator makes class member functions publicly visible, but has no use with data members.

18. C++ implements abstract data types through the use of classes with private and public sections.

Short Answers

1. Describe the following terms, and explain their use in a C++ program.

   a. constructors

   b. destructors

   c. abstraction

   d. user-defined type

   e. class

   f. objects

   g. instances

   h. class methods

   i. private and public

   j. access control

   k. data hiding

   l. encapsulation

   m. scope resolution operator

   n. class scope

   o. qualified name

   p. rewrite rule

   q. default constructor

   r. `#ifndef`, `#endif`

   s. `#define`

   t. `const` member function

   u. `this`

   v. abstract data types

   w. `typedef`

2. Explain the difference between procedural and object-oriented programming.

3. A metropolitan area consists of millions of people, hundreds of thousands of buildings, hundreds of miles of roads and utility lines, perhaps a dozen cities, and a handful of counties. How might you frame simplifying abstractions to cope with this complexity?

4. Why is OOP so strong in emphasizing hiding the implementation details of a class?

5. How do you decide whether to make class member functions public or private?

6. In Listing 9.3, stocks.cpp, there is no constructor defined. Yet the program works and objects are created and used. How is this possible? Also, why was the initialization of `stock1` in `main()` on a separate line from the object declaration? Could it have been done together in a single statement?

7. What specifically do each of these statements do, given a class `Moderate`? What functions are called, if any? (Assume that the declaration of `Moderate` may be different for each.)

   a. `Moderate board;`

   b. `Moderate argue("Peabody & Co.", 1200);`

   c. `Moderate feature();`

   d. `Moderate * ideal();`

   e. `Moderate group = 16, hierarchy;`

   f. `Moderate international = 12;`

8. What will be the output of this program?

```
//clascons.cpp

#include <iostream>
using namespace std;

class Zoo
{
    int julia;
```

```
public:
    Zoo();
    Zoo(int);
    ~Zoo();
};
int main(void)
{
    Zoo phil = 5, ted, harry = 3;
    return 0;
}
Zoo::Zoo()
{
    cout << "Default constructor\n";
}
Zoo::Zoo(int sam)
{
    cout << "Default constructor with int\n";
}
Zoo::~Zoo()
{
    cout << "Destructor running\n";
}
```

Programming Projects

Use `inline` functions wherever appropriate.

1. Rewrite the personal information manager (PIM) from Chapter 5, this time utilizing the concepts in this chapter. Include information about people you know, including, at a minimum, their name, address, city, state, ZIP, phone number, and year of birth. Using an array of objects, input at least five people, and output the information to the screen. Use separate files for compilation. Include a function to display a particular record when the last name is input (assume no duplicate last names). Hint: have different first and last name fields. Include explicit constructor(s) and a destructor.

For Further Discussion

1. Why is object-oriented programming a better approach to software construction?

2. C++ allows you to make data members public, although private is the default. Why might you make class data public, if ever?

3. Why might you define a class member function in a separate member function definitions area rather than in the class declaration?

4. How might using the OOP client-server model change and enhance the development of a full-scale programming project?

Activities for Learning

1. For your compiler, how do you find out what header files you need to `#include` when you use library functions?

2. What class libraries (files of predefined and compiled class members that you can use) came with your compiler?

3. Run the example programs in this chapter. Experiment with changes to get a feel for how the different C++ constructs are used. Modify them to make them more general and more useful to you.

Answers to Text Programming Exercises

1. Write a short program illustrating all the features of the class described in Review Question 5.

   Answer is given in Appendix G, answer to Review Question 5.

2. Do Programming Exercise 3 from Chapter 8, but replace the code shown there with an appropriate `golf` class declaration.

```
// pe8-golf.h -- for pe8-3.cpp

const int Len = 40;
struct golf
{
    char fullname[Len];
    int handicap;
};

// function solicits name and handicap from user
// returns 1 if name is entered, 0 if name is empty string
int setgolf(golf & g);

// function sets golf structure to provided name, handicap
void setgolf(golf & g, const char * name, int hc);

// function resets handicap to new value
void handicap(golf & g, int hc);

// function displays contents of golf structure
void showgolf(const golf & g);

// pe8-golf.cpp -- for pe8-3.cpp

#include <iostream>
#include <cstring>
using namespace std;
#include "pe8-golf.h"


// function solicits name and handicap from user
// returns 1 if name is entered, 0 if name is empty string
int setgolf(golf & g)
{
    cout << "Please enter golfer's full name: ";
    cin.getline(g.fullname, Len);
    if (g.fullname[0] == '\0')
        return 0;  // premature termination
    cout << "Please enter handicap for " << g.fullname << ": ";
    while (!(cin >> g.handicap))
    {
        cin.clear();
        cout << "Please enter an integer: ";
    }
    while (cin.get() != '\n')
        continue;
    return 1;
}

// function sets golf structure to provided name, handicap
void setgolf(golf & g, const char * name, int hc)
{
    strcpy(g.fullname, name);
    g.handicap = hc;
```

```
    }

    // function resets handicap to new value
    void handicap(golf & g, int hc)
    {
        g.handicap = hc;
    }

    // function displays contents of golf structure
    void showgolf(const golf & g)
    {
        cout << "Golfer:   " << g.fullname << "\n";
        cout << "Handicap: " << g.handicap << "\n\n";
    }

    // pe9-2.cpp

    #include <iostream>
    using namespace std;

    #include "pe9-golf.h"
    // link with pe9-golf.cpp
    const int Mems = 5;
    int main(void)
    {
        golf team[Mems];

        cout << "Enter up to " << Mems << " golf team members:\n";
        for (int i = 0; i < Mems; i++)
            if (team[i].setgolf() == 0)
                break;
        for (int j = 0; j < i; j++)
            team[j].showgolf();
        team[0] = golf("Fred Norman", 5);
        team[0].showgolf();
        team[0].handicap(3);
        team[0].showgolf();

        return 0;
    }
```

3. Consider the following structure declaration:
```
    struct customer {
        char fullname[35];
        double payment;
    };
```

Write a program that adds and removes **customer** structures from a stack, represented by a class declaration. Each time a customer is removed, his payment is added to a running total and the running total is reported.
```
    // pe9stack.h -- class definition for the stack ADT
    #ifndef _STACK_H_
    #define _STACK_H_

    struct customer {
        char fullname[35];
        double payment;
    };

    typedef customer Item;

    class Stack
    {
    private:
```

continues

```cpp
        enum {MAX = 10};      // constant specific to class
        Item items[MAX];      // holds stack items
        int top;          // index for top stack item
    public:
        Stack();
        bool isempty() const;
        bool isfull() const;
        // push() returns false if stack already is full, true otherwise
        bool push(const Item & item);     // add item to stack
        // pop() returns false if stack already is empty, true otherwise
        bool pop(Item & item);     // pop top into item
    };
    #endif

    // pe9-3.cpp

    #include <iostream>
    #include <cctype>
    using namespace std;
    #include "pe9stack.h"      // modified to define customer structure
    // link with pe9stack.cpp
    void get_customer(customer & cu);
    int main(void)
    {
        Stack st; // create a stack of customer structures
        customer temp;
        double payments = 0;
        char c;

        cout << "Please enter A to add a customer,\n"
             << "P to process a customer, and Q to quit.\n";
        while (cin >> c && (c = toupper(c)) != 'Q')
        {
            while (cin.get() != '\n')
                continue;
            if (c != 'A' && c != 'P')
            {
                cout << "Please respond with A, P, or Q: ";
                continue;
            }
            switch (c)
            {
                case 'A'   :   if (st.isfull())
                                   cout << "stack already full\n";
                               else
                               {
                                   get_customer(temp);
                                   st.push(temp);
                               }
                               break;
                case 'P'   :   if (st.isempty())
                                   cout << "stack already empty\n";
                               else {
                                   st.pop(temp);
                                   payments += temp.payment;
                                   cout << temp.fullname << " processed. ";
                                   cout << "Payments now total $"
                                        << payments << "\n";
                               }
                               break;
                default    :   cout << "Whoops! Programming error!\n";
            }
            cout << "Please enter A to add a customer,\n"
                 << "P to process a customer, and Q to quit.\n";
        }
        cout << "Done!\n";
```

```
            return 0;
    }

    void get_customer(customer & cu)
    {
        cout << "Enter customer name: ";
        cin.getline(cu.fullname,35);
        cout << "Enter customer payment: ";
        cin >> cu.payment;
        while (cin.get() != '\n')
            continue;
    }
```

4. Here's a class declaration:

```
    class Move
    {
    private:
        double x;
        double y;
    public:
        Move(double a = 0, double b = 0); // sets x, y to a, b
        showmove() const;       // shows current x, y values
        Move add(const Move & m) const;
    // this function adds x of m to x of invoking object to get new x,
    // adds y of m to y of invoking object to get new y, creates a new
    // Move object initialized to new x, y values and returns it
        reset(double a = 0, double b = 0); // resets x,y to a, b
```

Supply member function definitions and a program that exercises the class.

```
    //pe9-4.cpp
    #include <iostream>
    using namespace std;
    class Move{
    private:
        double x;
        double y;
    public:
        Move(double a = 0, double b = 0) {x = a; y = b;};
        void show() { cout << "(x,y) = (" << x << ',' << y << ")\n";}
        void reset(double a = 0, double b = 0) {x = a; y = b;};
        Move add(Move & m);
    };

    Move Move::add(Move & m)
    {
        double nx = x + m.x;
        double ny = y + m.y;
        Move xy(nx, ny);
        return xy;
    }

    int main(void)
    {
        Move a(10.0, 20.0);
        Move b(2.5, 3.5);
        a.show();
        b.show();
        a.add(b).show();
        return 0;
    }
```

5. We can describe a simple list as follows

• A simple list can hold zero or more items of some particular type

- One can create an empty list

- One can add items to a list

- One can determine if the list is empty

- One can determine if the list is full

- One can visit each item in a list and perform some action upon it

As you can see, this list really is simple, not allowing insertion or deletion for example. The main use of such a list is to provide a simplified programming project. In this case, create a class matching this description. You can implement the list as an array or, if you're familiar with the data type, as a linked list. But the public interface should not depend on your choice. That is, the public interface should not have array indices, pointers to nodes, and so on. It should be expressed in the general concepts of creating a list, adding an item to the list, and so on. The usual way to handle visiting each item and performing an action is to use a function that takes a function pointer as an argument:

```
void visit(void (*pf)(Item &));
```

Here pf points to a function that takes a reference to Item argument, where Item is the type for items in the list. The visit() function would apply this function to each item in the list.

You also should provide a short program utilizing your design.

```
// pe9-5arr.h -- header file for a simple list class

// program-specific declarations
const int TSIZE = 45;        // size of array to hold title
struct film
{
    char title[TSIZE];
    int rating;
};

// general type definitions
typedef struct film Item;

const int MAXLIST = 10;
class simplist
{
private:
    Item items[MAXLIST];
    int count;
public:
    simplist(void);
 bool isempty(void);
 bool isfull(void);
    int itemcount();
 bool additem(Item item);
    void transverse( void (*pfun)(Item item));
};
// pe9-5arr.cpp — functions supporting simple list operations
#include "pe9-5arr.h"

simplist::simplist(void)
{
    count = 0;
}

bool simplist::isempty(void)
{
    return count == 0;
}

bool simplist::isfull(void)
```

```
{
    return count == MAXLIST;
}

int simplist::itemcount()
{
    return count;
}
bool simplist::additem(Item item)
{
    if (count == MAXLIST)
        return false;
    else
        items[count++] = item;
    return true;
}

void simplist::transverse( void (*pfun)(Item item))
{
    for (int i = 0; i < count; i++)
        (*pfun)(items[i]);
}
// pe9-5a.cpp -- using a class definition

#include <iostream>
#include <cstdlib>          // prototype for exit()
using namespace std;
#include "pe9-5arr.h"       // simple list class declaration
                            // array version
void showmovies(Item item); // to be used by transverse()

int main(void)
{
    simplist movies;        // creates an empty list
    Item temp;

    if (movies.isfull())    // invokes isfull() member function
    {
        cout << "No more room in list! Bye!\n";
        exit(1);
    }
    cout << "Enter first movie title:\n";
    while (cin.getline(temp.title,TSIZE) && temp. title[0] != '\0')
    {
        cout << "Enter your rating <0-10>: ";
        cin >> temp.rating;
        while(cin.get() != '\n')
            continue;
        if (movies.additem(temp) == false)
        {
            cout << "List already is full!\n";
            break;
        }
        if (movies.isfull())
        {
            cout << "You have filled the list.\n";
            break;
        }
        cout << "Enter next movie title (empty line to stop):\n";
    }
    if (movies.isempty())
        cout << "No data entered. ";
    else
    {
        cout << "Here is the movie list:\n";
        movies.transverse(showmovies);
```

```
        }
        cout << "Bye!\n";
        return 0;
}

void showmovies(Item item)
{
        cout << "Movie: " << item.title << "  Rating: "
             << item.rating << '\n';
}
```

Answers to Additional Questions

True or False

1.	T	10.	F—inline functions
2.	T	11.	F—**public** only
3.	F	12.	T
4.	T	13.	T
5.	T	14.	F
6.	F	15.	F—can't reassign
7.	T	16.	F—call constructor
8.	T	17.	T
9.	F	18.	T

Short Answers

1.

a) A constructor is a special member function used to construct new objects and assign values to their data members.

b) A destructor is a special member function that is called automatically when an object is finished. It cleans up memory used by the object.

c) Abstraction is the crucial step of representing information in terms of its interface with the user.

d) A user-defined data type is a design that implements an abstraction.

e) A class in C++ is the vehicle for the translation of an abstraction to a user-defined type. It combines data representation and methods for manipulating that data into one package.

f) When the constructor is invoked, it uses the class design to create a specific object that occupies computer memory.

g) An instance is a specific object. There can be many instances of the same class, but each one is a different and unique object.

h) Class methods are functions belonging to a class and manipulate data within that class. Class methods are also called member functions.

i) Class data items and member functions can be declared as private or public. Public data items can be accessed from outside the class. Private data items are hidden from view within the class and can only be accessed via public member function.

j) Access control describes whether a data item is public or private.

k) If class data is declared as private, it is hidden within a class and cannot be directly accessed. It can only be indirectly accessed through a member function. This is known as data hiding.

l) The grouping of data and functions that manipulate that data into a class is known as encapsulation.

m) The scope resolution operator has the symbol ::. It is used to resolve the identity of the class to which it belongs.

n) Any data item that is declared within a class has class scope.

o) When the full class and member function name are specified using the scope resolution operator such as `Bozo::Retort()`, this is a qualified name.

p) The rewrite rule states, "Defining a method in a class declaration is equivalent to replacing the method definition with a prototype and then rewriting the definition as an `inline` function immediately after the class declaration."

q) The default constructor is created by C++ if you don't provide an explicit constructor.

r) `#ifndef` (meaning if not defined)and `#endif` are preprocessor directives normally used to avoid multiple inclusion of header files.

s) `#define` is a preprocessor directive used to define symbolic constants.

t) The `const` modifier is used to prevent data being altered by the program after it has been initialized.

u) C++ provides a pointer referred to as `this`, which points to the invoking object.

v) An abstract data type (or ADT) describes a data type in a general fashion without bringing in language or implementation details.

w) The `typedef` directive assigns an alternative name to a type definition. It can aid the clarity of a program.

2. A full description of procedural and object-oriented programming is given on page 372. Basically procedural programming describes data and functions as separate entities that can interact with each other if specifically told to do so. OOP describes data and functions that manipulate that data as one single encapsulated item.

3. One possible solution is the following ADT.

The metropolitan area is an object that contains data items.

    The items in the metropolitan area are

Counties, cities, buildings, people.

    The data items are related by

Roads and utilities.

4. Hiding the implementation details of a class simplifies programming because you don't have to know how data is stored. Making changes to the implementation can be done without affecting the operation of the calling program (unless the public interface changes).

5. A member function should be made `public` if it is part of the public interface of the class, that part of the class that the external program calls to get information about the class or manipulate the data. A member function should be `private` if it is solely part of the implementation of the class and not part of the public interface.

6. When a constructor is not explicitly defined, the compiler creates one automatically. This function does nothing, however, not even to initialize data members. The initialization is on a different line from the object declaration because the class used the default constructor, which doesn't initialize data members. That is the purpose of the `acquire()` function.

7. a. Creates a `Moderate` object board, with default constructor

   b. Creates a `Moderate` object argue, calling constructor with two arguments

   c. Declares a function `feature()` of type `Moderate`

   d. Declares a function `ideal()` of type pointer to `Moderate`

   e. Creates two `Moderate` objects group and hierarchy, calling single argument constructor for group and the default constructor for hierarchy

   f. Creates a `Moderate` object international, calling a constructor with a single argument

8.

```
Default constructor with int
Default constructor
Default constructor with int
Destructor running
Destructor running
Destructor running
```

Programming Projects

1.

```cpp
//pimclass.h
const int ArSize = 30;
class People {
private:
    char nameFirst[ArSize];
    char nameLast[ArSize];
    char address[ArSize];
    char city[ArSize];
    char state[ArSize];
    char zip[ArSize];
    char phone[ArSize];
    int birth;
public:
    People(char *, char *, char *, char *, char *, char *, char *, int);
    People();
    ~People();
    void show();
    char * getName();
};
//pimclass.cpp--member function definitions
#include <iostream>
#include <cstring>
using namespace std;

#include "pimclass.h"

//constructors
People::People() {}

People::People(char * fN, char * lN, char * add, char * cit,
    char * st, char * zp, char * ph, int year)
{
    strcpy(nameFirst, fN);
    strcpy(nameLast, lN);
    strcpy(address, add);
    strcpy(city, cit);
    strcpy(state, st);
    strcpy(zip, zp);
    strcpy(phone, ph);
    birth = year;
}
```

```cpp
//destructor
People::~People() {}

//other member functions
void People::show()
{
    cout << "\n";
    cout << nameFirst << " " << nameLast << "\n";
    cout << "    " << address << "\n";
    cout << "    " << city << ", " << state << "   " << zip << "\n";
    cout << "    " << phone << "\n";
    cout << "    " << birth;
}
char * People::getName()
{
    return nameLast;
}
// pimcl.cpp

#include <iostream>
#include <cstring>
using namespace std;
#include "pimclass.h"
const int numName = 5;

void showall(People *, int size);
int main (void)
{
    char find[30];
    People mail[numName] = {
        People("Don", "Kiely", "123 N. Main", "Irvine", "CA", "92715",
            "714-555-5487", 1957),
        People("Sam", "Malone", "8 Hazelnut", "Boston", "MA", "04589",
            "313-555-7928", 1949),
        People("John", "McKinney", "23 Misty", "Lake", "WI", "35409",
            "209-555-1717", 1962),
        People("Sally", "Jones", "2399 Valley", "Spring", "TX", "40908",
            "808-555-3252", 1956),
        People("Beth", "DeFrancis", "45 Medrow", "Dayton", "OH", "53298",
            "412-555-9795", 1958)
    };
    showall(mail, numName);
    cout << "\n\nEnter last name of person to find: ";
    cin.get(find, 30);
    for (int i = 0; i < numName; i++)
    {
        if (strcmp(mail[i].getName(), find) == 0)
        {
            mail[i].show();
            break;
        }
    }
    if (i == numName)
        cout << "Sorry, person not found!";
    return 0;
}

void showall(People * list, int number)
{
    cout << "Full Mailing List:\n";
    cout << "----------";
    for (int i = 0; i < number; i++)
        list[i].show();
}
```

WORKING WITH CLASSES

Statement of Purpose

This chapter expands the concepts of C++ classes, showing some of the ways they can be used to customize the language to fit the object. The features of the C++ language can be used by the programmer to make a flexible and productive programming environment. Operator overloading and automatic conversions provide a way for a program to handle much of the work of a class, invisible to the user.

Objectives

By the end of Chapter 10, the student should understand the following concepts:

- Operator overloading, the details of its use, and why it is a useful tool

- Overloading of +, -, and * operators

- Overloading of ostream objects, << in particular

- Using friend functions to extend the flexibility of class definitions

- State members used to add intelligence to classes

- Generating random numbers and the use of the system clock as a seed

- Decisions a compiler can make in converting data and how to give it guidance

- Conversion functions to explicitly define conversions involving objects

- The difference between explicit and implicit conversions

- Vector arithmetic and random walks

Lecture Outline

Operator overloading

Many of the C++ operators are overloaded in standard C++, and a programmer can use the same techniques with user-defined classes.

Sample program

mytime0.h—**Time** class before operator overloading

mytime0.cpp—implement **Time** methods

usetime0.cpp—use first draft of **Time** class

mytime1.h—**Time** class after operator overloading

mytime1.cpp—implement **Time** methods

usetime1.cpp—use second draft of **Time** class

usetime2.cpp—use third draft of **Time** class

- Another example of C++ polymorphism
- Similar to function overloading
- Allows assigning multiple meanings to most operators
- Many standard C++ operators are overloaded
- Compiler uses number and type of operands to decide which operator to use
- Operator function: `operator+(arguments)`
- Overload existing operators only; no new ones
- First operand must be the class object
- Need both prototype and definition, like regular member functions
- Overloading overloaded operators

    Binary operator has two operators

    Unary operator has one operator

    Different signatures required for multiple overloading

    Must have same number of operands as the built-in operator

- Overloading the addition operator
- Function notation for the addition
- Operator notation for the addition
- Stick with operations that are similar to built-in use of operator
- Restrictions on overloading

    Must have at least one operand that is a user-defined type

    Can't violate syntax rules for original operator

    Can't alter operator precedence

Can't create new operator symbols

Can't overload some operators

`sizeof`

membership operator (`.`)

pointer-to-member operator (`.*`)

scope resolution operator (`::`)

conditional operator (`?:`)

RTTI operator (`typeid`)

Type cast operator (`const_cast`)

Type cast operator (`dynamic_cast`)

Type cast operator (`reinterpret_cast`)

Type cast operator (`static_cast`)

- Operators that can be overloaded

Discussion of Table 10.1

Member function overload

Nonmember function overload

`friend` functions

When all else fails, C++ programmers always have `friend`s. Using `friend` functions helps to add functionality to classes when member functions can't be used.

Sample programs	These programs are the modified version as described in the text.
	mytime1.h—header with operator overloading
	mytime1.cpp—implement `Time` methods
	usetime1.cpp—use second draft of `Time` class

- Nonmember function allowed access to object's private section
- `friend` functions have same access privileges as member functions
- Allows duplicate operator definitions with same signature
- Since nonmember function, don't need an object to invoke
- For nonmember functions, first operand is the left operand of the operator, and the second is right operand
- Use `friend` keyword only in prototype
- Must explicitly supply an object
- Use to allow first operand to be a nonclass term

- Always requires one more argument than equivalent member function

  Member: `a = b.operator*(c);`

  friend: `a = operator*(b, c);`

  Both: `a = b * c;`

- `friend` functions extend functionality of class

Overloading the << operator

One of the most overloaded C++ operators is `<<`. Overloading it more allows classes to be output with ease.

Sample programs   mytime3.h—`Time` class with friends

           mytime3.cpp—implement `Time` methods

           usetime3.cpp—use fourth draft of `Time` class

- Useful to be able to use `<<` to output classes
- Most basic use is a bit manipulation operator
- `ostream` overloads `<<` to use with different basic data types
- Must use `friend` function because first operand is an `ostream` object
- Pass `ostream` object by reference so that actual object is used
- `operator <op> (argument list)` function should return an `ostream` function to allow combining operators

  `cout << A << endl;`

- Can avoid using `friend` function if class has methods that return data members

More on overloading: A Vector class

This section provides another chance to discuss and review overloading and friends by investigating the `Vector` class.

Sample programs   vector.h—`Vector` class with `<<`, mode state

           vector.cpp—methods for `Vector` class

           randwalk.cpp—use the `Vector` class

- Same class principles as `Time`
- Same friend principles as `Time`
- Same overload principles as `Time`
- State member and multiple class data representations

  Variable that affects how the object behaves

  A way to get around restrictions on function signatures

  Class data member contains value for current state

  Set state default in constructor or pass choice as argument

  Using `friend` function does not make it a `friend` to `ostream`

- When developing a new class, best to

  Start with simple implementation to get up and running

  Expand to add functionality

Automatic conversions and type casts

C++ works hard to make things work, converting data any way that is reasonable.

Sample programs   stonewt.h—header for `Stonewt` class

         stonewt.cpp—class methods

         stone.cpp—using user-defined conversions

         stonewt1.h—header for conversion function

         stonewt1.cpp—class methods and conversion functions

         stone1.cpp—new user-defined conversion functions

- Built-in types are automatically converted, if compatible

- Explicit versus implicit conversion

- Instruct C++ how to convert a class member

- Constructor taking one argument defines a **type** conversion

- Compiler uses the conversion from **type** to **object** when

  Initializing class **object** to **type**

  Assigning **type** to **object**

  Passing **type** to function expecting **object**

  Function that is declared to return **object** tries to return **type**

  When any of these situations uses **object** that can be converted to **type**

- For the last of above situations, choice must be unambiguous

- Forms that work for automatic conversion

  ```
  Stonewt pavarotti = 260;
  ```

  ```
  Stonewt pavarotti(260);
  ```

  ```
  Stonewt pavarotti = Stonewt(260);
  ```

  Last two forms work for multiple arguments

- Constructors work for conversions only to the class type

  To convert from the class type, use conversion functions

  Resemble user-defined type casts

  ```
  double thinker = (double)wolfe
  ```

  ```
  double thinker = double(wolfe)
  ```

  Or, let compiler look to see whether a conversion function is defined

  ```
  Stonewt wells(20, 3);
  ```

  ```
  double star = wells;
  ```

Definition form: `operator typename();`

    Function must be class method

    Must not specify a return type

    Must have no arguments

Compiler must be able to determine unambiguously what type to convert to

    Eliminate one of the multiple possibilities, or

    Use explicit type cast

Using a `friend` function makes it easier for compiler to make automatic conversions

    Both operands become function arguments

    Only a class object can invoke member function

    Using `friend` allows compiler to use conversions even if not called by class object

Programming techniques

New C++ functions and concepts are introduced throughout the chapter.

- C++ classes are ideal for objects having multiple representations (vector example)

  Conversions can be handled internally

  Issue of speed and size: which is more important?

- Using `rand()`, `srand()`, and `time()` to generate random numbers

  `time(0)` provides a dynamic seed for generator

  Each random value becomes seed for next call

  Actually pseudorandom numbers

  Use `stdlib.h` for random functions and `ctime` for `time()`

- Using `enum` to provide integer constants in classes

Additional Questions

True or False

1. Operator overloading is another form of polymorphism.

2. A C++ compiler uses the number and type of arguments and the return type of the **operator** function to determine which version of an overloaded operator to use.

3. C++ does not allow overloading the ^ symbol.

4. When using a member function to overload an operator, the function is implicitly invoked by whichever argument is a member of that class.

5. One benefit of using classes in C++ is that you can have the class take care of maintenance functions, such as updating data members, so the user doesn't have to.

6. Representing data in two different but equivalent forms makes sense when the program will be running in tight memory on slow hardware.

7. Multiple representations of data and private member conversion functions are object-oriented programming features of C++.

8. A `friend` becomes useful when the access controls of C++ classes are too restrictive.

9. A `friend` function must be used when you want to use a nonclass term as the first operand of an overloaded operator.

10. `cout << "Procedure 1A";` returns an object of the `ostream` class.

11. An easy and recommended way to make global changes to the types of objects that work with the `<<` operator is to add the new definition to the `ostream.h` file.

12. Using a member function to overload an operator is exactly the same as using a nonmember `friend` function.

13. A state member can be used to control the actions that a class's member functions take in manipulating the data members.

14. Any constructor that takes a single argument can provide the compiler with enough information to do at least some conversions.

15. Constructors can be used for conversions only to convert to the class type, not to another type.

Short Answers

1. Describe the following terms, and explain their use in a C++ program.

   a. operator overloading

   b. operator function

   c. binary operator

   d. unary operator

   e. `friend` function

   f. state member

   g. `rand()`

   h. `srand()`

   i. `time()`

   j. conversion function

2. Why might you include the same data in different forms in a class object? Why might you not?

3. Consider this function prototype and definition:

```
Building & operator+(const Building & lapalma) const;
Building & Building::operator+(const Building & lapalma) const
{
    long x1, x2, x3;
    x1 = area + lapalma.area;
    x2 = value + lapalma.value;
    x3 = debt + lapalma.debt;
    Building total = Building(x1, s2, x3);
    return &total;
}
```

Area, value, and debt are data members of `Building`. Unit1 and unit2 are `Building` objects. What happens when this code runs?

```
Building sum = unit1 + unit2;
```

4. Given this partial class definition

```
class TvShow
{
    double cost;
    char * name[50];
    double revenue;
    ...
public:
    TvShow();
    TvShow(long);
    TvShow(int);
    TvShow(char);
    ~TvShow();
    double annualrev();
    double profit();
    ...
};
```

which of the following are valid function prototypes when included in the class declaration?

a. `TvShow operator+(const TvShow & a) const;`

b. `TvShow operator*(TvShow & a, TvShow & b) const;`

c. `TvShow operator-(const TvShow & a) const;`

d. `friend TvShow operator+(const TvShow & a);`

e. `TvShow operator/(TvShow & a);`

f. `friend TvShow operator*(double a, double b);`

g. `TvShow operator#(const TvShow & a) const;`

h. `friend TvShow operator*(TvShow & a);`

5. When using a `friend` function to overload the `<<` operator, why do you not need to make modifications to the `ostream` class, even though the `operator<<()` function both calls and returns an object of the `ostream` class?

6. Will C++ make the following conversions automatically? Will there be any side effects?

```
int x;
int y;
double z;
char ch;
float fl;
```

a. `x = 5.345e78;`

b. `x = 0L;`

c. `fl = 'd';`

d. `fl = 10;`

e. `ch = 0L;`

f. `double * a = double(5);`

7. What does the following code do?

```
double fence = 45.62;
float fl = fence--int(fence);
```

8. Constants are not allowed in the declaration of a class. If possible, how could the following be included in the declaration?

```
const float fl = 1.23;
```

9. Given the `TvShow` class declaration above in question 4, what will the compiler do with the following?

   a. `TvShow allFamily;`

   b. `TvShow cosby = 14.2;`

   c. `TvShow simpsons = 10;`

   d. `TvShow twenty = 'X';`

   e. `TvShow starTrek = &allFamily;`

   f. `TvShow tonight = 170000L;`

Programming Projects

1. Create the declarations in a header file for a `Rectangle` class. Use a structure `point` to store two integer values representing the x and y coordinates that can be used as the corner of a rectangle. Store as data members the following items:

   ```
   point uLeft;     //location of upper left point
   point lRight;    //location of lower right point
   int hght;        //rectangle height
   int wdth;        //rectangle width
   long area;       //rectangle area
   ```

   Include two constructors: one taking the locations of the top, bottom, left, and right sides of the rectangle, and a default constructor. Include preprocessor directives to make sure that the same declarations aren't repeated.

2. Expand the `Rectangle` declaration by adding the following private member functions:

`setHeight()`	void function that sets the object's height, calculated from `uLeft` and `lRight`
`setWidth()`	void function that sets the width, calculated from `uLeft` and `lRight`
`setArea()`	void function that sets the area, calculated from the height and width

   Include the following public members:

`showULeft()`	void function that prints the upper-left coordinates; doesn't modify data
`showLLeft()`	void function that prints the lower-left coordinates; doesn't modify data
`showURight()`	void function that prints the upper-right coordinates; doesn't modify data
`showLRight()`	void function that prints the lower-right coordinates; doesn't modify data
`showHeight()`	void function that prints the height of the rectangle; doesn't modify data
`showWidth()`	void function that prints the width of the rectangle; doesn't modify data
`showArea()`	void function that prints the area of the rectangle; doesn't modify data

   Use `const` wherever possible.

3. Write the functions to implement the above class `Rectangle`.

   a. Check in the constructors that no point is greater than **500** or less than **0** to keep things simple. In other words, substitute **0** for bottom and left if they are negative, and **500** if top and right are greater than **500**. Also make sure that top > bottom and right > left; swap them if they aren't.

   b. Implement the constructors, setting all data members and calculating the height, width, and area with the appropriate member function. Define a default constructor that sets the top to **60**, bottom to **30**, left to **25**, and right to **75**.

   c. Define `setArea()` so that it first calculates the height and width.

d. Define the show functions so that they collectively produce this format of output:

```
Upper left at (20,75).
Lower left at (20,25).
Upper right at (80,75).
Lower right at (80,25).
Height is 50.
Width is 60.
Area is 3000.
```

4. Write a test program to create and print two Rectangle objects as shown above, one by explicitly calling the constructor with specific values, and one using the default constructor.

5. Add the capability to add Rectangle objects. Addition returns a rectangle whose width is the sum of the two rectangles' widths, whose height is the sum of the two rectangles' heights, and whose lower left corner is at (0,0). Make all changes necessary, implementing it as a member function.

6. Write a test program to create and print two Rectangle objects as shown above, one by explicitly calling the constructor with specific values, and one using the default constructor, and another to contain the sum of the first two. Also include a showAll() member function to allow a single function call to print all the data about a rectangle.

7. Add the capability to multiply Rectangle objects by an integer. When multiplied by an integer, the result is a new rectangle whose width and height are larger by a factor of the integer. Implement a test program that prints both the original and new rectangle's data.

8. Modify the program so that it can multiply both (integer * Rectangle) as well as (Rectangle * integer), and modify the test program to show the solution works.

9. Last, and most fun, modify the Rectangle program to allow a double to be assigned to a Rectangle object. When that happens, a square is created with area equal to the double. Use the library function

```
double sq = sqrt(area)
```

to calculate the sides of the square. The prototype for the sqrt() function is in math.h. Again, modify the test program. Be *very* careful with type conversions!

Activities for Learning

1. What libraries are available to your compiler? What libraries does your compiler automatically search when linking? If you need to have an additional library searched, how do you let the compiler know?

2. Look at the ostream.h, file included with your compiler. How many operator<< prototypes are there? What data types can be used with the << operator?

3. Run the example programs in this chapter. Experiment with changes to get a feel for how the different C++ constructs are used. Modify them to make them more general and more useful to you.

Answers to Text Programming Exercises

1. Modify Listing 10.7 so that, instead of reporting the results of a single trial for a particular target-step combination, it reports the highest, lowest, and average number of steps for *N* trials, where *N* is an integer entered by the user.

```
// pe10-1.cpp -- use the revised Vector class
// compile with the vector2.cpp file
// place original calculation inside a loop
```

```cpp
#include <iostream>
#include <ctime>
using namespace std;

#include <stdlib.h>       // rand(), srand() prototypes
#include "pe10vec2.h"

int main(void)
{
    srand(time(0));            // seed random-number generator
    double direction;
    Vector step;
    Vector result(0.0, 0.0);
    unsigned long steps = 0;
    double target;
    double dstep;
    unsigned long trials;
    unsigned long min, max, average;
    cout << "Enter target distance (q to quit): ";
    while (cin >> target)
    {
        cout << "Enter step length: ";
        if (!(cin >> dstep))
            break;
        cout << "Enter number of trials: ";
        if (!(cin >> trials))
            break;
        average = 0;
        for (int n = 0; n < trials; n++)    // new loop
        {
            while (result.magval() < target)
            {
                direction = rand() % 360;
                step.set(dstep, direction, 'p');
                result = result + step;
                steps++;
            }
            if ( n == 0)
                min = max = steps;
            else
            {
                if (steps > max) max = steps;
                if (steps < min) min = steps;
            }
            average += steps;
            steps = 0;
            result.set(0.0, 0.0);
        }                              // end new loop
        if (trials < 1)
        {
            cout << "No trials\n";
            continue;
        }
        average /= trials;

        cout << "Trials: " << trials << '\n';
        cout << "Average number of steps: " << average << '\n';
        cout << "Minimum number of steps: " << min << '\n';
        cout << "Maximum number of steps: " << max << '\n';
        steps = 0;
        result.set(0.0, 0.0);
        cout << "Enter target distance (q to quit): ";
    }
    cout << "Bye!\n";

    return 0;
}
```

2. Rewrite the `Stonewt` class so that it has a state member governing whether the object is interpreted in stone form, integer pounds form, or floating-point pounds form. Overload the `<<` operator to replace the `show_stn()` and `show_lbs()` methods. Overload the addition, subtraction, and multiplication operators so that one can add, subtract, and multiply `Stonewt` values. Test your class with a short program.

```
// pe10ston.h -- definition for Stonewt class
#ifndef _STONEWT_H_
#define _STONEWT_H_
class Stonewt
{

private:
    enum {Lbs_per_stn = 14};    // pounds per stone
    int stone;     // whole stones
    double pds_left;    // fractional pounds
    double pounds;     // entire weight in pounds
    char mode;      // display mode for weight
                    // 's' = stone, 'f' = float, 'w' = whole pounds
public:
    Stonewt(double lbs);     // constructor for double pounds
    Stonewt(int stn, double lbs);     // constructor for stone, lbs
    Stonewt();     // default constructor
    ~Stonewt();
    void set_mode(char m) {mode = m; }
    Stonewt operator+(const Stonewt & sw) const;
    Stonewt operator-(const Stonewt & sw) const;
    Stonewt operator*(double m) const;
    friend Stonewt operator*(double m, const Stonewt & sw)
        { return sw * m; }
    friend ostream & operator<<(ostream & os, const Stonewt & sw);
};
#endif

// stonewt.cpp -- Stonewt class methods
#include <iostream.h>
#include "pe10ston.h"

// construct Stonewt object from double value
Stonewt::Stonewt(double lbs)
{
    stone = int (lbs) / Lbs_per_stn;     // integer division
    pds_left = int (lbs) % Lbs_per_stn + lbs--int(lbs);
    pounds = lbs;
    mode = 'f';
}

// construct Stonewt object from stone, double values
Stonewt::Stonewt(int stn, double lbs)
{
    stone = stn;
    pds_left = lbs;
    pounds =  stn * Lbs_per_stn +lbs;
    mode = 's';
}

Stonewt::Stonewt()     // default constructor, wt = 0
{
    stone = pounds = pds_left = 0;
    mode = 's';
}

Stonewt::~Stonewt()     // destructor
{
}

ostream & operator<<(ostream & os, const Stonewt & sw)
```

```
{
// show weight in stones
    if (sw.mode == 's')
        os << sw.stone << " stone, " << sw.pds_left << " pounds\n";
// show weight in pounds
    else if (sw.mode == 'f')
        os << sw.pounds << " pounds\n";
// show weight in whole pounds
    else if (sw.mode == 'w')
        os << (int) sw.pounds << " pounds\n";
    else
        os << "Programming flaw in operator<<()\n";
    return os;
}

Stonewt Stonewt::operator+(const Stonewt & sw) const
{
    double wt = pounds + sw.pounds;
    Stonewt temp(wt);
    return temp;
}

Stonewt Stonewt::operator-(const Stonewt & sw) const
{
    double wt = pounds--sw.pounds;
    Stonewt temp(wt);
    return temp;
}

Stonewt Stonewt::operator*(double m) const
{
    double wt = m * pounds;
    Stonewt temp(wt);
    return temp;
}

// pe10-2.cpp
#include <iostream.h>
#include "pe10ston.h"
// link with pe10ston.cpp
int main(void)
{
    Stonewt fullback(245.5);
    Stonewt cornerback(13, 5.2);
    cout << fullback;
    cout << cornerback;
    cornerback.set_mode('w');
    cout << cornerback;
    Stonewt lump;
    lump = fullback + cornerback;
    cout << lump;
    fullback = fullback * 1.1;
    cout << fullback;
    lump = lump--fullback;
    cout << lump;
    lump = 1.3 * lump;
    lump.set_mode('s');
    cout << lump;

    return 0;
}
```

3. A complex number has two parts: a real part and an imaginary part. One way to write an imaginary number is this: (**3.0**, **4.0i**). Here **3.0** is the real part and **4.0** is the imaginary part. Suppose **a** = (**A,Bi**) and **c** = (**C,Di**). Here are some complex operations:

Addition: a + c = (A + C, (B + D)i)

Subtraction: a–c = (A–C, (B–D)i)

Multiplication: a * c = (A * C–B*D, (A*D + B*C)i)

Multiplication: (x a real number): x * c = (x*C,x*Di)

Conjugation: ~a = (A, -Bi)

Define a complex class so that the following program can use it with correct results. Note that you have to overload the << and >> operators. Many systems already have complex support in a **complex.h** header file, so use **complex0.h** to avoid conflicts. Use **const** whenever warranted.

```cpp
#include <iostream>
using namespace std;
#include "complex0.h"    // to avoid confusion with complex.h
int main(void)
{
    complex a(3.0, 4.0);    // initialize to (3,4i)
    complex c;
    cout << "Enter a complex number (q to quit):\n";
    while (cin >> c)
    {
        cout << "c is " << c << '\n';
        cout << "complex conjugate is " << ~c << '\n';
        cout << "a + c is " << a + c << '\n';
        cout << "a * c is " << a * c << '\n';
        cout << "2 * c is " << 2 * c << '\n';
        cout << "Enter a complex number (q to quit):\n";
    }
    cout << "Done!\n";
    return 0;
}
```

Here is a sample run. Note that cin >> c, through overloading, now prompts for real and imaginary parts:

```
Enter a complex number (q to quit):
real: 10
imaginary: 12
c is (10,12i)
complex conjugate is (10,-12i)
a + c is (13,16i)
a * c is (-18,76i)
2 * c is (20,24i)
Enter a complex number (q to quit):
real: q
Done!

// pe10cmlx.h
#include <iostream.h>

class complex
{
private:
    double r;
    double i;
public:
    complex();
    complex(double real);
    complex(double real, double imag);
    double magnitude();
    complex operator+(const complex & z) const;
```

```cpp
    complex operator-(const complex & z) const;
    complex operator~() const;
    friend complex square(const complex & z);
    friend complex operator*(const complex & z, const complex & w);
    friend ostream & operator<<(ostream & os, const complex & z);
    friend istream & operator>>(istream & is, complex & z);
};

// pe10cmlx.cpp
#include <iostream>
#include <cmath>
using namespace std;
#include "pe10cmlx.h"


complex::complex()
{
    r = i = 0.0;
}

complex::complex(double real)
{
    r = real;
    i = 0.0;
}

complex::complex(double real, double imag)
{
    r = real;
    i = imag;
}

double complex::magnitude()
{
    return sqrt(r*r + i*i);
}
complex complex::operator+(const complex & z) const
{
    complex sum;
    sum.r = r + z.r;
    sum.i = i + z.i;
    return sum;
}

complex complex::operator-(const complex & z) const
{
    complex sum;
    sum.r = r + z.r;
    sum.i = i + z.i;
    return sum;
}

complex complex::operator~() const
{
    complex conjugate;
    conjugate.r = r;
    conjugate.i = -i;
    return conjugate;
}
complex square (const complex & z)
{
    complex sq;
    sq.r = z.r * z.r--z.i * z.i;
    sq.i = 2.0 * z.r * z.i;
    return sq;
}
```

```
complex operator*(const complex & z, const complex & w)
{
    complex sq;
    sq.r = w.r * z.r--w.i * z.i;
    sq.i = w.r * z.i + w.i * z.r;
    return sq;
}

ostream & operator<<(ostream & os, const complex & z)
{
    os << '(' << z.r << ',' << z.i << "i)";
    return os;
}

istream & operator>>(istream & is, complex & z)
{
    cout << "real: ";
    if (is >> z.r)
    {
        cout << "imaginary: ";
        is >> z.i;
    }
    return is;
}
```

Answers to Additional Questions

True or False

1. T	6. F	11. F
2. F—no return	7. T	12. F
3. T	8. T	13. T
4. F	9. T	14. T
5. T	10. T	15. T

Short Answers

1.

   a) Operator overloading is described on page 422.

   b) Operator function is described on page 423.

   c) Binary operator requires two operands; for example, A and B.

   d) Unary operator requires a single operand; for example, A.

   e) `Friend` function is described on page 432.

   f) State member is described on page 450.

   g) `rand()` is contained in `cstdlib` and returns a random number.

   h) `srand()` is contained in `cstdlib` and seeds the random number generator used by `rand()`.

   i) `time()` is contained in the `ctime` library and returns the current system time and date to variable of type `time_t`.

   j) Conversion functions are described on page 464.

2. Use multiple data representations when both forms are needed frequently. If they aren't needed frequently, store just one version and include conversion member functions.

3. The addition of `Buildings` returns a reference to nothing, since total doesn't exist at completion of the `operator` function.

4. a. Valid

    b. Invalid—this is member function, so operator will have three operands

    c. Valid

    d. Valid

    e. Valid

    f. Invalid—at least one operand must be a class object

    g. Invalid—# is not a valid operator

    h. Valid

5. There is a good description of the answer to this question on page 436 under the heading "Friend or No Friend?".

6. a. Yes, but large loss of precision

    b. Yes

    c. Yes

    d. Yes

    e. Yes

    f. No, assigning `double` to pointer

7. Makes `fl` equal to the fractional part of `fence`, in this case 0.62.

8. It can't be used, unless an integer can be substituted. Using `enum` works with integers, but not `float`.

9. a. Creates a `TvShow` object `allFamily` using default constructor

    b. Gives error for ambiguous conversion

    c. Creates a `TvShow` object `simpsons` using `int` constructor

    d. Creates a `TvShow` object `twenty` using `char` constructor

    e. Error—initializing with an address

    f. Creates a `TvShow` object `tonight` using `long` constructor

Programming Projects

1. Here is the complete header file:

```
// rect.h—class declarations
#ifndef _RECT_H_
#define _RECT_H_
struct point
{
    int xcoord;
    int ycoord;
};

class Rectangle
{
```

continues

```
private:
    point uLeft;        //location of upper left point
    point lRight;       //location of lower right point
    int hght;           //rectangle height
    int wdth;           //rectangle width
    long area;          //rectangle area
public:
    //constructors
    Rectangle(int top, int left, int bottom, int right);
    Rectangle();

    //destructor
    ~Rectangle () {}

#endif
```

2. Modified to include member functions.

```
// rect.h--class declarations
#ifndef _RECT_H_
#define _RECT_H_
struct point
{
    int xcoord;
    int ycoord;
};

class Rectangle
{
private:
    point uLeft;        //location of upper left point
    point lRight;       //location of lower right point
    int hght;           //rectangle height
    int wdth;           //rectangle width
    long area;          //rectangle area
    void setHeight();
    void setWidth();
    void setArea();
public:
    //constructors
    Rectangle(int top, int left, int bottom, int right);
    Rectangle();

    //destructor
    ~Rectangle () {}

    void showULeft() const;
    void showLLeft() const;
    void showURight() const;
    void showLRight() const;

    void showHeight() const;
    void showWidth() const;
    void showArea() const;
};
#endif
```

3. Okay, most of the work is done!

```
// rect.cpp—implementation of public interface
#include <iostream>
using namespace std;

#include "rect.h"
// private members
Rectangle::Rectangle(int top, int left, int bottom, int right)
{
```

```
        top = (top > 100 ? 100 : top);
        left = (left < 0 ? 0 : left);
        bottom = (bottom < 0 ? 0 : bottom);
        right = (right > 100 ? 100 : right);
        uLeft.ycoord = (top > bottom ? top : bottom);
        uLeft.xcoord = (right > left ? left : right);
        lRight.ycoord = (top > bottom ? bottom : top);
        lRight.xcoord = (right > left ? right : left);
        setArea();
}
Rectangle::Rectangle()
{
        uLeft.ycoord = 60;
        uLeft.xcoord = 25;
        lRight.ycoord = 30;
        lRight.xcoord = 75;
        setArea();
}
void Rectangle::setHeight()
{
        hght = uLeft.ycoord--lRight.ycoord;
}
void Rectangle::setWidth()
{
        wdth = lRight.xcoord--uLeft.xcoord;
}
void Rectangle::setArea()
{
        setHeight();
        setWidth();
        area = hght * wdth;
}

//public members
void Rectangle::showULeft() const
{
        cout << "Upper left at (" << uLeft.xcoord;
        cout << "," << uLeft.ycoord << ").\n";
}
void Rectangle::showLLeft() const
{
        cout << "Lower left at (" << uLeft.xcoord;
        cout << "," << lRight.ycoord << ").\n";
}
void Rectangle::showURight() const
{
        cout << "Upper right at (" << lRight.xcoord;
        cout << "," << uLeft.ycoord << ").\n";
}
void Rectangle::showLRight() const
{
        cout << "Lower right at (" << lRight.xcoord;
        cout << "," << lRight.ycoord << ").\n";
}
void Rectangle::showHeight() const
{
        cout << "Height is " << hght << ".\n";
}
void Rectangle::showWidth() const
{
        cout << "Width is " << wdth << ".\n";
}
void Rectangle::showArea() const
{
        cout << "Area is " << area << ".\n";
}
```

4.

```
// userect.cpp--test function for rectangle
#include "rect.h"
int main(void)
{
    Rectangle rct(75, 20, 25, 80);
    rct.showULeft();
    rct.showLLeft();
    rct.showURight();
    rct.showLRight();

    rct.showHeight();
    rct.showWidth();
    rct.showArea();

    rct = Rectangle();
    rct.showULeft();
    rct.showLLeft();
    rct.showURight();
    rct.showLRight();

    rct.showHeight();
    rct.showWidth();
    rct.showArea();
    return 0;
}
```

5. Here is the full program through question 9, showing additions:

```
// rect.h--class declarations
#ifndef _RECT_H_
#define _RECT_H_
struct point
{
    int xcoord;
    int ycoord;
};

class Rectangle
{
private:
    point uLeft;        //location of upper left point
    point lRight;       //location of lower right point
    int hght;           //rectangle height
    int wdth;           //rectangle width
    long area;           //rectangle area
    void setHeight();
    void setWidth();
    void setArea();
public:
    //constructors
    Rectangle(int top, int left, int bottom, int right);
    //new constructor added for question 9:
    Rectangle(double Area);
    Rectangle();

    //destructor
    ~Rectangle () {}

    void showULeft() const;
    void showLLeft() const;
    void showURight() const;
    void showLRight() const;

    void showHeight() const;
    void showWidth() const;
    void showArea() const;
```

```cpp
    //added for question 5:
    Rectangle operator+(Rectangle & a) const;
    //added for question 6:
    void showAll() const;
    //added for question 7:
    Rectangle operator*(int a) const;
    //added for question 8:
    friend Rectangle operator*(int a, const Rectangle & b);
};
#endif

// rect.cpp--implementation of public interface
#include <iostream>
#include <cmath>
using namespace std;

#include "rect3.h"

// private members
Rectangle::Rectangle(int top, int left, int bottom, int right)
{
    top = (top > 500 ? 500 : top);
    left = (left < 0 ? 0 : left);
    bottom = (bottom < 0 ? 0 : bottom);
    right = (right > 500 ? 500 : right);
    uLeft.ycoord = (top > bottom ? top : bottom);
    uLeft.xcoord = (right > left ? left : right);
    lRight.ycoord = (top > bottom ? bottom : top);
    lRight.xcoord = (right > left ? right : left);
    setArea();
}
Rectangle::Rectangle()
{
    uLeft.ycoord = 60;
    uLeft.xcoord = 25;
    lRight.ycoord = 30;
    lRight.xcoord = 75;
    setArea();
}
void Rectangle::setHeight()
{
    hght = uLeft.ycoord--lRight.ycoord;
}
void Rectangle::setWidth()
{
    wdth = lRight.xcoord--uLeft.xcoord;
}
void Rectangle::setArea()
{
    setHeight();
    setWidth();
    //cast to longs for question 9:
    area = long(hght) * long(wdth);
}

//public members
void Rectangle::showULeft() const
{
    cout << "Upper left at (" << uLeft.xcoord;
    cout << "," << uLeft.ycoord << ").\n";
}
void Rectangle::showLLeft() const
{
    cout << "Lower left at (" << uLeft.xcoord;
    cout << "," << lRight.ycoord << ").\n";
}
```

continues

```cpp
void Rectangle::showURight() const
{
    cout << "Upper right at (" << lRight.xcoord;
    cout << "," << uLeft.ycoord << ").\n";
}
void Rectangle::showLRight() const
{
    cout << "Lower right at (" << lRight.xcoord;
    cout << "," << lRight.ycoord << ").\n";
}
void Rectangle::showHeight() const
{
    cout << "Height is " << hght << ".\n";
}
void Rectangle::showWidth() const
{
    cout << "Width is " << wdth << ".\n";
}
void Rectangle::showArea() const
{
    cout << "Area is " << area << ".\n";
}
//added for question 5:
Rectangle Rectangle::operator+(Rectangle & a) const
{
    int top, left, bottom, right;
    top = hght + a.hght;
    left = 0;
    bottom = 0;
    right = wdth + a.wdth;
    Rectangle b(top, left, bottom, right);

    return b;
}
//added for question 6:
void Rectangle::showAll() const
{
    showULeft();
    showLLeft();
    showURight();
    showLRight();

    showHeight();
    showWidth();
    showArea();
    cout << "\n";
}
//added for question 7:
Rectangle Rectangle::operator*(int a) const
{
    int top, left, bottom, right;
    top = hght * a;
    left = 0;
    bottom = 0;
    right = wdth * a;
    Rectangle b(top, left, bottom, right);

    return b;
}
//added for question 8:
Rectangle operator*(int a, const Rectangle & b)
{
    return b * a;
}
//added for question 9
```

```
Rectangle::Rectangle(double Area)
{
    hght = wdth = sqrt(Area);
    uLeft.ycoord = hght;
    uLeft.xcoord = 0;
    lRight.ycoord = 0;
    lRight.xcoord = wdth;
    setArea();
}
```

6. And here is a new userect1.h:

```
// userect1.cpp--test function for rectangle
#include "rect1.h"
int main(void)
{
    Rectangle a(75, 20, 25, 80);
    Rectangle b(60, 10, 0, 80);
    Rectangle rct = a + b;

    a.showAll();
    b.showAll();
    rct.showAll();

    return 0;
}
```

7. And here is a new userect2.h:

```
// userect1.cpp--test function for rectangle
#include "rect2.h"
int main(void)
{
    Rectangle a(75, 20, 25, 80);
    Rectangle rct = a * 3;

    a.showAll();
    rct.showAll();

    return 0;
}
```

8. New test function:

```
// userect2.cpp--test function for rectangle
#include "rect2.h"
int main(void)
{
    Rectangle a(75, 20, 25, 80);
    Rectangle rct = a * 3;
    Rectangle rct1 = 3 * a;

    a.showAll();
    rct.showAll();
    rct1.showAll();
    return 0;
}
```

9. And yet another test program:

```
// userect3.cpp--test function for rectangle
#include "rect3.h"
int main(void)
{
    double Area = 100000.0;
```

```
        Rectangle a = Area;

        a.showAll();
        return 0;
}
```

CLASSES AND DYNAMIC MEMORY ALLOCATION

Statement of Purpose

Building on the class concepts introduced so far, this chapter teaches how to make classes far more useful while dealing with some of the dangers of their power. Using dynamic memory with classes enables their use for a wide variety of programming problems, in particular the queue simulation presented. `new` and `delete` present their own issues that must be addressed in the design of a class to ensure both that a program works correctly and that memory is not corrupted. A lot of information is presented for the student to absorb, but only by using C++ can the concepts be made useful.

Objectives

By the end of Chapter 11, the student should understand the following concepts:

- Using dynamic memory with `new` and `delete` and classes

- How to use classes to make the free store to hold data

- `static` class members to hold data about all the objects in a class

- Constructors and destructors to manage dynamic memory

- Freeing dynamic memory versus freeing memory used by an object

- Default member functions provided by C++ and what can go wrong

- Default memberwise copying and deep copying in constructors and assignment operators

- Deleting memory multiple times—why it is a problem and how to avoid it

- Effectively using pointers to objects

- How a queue simulation works and implementing classes with dynamic memory

- Nesting structures and classes within a class

- Initializing `const` and reference data members using an initializer list

- Using dummy private methods to prevent future problems

Lecture Outline

Dynamic memory and classes

Here is another big step forward for the student's understanding of C++. A clear understanding of using **new** and **delete** is necessary to use classes effectively.

Sample programs
strng1.h—**String** class declaration

strngs1.cpp—**String** class methods

vegnews.cpp—using **new** and **delete** with classes for veggie news

- Key to making memory allocation decisions during runtime
- Using **new** and **delete** with classes raises new issues
- New technique: using a pointer to **char** rather than **char** array in class

  Declaration specifies memory for pointer only, not the string

  Removes limitations to string length
- **static** class member

  C++ creates one copy of **static** class variable no matter how many objects created

  Variable then shared among all members of class

  Useful for data private to a class, but has same value for all objects

  Must initialize outside of class declaration

  Form: **int String::num_strings = 0;**

  Put initialization in methods file, so only have one initialization

  Actual storage is separate from class objects
- Constructor allocates memory for the string object using **new**
- Destructor **delete**s the allocated memory
- Freeing memory object is *not* the same as freeing the memory pointed to by a member

  Must release both

  Must explicitly release dynamic memory with **delete**

  new and **delete** must be same form

    new with brackets, **delete** with brackets

    new without brackets, **delete** without brackets

Issues using **new** and **delete** with classes

Here the dangers of **new** and **delete** are explained in detail so that the student knows what to watch for and how to code classes properly.

- Two levels of usage

  Memory allocation for name strings pointed to by a data member

  Memory allocation for object itself, including pointer to the name string

- Destructor is called

  Automatic variable: when program block is exited

  `static` variable: when program terminates

  Object allocated with `new`: when explicitly deleted

- Creating with `new` in one function and deleting in another is potential source of programming errors

  Need to remember to put `delete` someplace

  Can cause memory leaks if loses track of objects

Another level of dynamic memory and classes

In this section, solutions are provided by introducing copy constructors and new behaviors of member functions.

Sample programs

problem1.cpp—deleting too many objects and null pointers

problem2.cpp—problem initializing one `String` object with another

problem3.cpp—null pointer assignment

strng2.h—revised `String` class declaration

strng2.cpp—revised `String` class methods

sayings1.cpp—test new `String` class by inputting sayings

- Member functions automatically provided by C++:

  Default constructor if none defined

  Copy constructor if none defined

  Assignment operator if none defined

  Address operator if none defined (`this` pointer)

- Default constructor

  No arguments and does nothing

  Required because creating an object always invokes constructor

  If you define constructor, no default constructor defined automatically

  Constructor with arguments can be default if all arguments have defaults

  Only one default constructor allowed

- Copy constructor

  Used to copy an object to a newly created object

  Prototype: `class_name(const Class_name &);`

  Single argument is a constant reference to a class object

  Used when new object is created and initialized to existing object of same type

    Not used for assignment

    During explicit initialization

    When passing object by value

    When returning an object

    Temporary object created

Good reason to pass objects by reference to avoid overhead

Memberwise copying is default

    Each member copied by value

    Member that is class object uses that class's copy constructor

    `static` members are unaffected

- Weirdness of problem1.cpp and problem2.cpp

One object constructed, two destroyed

    Second object created with copy constructor

    Doesn't affect reliability of program

-1 objects left

    Default constructor doesn't affect `static` members

    Copy constructor didn't affect `num_strings` count

    Solution: provide explicit copy constructor

Null pointer assignment—most dangerous

    Implicit copy constructor passes by value

    Copies the pointer, not the string itself

    Result: both objects point to same string

    Memory is `delete`d twice—big problem

    Solution: make a deep copy by allocating new memory for string copy

- Assignment operator

String corrupted in memory: memory mismanagement

C++ automatically overloads assignment operator for class object assignment

Used when assigning one object to another existing object

Not necessarily used when initializing

Implementations *may* use for initializing

So, default assignment operator uses member-to-member copying

Problem3.cpp again `delete`s string twice

    Undefined behavior

    Anything can happen

Solution: provide assignment operator that uses deep copying

Similar to copy constructor, except

    Use `delete` to free former obligations

    Protect against assigning to itself

    Return a reference to invoking object

    Last item allows chaining `a = b = c;`

- Copying ordinary string to `String` object

    If do often, may be better to not use conversion constructor

      Creates temporary object with the overhead

      Instead, overload assignment operator

- Recap of using `new` in constructors

    If use `new` to initialize a pointer member, use `delete` in destructor

    Make `new` and `delete` compatible—both with or without brackets

    If multiple constructors, all uses of `new` must be compatible with each other and with destructor

      Okay to initialize pointer in one and to NULL in another

    Define copy constructor using deep copying

    Define assignment operator using deep copying

Using pointers to objects

Expanding on the uses of classes and dynamic memory, the topic of using pointers to keep track of data in memory is introduced.

Sample program   sayings2.cpp—input sayings using pointers to keep track

- Object initialization with `new`

    Invokes constructor with same type argument

    Uses trivial conversions as long as no ambiguity

- When using pointers to objects

    Declare as usual: `String * glamour;`

    Can initialize pointer to existing object: `String * first = &sayings[0];`

    Can create new object using `new`: `String * favorite = new String(sayings[choice]);`

    Using `new` invokes appropriate class constructor

    Use the `->` operator to access class method via pointer

    Apply dereferencing operator (`*`) to a pointer to obtain object

Review of techniques used for classes

To cement the understanding of the extensive lessons so far, here is a recap of the techniques presented thus far.

- Overloading the `<<` operator

    Use a `friend` function with `ostream` argument that returns `ostream` object

- Conversion functions

    Use constructor with single argument of that type

    Use `operator typename();` to convert object to `typename` and return that type

- Classes whose constructors use **new**

  Use **delete** on any class member pointing to memory allocated by **new**

  If destructor frees memory with **delete** on a pointer class member, use **new** or set pointer to **null** in every constructor

  Use **new** and **delete** consistently in all constructors and destructors

  Define copy constructor that allocates **new** memory rather than copying pointer

  Overload an assignment operator using deep copying

Queue simulation

The queue simulation provides an opportunity to bring together everything learned about classes through this chapter, besides introducing a fundamental programming problem.

Sample programs   queue.h—queue interface

queue.cpp—queue and customer methods

bank.cpp—simulating the queue

- Queue is an abstract data type holding an ordered sequence of items

  New items added to rear of queue

  Items removed from the front

  First-in, first-out structure (FIFO)

  Simulates line at checkout counter

- Attributes of a queue class

  Holds ordered sequence of items

  Has limit of number of items can hold

  Is able to create an empty queue

  Is able to check if queue is empty

  Is able to check if queue is full

  Is able to add item to end of queue

  Is able to remove an item from front of queue

  Is able to determine number of items in queue

- Use **new** to dynamically allocate memory for queue items

  Singly linked list consisting of sequence of nodes

  Each node contains data plus pointer to next item

  Last node set to **null** to indicate end of list

  Use an object to keep track of front and rear of list

- Nesting a structure or class declaration within an object

  Has class scope

  Not all compilers support yet

  Doesn't of itself allocate memory

  Specifies type that can be used internally

- Initializing `const` data member

  Constructor cannot assign value

  Calling constructor creates object before code within brackets is executed

  So, must initialize before brackets using initializer list

    Comma-separated list of initializers preceded by colon

    Form: `Queue::Queue(int qs) : qsize(qs)`

  Can initialize all variables this way

  Usable only by class constructor

  Use also for members declared as references

  Members initialized in order listed in declaration, not initializer list

- Steps to add item to queue

  Terminate if queue is full

  Create a new node, terminating if unable

  Place proper values into node

  Increase item count

  Attach node to rear of queue

    Link to other nodes

    Set `rear` to point to new node

    If queue is empty, set `front` to point to it

- Steps to remove item from front of queue

  Terminate if queue is empty

  Provide first item to calling function

  Decrease item count

  Save location of front for deletion

  Remove item by setting `front` to second item in list

  Delete former first node

  If list is empty, set `rear` to `null`

- Define explicit destructor for nodes remaining in queue

- Provide dummy private members for copy constructor and overloaded assignment operator

  Overrides implicit method definitions

  If program attempts to use, error results

- Simulation

  If new customer arrives, add to queue if room or turn away

  If no one being processed, take first customer, and update waiting time

  If customer is being processed, decrement wait time counter

  Track number of customers served, turned away, cumulative waiting time, and cumulative queue length

Additional Questions

True or False

1. The following statement creates a unique class member occupying one memory location no matter how many objects of the class are created:

   ```
   static long baseballs;
   ```

2. The following statement initializes `baseballs` when it is within a class declaration:

   ```
   static short baseballs = 5;
   ```

3. The same statement included in the class default constructor sets `baseballs` to **5** each time a new object is created with the default constructor.

4. Freeing the memory occupied by an object is not the same as freeing the dynamic memory that a class member points to.

5. The destructor for an object that is an automatic variable is called when the function block ends, and the destructor for an object that is a `static` variable is called when the entire program terminates.

6. A very serious potential problem is creating an object with `new` in one function and using `delete` to free it in another function, unless the different functions are class constructors and a destructor.

7. A copy constructor must have a single argument that is a constant reference to a class object, and a default assignment operator must return a reference to the object to work properly with chaining.

8. By default, C++ uses only the default assignment operator when it generates temporary objects.

9. Once deep copying is complete on an object, there exist in memory two identical strings pointed to by class data members.

10. If an object invokes the implicit copy constructor, there exist in memory two identical strings pointed to by class data members.

11. The results of using `delete` twice to free the same memory is that it will be duplicated each time you take such action, so that you can count on that behavior and use it in programming classes.

12. Class object assignment and conversions to a class object are both implemented by overloading the assignment operator.

13. Assignment and initialization of an object always invoke the copy constructor.

14. When using `new` and `delete`, it is critical that the same form be used in all class constructors and destructors.

15. A linked list is one way to keep track of dynamically allocated objects in memory when it is unknown at compile time how many objects there will be.

16. The following code allocates memory in the `Menu` class for `Food`.

    ```
    class Food
    {
        char * name;
        double price;
        int vendor;
    }
    class Menu
    {
        Food * dish;
        double price;
        char * cook;
    }
    ```

17. An initializer list can only be used for class member functions.

18. Data members are initialized in the order in which they appear in an initializer list.

Short Answers

1. Describe the following terms, and explain their use in a C++ program.

    a. `static` class member

    b. memory leak

    c. deep copying

    d. queue

    e. linked list

    f. node

    g. singly linked list

    h. initializer list

    i. enqueue

    j. dequeue

    k. `RAND_MAX`

    l. `INT_MAX`

2. Run Listing 11.4 in the text. Do you get the same results? If not, how do you explain the difference?

3. Unless you specifically define these member functions, what implicit member functions does C++ provide?

4. Given this partial class declaration, what implicit member functions does C++ provide?

```
class Beans
{
    ...
public:
    Beans(int count);
    update(char * mfg, int year);
    ...
}
```

5. For a class `Patriot`, what type of member function is each of the following?

    a. `Patriot() {};`

    b. `~Patriot();`

    c. `Patriot(const Patriot &);`

    d. `Patriot & Patriot::operator=(const Patriot & p);`

6. For a class `Humblepie` and class objects `baked` and `unbaked`, do each of the following statements necessarily invoke the copy constructor?

    a. `Humblepie baked(unbaked);`

    b. `Humblepie * pride = new Humblepie(unbaked);`

    c. `bakepie(unbaked);`

    d. `Humblepie sherwood = baked + unbaked;`

    e. `baked = unbaked;`

    f. `Humblepie forest = baked;`

    g. `return unbaked;`

7. How does the implementation of an assignment operator differ from a copy constructor for objects that allocate memory using `new`?

8. Given objects `first`, `second`, `third`, and the following statement, which object first invokes the assignment operator?

   ```
   first = second = third;
   ```

9. Write a `Census` class constructor that has the following private data members: pointer to the front of a linked list of `City` objects, a pointer to the rear of the linked list, a constant `int num_cities`, a `double avg_pop`, and a `double avg_budget`. Initialize front and rear to NULL, `num_cities` to `50`, and the others to zero. (A file `census.dat` is included on the disk included with the text.)

10. Why are dummy private methods made private?

Programming Projects

1. Modify vector2.h, vector2.cpp, and randwalk.cpp in Chapter 10 to use dynamic memory allocation for the `Vector` class. Specifically,

   a. Include a structure VData as follows for the vector's data, and use it as a member of the Vector class.
   ```
   struct VData
   {
       double x;
       double y;
       double mag;
       double ang;
   };
   ```

   b. Include a new vName string member of the Vector class to hold a name of each vector object. Allocate only enough memory for the actual length of the string.

2. Write a program to record and report census data for the top 20 cities in the United States. Define a `Census` class that uses a linked list of `City` objects to record the information shown below:

   ```
   City Census Listing (1990):
   ```

Name	Pop.	Rank	Area
Baltimore	736014	13	80.30
Boston	574283	20	47.20
Chicago	2783726	3	228.47
Columbus	632910	16	197.81
Dallas	1006877	8	378.00
Detroit	1027974	7	143.00
Houston	1630553	4	581.44
Indianapolis	744952	12	352.00
Jacksonville	672971	15	759.60
Los Angeles	3485398	2	467.40
Memphis	610337	18	281.00
Milwaukee	628088	17	95.80
New York	7322564	1	321.80
Philadelphia	1585577	5	136.00
Phoenix	983403	9	427.80
San Antonio	935933	10	342.17
San Diego	1110549	6	330.70
San Francisco	723959	14	46.10
San Jose	782248	11	173.6
Washington D.C.	606900	19	68.25

Include a calculation of the average population and area in square miles. Hint: Used a fixed array to record the city name.

Activities for Learning

1. Does your compiler support nested structures and classes? How do you know?

2. Does your compiler define `RAND_MAX`?

3. Run the example programs in this chapter. Experiment with changes to get a feel for how the different C++ constructs are used. Modify them to make them more general and more useful to you.

Answers to Text Programming Exercises

1. Enhance the `String` class declaration (the strng2.h version) by doing the following:

   a. Overload the + operator to allow you to join two strings into one.

   b. Provide a `stringlow()` member function that converts all alphabetic characters in a string to lowercase.

   c. Provide a `stringup()` member function that converts all alphabetic characters in a string to uppercase.

   d. Provide a member function that takes a `char` argument and which returns the number of times that character appears in the string.

   Test your work in the following program:

```
// pe11_1.cpp

#include <iostream>
using namespace std;

#include "strng2.h"

int main(void)
{
    String s1(" and I am a C++ student.");
    String s2 = "Please enter your name: ";
    String s3;
    cout << s2;                     // overloaded << operator
    cin >> s3;                      // overloaded >> operator
    s2 = "My name is " + s3         // overloaded =, + operators
    cout << s2 << ".\n";
    s2 = s2 + s1;                   // + concatenates strings
    s2.stringup();                  // converts string to uppercase
    cout << "The string\n" << s2 << "\nconstains " << s2.has('A')
        << " 'A' characters in it.\n";
    s1 = "red";
    String rgb[3] = {String(s1), String("green"), String("blue")};
    cout << "Enter the name of a primary color for mixing light: ";
    String ans;
    int success = 0;
    while (cin >> ans)
    {
        ans.stringlow();            // converts string to lowercase
        for (int i = 0; i < 3; i++)
        {
            if (ans == rgb[i])      // overloaded == operator
            {
```

```
                    cout << "That's right!\n";
                    success = 1;
                    break;
                }
            }
        if (success == 1)
            break;
        else
            cout << "Try again!\n";
        }
    cout << "Bye\n";
    return 0;
}
```

Your output should look like this sample run.

```
 Please enter your name: Fretta Farbo
My name is Fretta Farbo.
The string
MY NAME IS FRETTA FARBO AND I AM A C++ STUDENT.
contains 6 'A' characters in it.
Enter the name of a primary color for mixing light: yellow
Try again!
BLUE
That's right!
Bye
```

```cpp
// pe11strg.h

#include <iostream>
using namespace std;

class String {
private:
    char * str;            // pointer to a string
    int chars;             // number of characters
    static int strings;    // total number of strings
public:
    String();
    String(const char * ps); // converts C++ string to String
    String(const String & s);
        ~String();
    int numstrings();
    int len();
    void stringup();
    void stringlow();
    int has(char ch);
    String & operator=(const String & s);
    friend ostream & operator<<(ostream & os, const String & s);
    friend istream & operator>>(istream & os, String & s);
    friend String operator+(const String & s1, const String & s2);
    friend int operator==(const String & s1, const String & s2);
    friend int operator<(const String & s1, const String & s2);
    friend int operator>(const String & s1, const String & s2);
};

// pe11strg.cpp
#include <iostream>
#include <cctype>
using namespace std;

#include "pe11strg.h"
int String::strings = 0;

String::String()
{
```

```
        str = NULL;
        chars = 0;
        strings++;
}

String::String(const char * ps)
{
        chars = strlen(ps);
        str = new char [chars + 1];
        strcpy(str, ps);
        strings++;
}

String::String(const String & s)
{
        chars = s.chars;
        str = new char [chars + 1];
        strcpy(str, s.str);
        strings++;
}

String::~String()
{
        strings--;
        delete [] str;
}

int String::numstrings()
{
        return strings;
}

int String::len()
{
        return chars;
}

void String::stringup()
{
        for (int i = 0; i < chars; i++)
            str[i] = toupper(str[i]);
}

void String::stringlow()
{
        for (int i = 0; i < chars; i++)
            str[i] = tolower(str[i]);
}


String & String::operator=(const String & s) // allows chaining
{
        if (this == &s)        // assignment to self
            return * this;
        delete [] str;              // free old contents, if any
        chars = s.chars;
        str = new char [chars + 1];
        strcpy(str, s.str);
        return * this;
}

ostream & operator<<(ostream & os, const String & s)
{
        os << s.str;
        return os;
}
```

```
istream & operator>>(istream & is, String & s)
{
    char temp[80];
    is.getline(temp,80);
    s = temp;
    return is;
}

String operator+(const String & s1, const String & s2)
{
    int len = s1.chars + s2.chars;
    char * ps = new char [len + 1];
    strcpy(ps, s1.str);
    strcat(ps, s2.str);
    String temp(ps);
    return temp;
}

/*
String::operator char *()
{
    char * ps = new char [chars + 1];
    strcpy(ps,str);
    return ps;
}
*/

int String::has(char ch)
{
    int ct = 0;
    char * ps = str;
    while (*ps)
    {
        if (*ps++ == ch)
            ++ct;
    }
    return ct;
}

int operator==(const String & s1, const String & s2)
{
    if (s1.chars != s2.chars)
        return 0;
    else if (strcmp(s1.str, s2.str) == 0)
        return 1;
    else
        return 0;
}

int operator<(const String & s1, const String & s2)
{
    if (strcmp(s1.str, s2.str) < 0)
        return 1;
    else
        return 0;
}
int operator>(const String & s1, const String & s2)
{
    if (strcmp(s1.str, s2.str) > 0)
        return 1;
    else
        return 0;
}
```

2. Rewrite the **Stock** class, as described in Listings 9.7 and 9.8, so that it uses dynamically allocated memory instead of fixed arrays to hold the player names. Also, replace the **show()** member function with an overloaded **operator<<()** definition. Test the new definition using the program in Listing 9.9.

```
// pe11stok.h
#ifndef _STOCK2_H_
#define _STOCK2_H_

#include <iostream>
using namespace std;

class Stock
{
private:
    char * company;
    int shares;
    double share_val;
    double total_val;
    void set_tot() { total_val = shares * share_val; }
public:
    Stock();          // default constructor
    Stock(const char * co, int n, double pr);
    Stock(const Stock & st);     // copy constructor
    ~Stock() { delete [] company; }
    Stock & operator=(const Stock & st); // assignment
    void buy(int num, double price);
    void sell(int num, double price);
    void update(double price);
    friend ostream & operator<<(ostream & os, const Stock & st);
    const Stock & topval(const Stock & s) const;
};

#endif

// pe11stok.cpp     // Stock class methods

#include <iostream>
#include <cstring>  // for strcpy()
using namespace std;

#include <stdlib.h>      // for exit()

#include "pe11stok.h"

// constructors
Stock::Stock()
{
    company = new char [strlen("no name") + 1];
    strcpy(company, "no name");
    shares = 0;
    share_val = 0.0;
    total_val = 0.0;
}

Stock::Stock(const char * co, int n, double pr)
{
    company = new char [strlen(co) + 1];
    strcpy(company, co);
    shares = n;
    share_val = pr;
    set_tot();
}

Stock::Stock(const Stock & st)
{
    company = new char [strlen(st.company) + 1];
```

```cpp
        strcpy(company, st.company);
        shares = st.shares;
        share_val = st.share_val;
        set_tot();
}

Stock & Stock::operator=(const Stock & st)
{
    if (this == &st)
        return *this;
    delete [] company;
    company = new char [strlen(st.company) + 1];
    strcpy(company, st.company);
    shares = st.shares;
    share_val = st.share_val;
    set_tot();
    return *this;
}

void Stock::buy(int num, double price)
{
    shares += num;
    share_val = price;
    set_tot();
}

void Stock::sell(int num, double price)
{
    if (num > shares)
    {
        cerr << "You can't sell more than you have!\n";
        exit(1);
    }
    shares -= num;
    share_val = price;
    set_tot();
}

void Stock::update(double price)
{
    share_val = price;
    set_tot();
}

ostream & operator<<(ostream & os, const Stock & st)
{
    os << "Company: " << st.company
        << "  Shares: " << st.shares << '\n'
        << "  Share Price: $" << st.share_val
        << "  Total Worth: $" << st.total_val << '\n';
    return os;
}

const Stock & Stock::topval(const Stock & s) const
{
    if (s.total_val > total_val)
        return s;
    else
        return *this;
}// pe11-2.cpp -- use the Stock class with dynamic memory
// link with pe11stok.cpp
#include <iostream.h>
#include "pe11stok.h"

const int STKS = 4;
int main(void)
{
```

```
// create an array of initialized objects
    Stock stocks[STKS] = {
        Stock("NanoSmart", 12, 20.0),
        Stock("Boffo Objects", 200, 2.0),
        Stock("Monolithic Obelisks", 130, 3.25),
        Stock("Fleep Enterprises", 60, 6.5)
        };

    cout.precision(2);              // #.## format
    cout.setf(ios::fixed, ios::floatfield);      // #.## format
    cout.setf(ios::showpoint);      // #.## format

    cout << "Stock holdings:\n";
    for (int st = 0; st < STKS; st++)
        cout << stocks[st];

    Stock top = stocks[0];
    for (st = 1; st < STKS; st++)
        top = top.topval(stocks[st]);
    cout << "\nMost valuable holding:\n";
    cout << top;

    return 0;
}
```

3. Consider the following variation of the `Stack` class defined in Listing 9.10.

```
// stack.h -- class declaration for the stack ADT
typedef unsigned long Item;



class Stack
{
private:
    enum {MAX = 10};    // constant specific to class
    Item * pitems;      // holds stack items
    int size;           // number of elements in stack
    int top;            // index for top stack item
public:
    Stack(int n = 10);    // creates stack with n elements
    ~Stack();
    bool isempty() const;
    bool isfull() const;
    // push() returns false if stack already is full, true otherwise
    bool push(const Item & item);    // add item to stack
    // pop() returns false if stack already is empty, true otherwise
    bool pop(Item & item);    // pop top into item
};
```

As the private members suggest, this class uses a dynamically allocated array to hold the stack items. Rewrite the methods to fit this new representation, and write a program that demonstrates all the methods.

```
// pe11stak.h -- class definition for the stack ADT
#ifndef _STACK_H_
#define _STACK_H_

typedef unsigned long Item;

class Stack
{
private:
    enum {MAX = 10};    // constant specific to class
    Item * pitems;      // holds stack items
    int size;       // max number of elements in stack
    int top;            // index for top stack item
```

continues

```
        Stack(const Stack & st) { } // no copying of stacks
        Stack & operator=(const Stack & st) { return *this; } // no assignment
public:
        Stack(int n = MAX);
        ~Stack();
        bool isempty() const;
        bool isfull() const;
        // push() returns false if stack already is full, true otherwise
        bool push(const Item & item);    // add item to stack
        // pop() returns false if stack already is empty, true otherwise
        bool pop(Item & item);    // pop top into item
};
#endif

// pe11stak.cpp -- Stack member functions
#include "pe11stak.h"
Stack::Stack(int n)    // create an empty stack
{
        size = n;
        pitems = new Item [size];
        top = 0;
}
Stack::~Stack() { delete [] pitems; }

bool Stack::isempty() const
{
        return top == 0 ? true: false;
}

bool Stack::isfull() const
{
        return top == size ? true: false;
}

bool Stack::push(const Item & item)
{
        if (top < size)
        {
                pitems[top++] = item;
                return true;
        }
        else
                return false;
}

bool Stack::pop(Item & item)
{
        if (top > 0)
        {
                item = pitems[--top];
                return true;
        }
        else
                return false;
}


// pe9-3.cpp

#include <iostream>
#include <cctype>
using namespace std;
#include "pe11stak.h"    // modified to define customer structure
// link with pe11stak.cpp
int main(void)
{
        Stack st(3); // create a stack of po numbers
```

```
        unsigned long temp;
        char c;

        cout << "Please enter A to add a PO,\n"
             << "P to process a PO, and Q to quit.\n";
        while (cin >> c && (c = toupper(c)) ! = 'Q')
        {
            while (cin.get() != '\n')
                continue;
            if (c != 'A' && c != 'P')
            {
                cout << "Please respond with A, P, or Q: ";
                continue;
            }
            switch (c)
            {
                case 'A': if (st.isfull())
                        cout << "stack already full\n";
                    else
                    {
                        cout << "Enter PO number: ";
                        cin >> temp;
                        st.push(temp);
                    }
                    break;
                case 'P': if (st.isempty())
                        cout << "stack already empty\n";
                    else {
                        st.pop(temp);
                        cout << "Processing PO " << temp << '\n';
                    }
                    break;
                default: cout << "Whoops! Programming error!\n";
            }
            cout << "Please enter A to add a customer,\n"
                << "P to process a customer, and Q to quit.\n";
        }
        cout << "Done!\n";
        return 0;
    }
```

4. The Bank of Heather has performed a study showing that autoteller customers won't wait more than one minute in line. Using the simulation of Listing 11.13, find a value for number of customers per hour that leads to an average wait time of one minute. (Use at least a 100-hour trial period.) The Bank of Heather would like to know what would happen if they added a second automatic teller. Modify the simulation so it has two queues. Assume a customer will join the first queue if it has fewer people in it than the second queue and that he or she will join the second queue otherwise. Again, find a value for number of customers per hour that leads to an average wait time of one minute. (Note: this is a nonlinear problem in that doubling the number of machines doesn't double the number of customers that can be handled per hour with a one-minute wait maximum.)

   a. A 10-element queue yields a one-minute wait when the average number of customers per hour is about 18. You can simplify the investigation by adding a new loop that allows the user to enter various values for the customers per hour. Here's a quick modification:

```
// pe11-4.cpp -- use the Queue interface
// link to pe11que.cpp
// modify Listing 11.13 to put calculation in a loop to
// make it easier to test different values for customers
// per hour
#include <iostream>
#include <ctime>     // for time()
using namespace std;

#include <stdlib.h>     // for rand() and srand()
```

continues

```cpp
#include "pe11que.h"

const long MIN_PER_HR = 60L;

bool newcustomer(double x);          // is there a new customer?

int main(void)
{
// setting things up
    srand(time(0));                  // random initializing of rand()

    cout << "Case Study: Bank of Heather Automatic Teller\n";
    cout << "Enter maximum size of queue: ";
    int qs;
    cin >> qs;
    Queue line(qs);                  // line queue holds up to qs people

    cout << "Enter the number of simulation hours: ";
    int hours;                       // hours of simulation
    cin >> hours;
    // simulation will run 1 cycle per minute
    long cyclelimit = MIN_PER_HR * hours; // # of cycles
    Item temp;              // new customer data
    long turnaways;          // turned away by full queue
    long customers;          // joined the queue
    long served;            // served during the simulation
    long sum_line;          // cumulative line length
    int wait_time;          // time until autoteller is free
    long line_wait;         // cumulative time in line
    double min_per_cust;    // average time between arrivals

    cout << "Enter the average number of customers per hour: ";
    double perhour;          // average # of arrival per hour
    cin >> perhour;
    while ( perhour > 0 ) // begin new loop
    {
     min_per_cust = MIN_PER_HR / perhour;
     turnaways = 0;
     customers = 0;
     served = 0;
     sum_line = 0;
     wait_time = 0;
     line_wait = 0;

// running the simulation
    for (long cycle = 0; cycle < cyclelimit; cycle++)
    {
        if (newcustomer(min_per_cust))     // have newcomer
        {
            if (line.isfull())
                turnaways++;
            else
            {
                customers++;
                temp.set(cycle);     // cycle = time of arrival
                line.enqueue(temp);    // add newcomer to line
            }
        }
        if (wait_time <= 0 && !line.isempty())
        {
            line.dequeue (temp);       // attend next customer
            wait_time = temp.ptime(); // for wait_time minutes
            line_wait += cycle--temp.when();
            served++;
        }
```

```
            if (wait_time > 0)
                wait_time--;
            sum_line += line.queuecount();
        }

// reporting results
    if (customers > 0)
    {
        cout << "customers accepted: " << customers << '\n';
        cout << "  customers served: " << served << '\n';
        cout << "          turnaways: " << turnaways << '\n';
        cout << "average queue size: ";
        cout.precision(2);
        cout.setf(ios::fixed, ios::floatfield);
        cout.setf(ios::showpoint);
        cout << (double) sum_line / cyclelimit << '\n';
        cout << " average wait time: "
                << (double) line_wait / served << " minutes\n";
    }
    else
        cout << "No customers!\n";
    // clear queue
    while (!line.isempty())
        line.dequeue(temp);

    cout << "Enter new value for customers per hour (0 to quit): ";
    cin >> perhour;
    } // end of new loop
    cout << "Bye\n";

    return 0;
}

//  x = average time, in minutes, between customers
//  return value is true if customer shows up this minute
bool newcustomer(double x)
{
    if (rand() * x / RAND_MAX < 1)
        return true;
    else
        return false;
}
```

b. When adding a second queue, direct customers to the shorter line. Process each queue. With two 10-element queues, about 52 customers per hour lead to an average wait of one minute.

```
// pe11-4.cpp -- use the Queue interface
// link to pe11que.cpp
// modify Listing 11.13 to put calculation in a loop to
// make it easier to test different values for customers
// per hour
#include <iostream>
#include <ctime>      // for time()
using namespace std;

#include <stdlib.h>     // for rand() and srand()

#include "pe11que.h"

const long MIN_PER_HR = 60L;

bool newcustomer(double x);        // is there a new customer?

int main(void)
{
```

```
// setting things up
    srand(time(0));              //  random initializing of rand()

    cout << "Case Study: Bank of Heather Automatic Teller\n";
    cout << "Enter maximum size of each queue: ";
    int qs;
    cin >> qs;
    Queue line1(qs);             // line queue holds up to qs people
    Queue line2(qs);             // second queue

    cout << "Enter the number of simulation hours: ";
    int hours;                   //  hours of simulation
    cin >> hours;
    // simulation will run 1 cycle per minute
    long cyclelimit = MIN_PER_HR * hours; // # of cycles
    Item temp;                   //  new customer data
    long turnaways;              //  turned away by full queue
    long customers;              //  joined the queue
    long served;                 //  served during the simulation
    long sum_line;               //  cumulative line length
    int wait_time1;              //  time until autoteller1 is free
    int wait_time2;              //  time until autoteller2 is free
    long line_wait;              //  cumulative time in line
     double min_per_cust;        //  average time between arrivals

    cout << "Enter the average number of customers per hour: ";
    double perhour;              //  average # of arrival per hour
    cin >> perhour;
    while ( perhour > 0 ) // begin new loop
    {
     min_per_cust = MIN_PER_HR / perhour;
     turnaways = 0;
     customers = 0;
     served = 0;
     sum_line = 0;
     wait_time1 = wait_time2 = 0;
     line_wait = 0;

// running the simulation
    for (long cycle = 0; cycle < cyclelimit; cycle++)
    {
       if (newcustomer(min_per_cust))     // have newcomer
       {
           if (line1.isfull() && line2.isfull())
               turnaways++;
           else // at least one line is not full
           {
               customers++;
               temp.set(cycle);     // cycle = time of arrival
// add customer to shorter line
               if (line1.queuecount() <= line2.queuecount())
                   line1.enqueue(temp);    // add newcomer to line1
               else
                   line2.enqueue(temp);    // add newcomer to line2
           }
       }
// process customers in first queue
       if (wait_time1 <= 0 && !line1.isempty())
       {
           line1.dequeue (temp);       // attend next customer
           wait_time1 = temp.ptime(); // for wait_time minutes
           line_wait += cycle--temp.when();
           served++;
       }
       if (wait_time1 > 0)
           wait_time1--;
```

```
        sum_line += line1.queuecount();
// process customers in second queue
        if (wait_time2 <= 0 && !line2.isempty())
        {
            line2.dequeue (temp);        // attend next customer
            wait_time2 = temp.ptime(); // for wait_time minutes
            line_wait += cycle--temp.when();
            served++;
        }
        if (wait_time2 > 0)
            wait_time2--;
        sum_line += line2.queuecount();
    }
// reporting results
    if (customers > 0)
    {
        cout << "customers accepted: " << customers << '\n';
        cout << "  customers served: " << served << '\n';
        cout << "          turnaways: " << turnaways << '\n';
        cout << "average queue size: ";
        cout.precision(2);
        cout.setf(ios::fixed, ios::floatfield);
        cout.setf(ios::showpoint);
        cout << (double) sum_line / cyclelimit << '\n';
        cout << " average wait time: "
            << (double) line_wait / served << " minutes\n";
    }
    else
        cout << "No customers!\n";
    // clear queues
    while (!line1.isempty())
        line1.dequeue(temp);
    while (!line2.isempty())
        line2.dequeue(temp);

    cout << "Enter new value for customers per hour (0 to quit): ";
    cin >> perhour;
    } // end of new loop
    cout << "Bye\n";

    return 0;
}

//  x = average time, in minutes, between customers
//  return value is true if customer shows up this minute
bool newcustomer(double x)
{
    if (rand() * x / RAND_MAX < 1)
        return true;
    else
        return false;
}
```

Answers to Additional Questions

True or False

1. T	7. T	13. F
2. F	8. F—copy constructor	14. T
3. F	9. T	15. T
4. T	10. F	16. F
5. T	11. F	17. F
6. T	12. T	18. F

Short Answers

1.

   a) A `static` class member has a special property. A program creates only one copy of a `static` class variable regardless of the number of objects created. That `static` member is shared by all instances of the class. See pages 479 and 481.

   b) If an object is not deleted correctly it will still occupy memory that no longer can be accessed by the program. This memory is "lost" until the computer is reset.

   c) There is a good description of deep copying on page 496 and in Figure 11.5.

   d) A queue is a data structure based upon a sequence. Data can only be added at the back and leave from the front. A full description is given on page 514 and Figure 11.7.

   e) A linked list is an implementation of an ADT queue. A description is given on page 516 and Figure 11.8.

   f) A node is a data structure that can hold the information to be held in the list along with a pointer to the next node. See page 516.

   g) In a single linked list, each node has a single pointer that points to the next node in the list.

   h) An initializer list is used to initialize the list. The syntax is given on page 520.

   i) enqueue is a member function used to add an item to the back of the queue. See page 521.

   j) dequeue is a member function used to allow an item to leave from the front of the queue. See page 522.

   k) `RAND_MAX` is defined in cstdlib and represents the largest value that the function `rand()` can return.

   l) `INT_MAX` is defined in climits and represents the largest integer value that can be used in the system.

2. If results are different, it is because we are working with undefined behavior, which means that essentially anything can happen.

3. Default constructor

   Copy constructor

   Assignment operator

   Address operator (for `this`)

4. Assignment operator

   Address operator

5. a. Implicit default constructor

    b. Default destructor

    c. Copy constructor

    d. Assignment operator

6. a. Yes

    b. Yes

    c. Yes

    d. Maybe—temporary object might be created

    e. No

    f. Yes

    g. Yes

7. Use **delete** to free former obligations

    Protect against assigning to itself

    Return a reference to invoking object

8. **second** invokes the first assignment.

9.

```
Census::Census(int num_cities) : num_cities(50)
{
front = rear = NULL;
avg_pop = 0;
avg_budget = 0;
}
```

10. Dummy private methods are made private so that if they are called by the program, an error will alert the programmer to the fact that they are not yet implemented. That way, subtle bugs can be avoided.

Programming Projects

1.

```
// vector2.h -- Vector class with <<, mode state
#ifndef _VECTOR2_H_
#define _VECTOR2_H_
struct VData
{
    double x;           // horizontal value
    double y;           // vertical value
    double mag;         // length of vector
    double ang;         // direction of vector
};

class Vector
{
private:
    VData vect;
    char * vName;
    char mode;          // 'r' = rectangular, 'p' = polar
public:
    Vector(void);
    Vector(double n1, double n2, char * name = NULL, char form = 'r');
    Vector(const Vector & vct);
    void set(double n1, double n2, char form = 'r');
```

continues

```cpp
    ~Vector(void);
    void set_mag(void);
    void set_ang(void);
    void set_x(void);
    void set_y(void);
    double xval() const {return vect.x;} // report x value
    double yval() const {return vect.y;} // report y value
    double magval() const {return vect.mag;}    // report magnitude
    double angval() const {return vect.ang;}    // report angle
    char * getname();
    void polar_mode();
    void rect_mode();
    Vector & operator=(const Vector & vct);
    Vector operator+(const Vector & b) const;
    Vector operator-(const Vector & b) const;
    Vector operator-() const;
    Vector operator*(double n) const;

    friend Vector operator*(double n, Vector & a);
    friend ostream& operator<<(ostream& os, const Vector & v);
};
#endif

// vec_oops.cpp -- methods for Vector class

#include <iostream>
#include <cmath>
#include <cstring>
using namespace std;

#include "vec_oops.h"

const double Rad_to_deg = 57.2957795130823;

void Vector::set_mag(void)
{
    vect.mag = sqrt(vect.x * vect.x + vect.y * vect.y);
}

void Vector::set_ang(void)
{
    if (vect.x == 0.0 && vect.y == 0.0)
        vect.ang = 0.0;
    else
        vect.ang = atan2(vect.y, vect.x);
}
// set x from polar coordinate
void Vector::set_x(void)
{
    vect.x = vect.mag * cos(vect.ang);
}

// set y from polar coordinate
void Vector::set_y(void)
{
    vect.y = vect.mag * sin(vect.ang);
}
Vector::Vector(void)             // default constructor
{
    vect.x = vect.y = vect.mag = vect.ang = 0.0;
    vName = new char[1];
    vName[0] = '\0';
    mode = 'r';
}
Vector::Vector(double n1, double n2, char * name, char form)
{
    mode = form;
```

```
        vName = new char [strlen(name)+1];
        strcpy(vName, name);
        if (form == 'r')
        {
            vect.x = n1;
            vect.y = n2;
            set_mag();
            set_ang();
        }
        else if (form == 'p')
        {
            vect.mag = n1;
            vect.ang = n2 / Rad_to_deg;
            set_x();
            set_y();
        }
        else
        {
            cout << "Incorrect 3rd argument to Vector() -- ";
            cout << "vector set to 0\n";
            vect.x = vect.y = vect.mag = vect.ang = 0.0;
            mode = 'r';
        }
}
Vector::Vector(const Vector & vct)   //copy constructor
{
    mode = vct.mode;
    vName = new char [strlen(vct.vName)+1];
    strcpy(vName, vct.vName);

    vect.x = vct.vect.x;
    vect.y = vct.vect.y;
    set_mag();
    set_ang();
}
Vector::~Vector(void)    // destructor
{
    //cout << &vName << "\n";
    delete [] vName;
}

void Vector::set(double n1, double n2, char form)
{
    mode = form;
    if (form == 'r')
     {
        vect.x = n1;
        vect.y = n2;
        set_mag();
        set_ang();
    }
    else if (form == 'p')
    {
        vect.mag = n1;
        vect.ang = n2 / Rad_to_deg;
        set_x();
        set_y();
    }
    else
    {
        cout << "Incorrect 3rd argument to Vector() -- ";
        cout << "vector set to 0\n";
        vect.x = vect.y = vect.mag = vect.ang = 0.0;
        mode = 'r';
    }
```

continues

```
}
void Vector::polar_mode()          // set to polar mode
{
   mode = 'p';
}
void Vector::rect_mode()                        // set to rectangular mode
{
   mode = 'r';
}
char * Vector::getname()
{
    return vName;
}
// operator overloading
Vector & Vector::operator=(const Vector & vct)   //assignment operator
{
    if (this == &vct)
        return *this;
    mode = vct.mode;
    delete [] vName;
    vName = new char [strlen(vct.vName)+1];
    strcpy(vName, vct.vName);

    vect.x = vct.vect.x;
    vect.y = vct.vect.y;
    set_mag();
    set_ang();
    return *this;
}
// add two Vectors
Vector Vector:: operator+(const Vector & b) const
{
   double sx, sy;
   sx = vect.x + b.vect.x;
   sy = vect.y + b.vect.y;
   return (Vector (sx, sy, vName));
}

// subtract two Vectors
Vector Vector::operator-(const Vector & b) const
{
   double dx, dy;
   dx = vect.x--b.vect.x;
   dy = vect.y--b.vect.y;
   Vector diff = Vector(dx, dy);
   return diff;
}

// change sign of Vector
Vector Vector::operator-() const
{
   double nx, ny;
   nx = -vect.x;
   ny = -vect.y;
   Vector neg = Vector(nx, ny);
   return neg;
}

// multiply Vector by n
Vector Vector::operator*(double n) const
{
   double mx, my;
   mx = n * vect.x;
   my = n * vect.y;
   Vector mult = Vector(mx, my);
   return mult;
}
```

```cpp
// friend methods
// multiply n by Vector a
Vector operator*(double n, const Vector & a)
{
    return a * n;
}

// display rectangular coordinates if mode is r,
// else display polar coordinates if mode is p
ostream& operator<<(ostream & os, const Vector & v)
{
    if (v.mode == 'r')
        os << "(x,y) = (" << v.vect.x << ", " << v.vect.y << ")";
    else if (v.mode == 'p')
    {
        os << "(m,a) = (" << v.vect.mag << ", "
            << v.vect.ang * Rad_to_deg << ")";
    }
    else
        os << "Vector object mode is invalid";
    return os;
}

// randwalk.cpp -- use the revised Vector class
// compile with the vector2.cpp file
#include <iostream.h>
#include <iostream>
#include <ctime>    // time() prototype
using namespace std;

#include <stdlib.h>     // rand(), srand() prototypes


#include "vec_oops.h"

int main(void)
{
    srand(time(0));             // seed random-number generator
    double direction;
    Vector step;
    Vector result(0.0, 0.0, "Floyd");
    unsigned long steps = 0;
    double target;
    double dstep;
    cout << "Enter target distance (q to quit): ";
    while (cin >> target)
    {
        cout << "Enter step length: ";
        if (!(cin >> dstep))
            break;

        while (result.magval() < target)
        {
            direction = rand() % 360;
            step.set(dstep, direction, 'p');
            result = result + step;
            steps++;
        }
        cout << "\nResults for " << result.getname() << ":\n";
        cout << "After " << steps << " steps, the subject "
            "has the following location:\n";
        cout << result << "\n";
        result.polar_mode();
        cout << " or\n" << result << "\n";
```

continues

```
            cout << "Average outward distance per step = "
                << result.magval()/steps << "\n";
            steps = 0;
            result.set(0.0, 0.0);
            cout << "Enter target distance (q to quit): ";
        }
        cout << "Bye!\n";

        return 0;
    }
```

2.

```
    //census.h--interface for city linked list
    #ifndef _CENSUS_H_
    #define _CENSUS_H_


    #include <iostream>
    using namespace std;

    const int nameSize = 20;
    class City
    {
    private:
        char name[nameSize];
        long population;
        int rank;
        float area;
    public:
        City(char * cityname, long pop = 0, int rank = 0, float area = 0);
        City(const City & c);
        City();
        ~City();
        void setname(char * n);
        void setpop(long pop);
        void setrank(int rnk);
        void setarea(float ar);
        char * getname() const;
        long getpop() const;
        int getrnk() const;
        float getar() const;

        City & operator=(const City & c);
        City & operator+(const City & c);
        friend bool operator>(const City & c1, const City & c2);
        friend bool operator<(const City & c1, const City & c2);
        friend bool operator==(const City & c1, const City & c2);
        friend ostream & operator<<(ostream & os, const City & c);
    };

    typedef City Item;

    class Census
    {
        struct Node
        {
            Item item;
            struct Node * next;
        };
        enum {L_SIZE = 25};
    private:
        Node * front;
        Node * rear;
        int items;
        const int lsize;      //maximum number in list
        //any preemptive definitions?
```

```cpp
public:
    Census(int ls = L_SIZE);
    ~Census();
    bool isempty() const;
    bool isfull() const;
    int listcount() const;
    bool addCity(const Item & item);
    bool addCity(char * cityname, long pop, int rnk, float ar);
    long avgpop() const;
    float avgar() const;
    void showList() const;
};
#endif

//census.cpp--census interface

#include <cstring>
using namespace std;

#include "census.h"

//Census list methods
Census::Census(int ls) : lsize(ls)
{
    front = rear = NULL;
    items = 0;
}
Census::~Census()
{
    Node * temp;
    while (front != NULL)
    {
        temp = front;
        front = front->next;
        delete temp;
    }
}
bool Census::isempty() const
{
    return items == 0 ? true :  false;
}
bool Census::isfull() const
{
    return items == lsize ? true : false;
}
int Census::listcount() const
{
    return items;
}
bool Census::addCity(const Item & item)
{
    if (isfull())
        return false;
    Node * add = new Node;
    if (add == NULL)
        return false;
    add->item = item;
    add->next = NULL;
    items++;
    if (front == NULL)
        front = add;
    else
        rear->next = add;
    rear = add;
    return true;
```

continues

```
}
bool Census::addCity(char * cityname, long pop, int rnk, float ar)
{
    if (isfull())
        return false;
    Node * add = new Node;
    if (add == NULL)
        return false;
    add->item.setname(cityname);
    add->item.setpop(pop);
    add->item.setrank(rnk);
    add->item.setarea(ar);
    //add->item = item;
    add->next = NULL;
    items++;
    if (front == NULL)
        front = add;
    else
        rear->next = add;
    rear = add;
    return true;
}
long Census::avgpop() const
{
    if (front == NULL)
        return false;
    Node * pt = front;
    // calculating apop this way avoids overflowing population
    // particularly since we know how many items are in the list
    long apop = pt->item.getpop() / items;
    while (pt->next)
    {
        pt = pt->next;
        apop += pt->item.getpop() / items;
    }
    return apop;
}
float Census::avgar() const
{
    if (front == NULL)
        return false;
    Node * pt = front;
    float aar = pt->item.getar() / items;
    while (pt->next)
    {
        pt = pt->next;
        aar += pt->item.getar() / items;
    }
    return aar;
}
void Census::showList() const
{
    if (front == NULL)
        cout << "Empty list.\n";
    Node * pt = front;
    cout << "City Census Listing:\n";
    cout << "Name\t\t\t Pop.\t\tRank\t Area\n";
    do
    {
        cout << pt->item;
        pt = pt->next;
    }
    while (pt->next);

    cout << "Average population:  " << avgpop() << "\n";
    cout << "Average area (sq mi): " << avgar() << "\n";
}
```

```
//city.cpp—city interface

#include <cstring>
using namespace std;
#include "census.h"

//City list methods
City::City(char * cityname, long pop, int rnk, float ar)
{
    strcpy(name, cityname);
    population = pop;
    rank = rnk;
    area = ar;
}
City::City(const City & c)
{
    strcpy(name, c.name);
    population = c.population;
    rank = c.rank;
    area = c.area;
}
City::City()
{
    name[0] = '\0';
    population = 0;
    rank = 0;
    area = 0;
}
City::~City()
{
}
void City::setname(char * n)
{
    strcpy(name, n);
}
void City::setpop(long p)
{
    population = p;
}
void City::setrank(int b)
{
    rank = b;
}
void City::setarea(float a)
{
    area = a;
}
long City::getpop() const
{
    return population;
}
int City::getrnk() const
{
    return rank;
}
float City::getar() const
{
    return area;
}
char * City::getname() const
{
    return name;
}
// overloaded operators
```

continues

```
City & City::operator=(const City & ct)
{
    if (this == &ct)
        return *this;
    strcpy(name, ct.name);
    population = ct.population;
    rank = ct.rank;
    area = ct.area;
    return *this;
}
City & City::operator+(const City & ct)
{
    population += ct.population;
    rank += ct.rank;
    area += ct.area;
    strcpy(name, "Summation");
    return *this;
}
bool operator>(const City & c1, const City & c2)
{
    if (c1.population > c2.population)
        return true;
    else
        return false;
}
bool operator<(const City & c1, const City & c2)
{
    if (c1.population < c2.population)
        return true;
    else
        return false;
}
bool operator==(const City & c1, const City & c2)
{
    if (c1.population == c2.population)
        return true;
    else
        return false;
}
ostream & operator<<(ostream & os, const City & c)
{
    cout.precision(2);
    cout.setf(ios::fixed, ios::floatfield);
    cout.setf(ios::showpoint);
    os << c.name << " \t" << c.population;
    os << "  \t " << c.rank << " \t" << c.area << "\n";
    return os;
}

//city_cen.cpp—test program for city census

#include <iostream>
using namespace std;

#include "census.h"

int main(void)
{
    Census c1990 = 20;
    c1990.addCity("Baltimore        ", 736014, 13, 80.3);
    c1990.addCity("Boston           ", 574283, 20, 47.2);
    c1990.addCity("Chicago          ", 2783726, 3, 228.469);
    c1990.addCity("Columbus         ", 632910, 16, 197.81);
    c1990.addCity("Dallas           ", 1006877, 8, 378.0);
    c1990.addCity("Detroit          ", 1027974, 7, 143.0);
    c1990.addCity("Houston          ", 1630553, 4, 581.44);
```

```
c1990.addCity("Indianapolis    ", 744952, 12, 352.0);
c1990.addCity("Jacksonville    ", 672971, 15, 759.6);
c1990.addCity("Los Angeles     ", 3485398, 2, 467.4);
c1990.addCity("Memphis         ", 610337, 18, 281.0);
c1990.addCity("Milwaukee       ", 628088, 17, 95.8);
c1990.addCity("New York        ", 7322564, 1, 321.8);
c1990.addCity("Philadelphia    ", 1585577, 5, 136.0);
c1990.addCity("Phoenix         ", 983403, 9, 427.8);
c1990.addCity("San Antonio     ", 935933, 10, 342.17);
c1990.addCity("San Diego       ", 1110549, 6, 330.7);
c1990.addCity("San Francisco   ", 723959, 14, 46.1);
c1990.addCity("San Jose        ", 782248, 11, 173.6);
c1990.addCity("Washington, D.C.", 606900, 19, 68.25);

//show the list
c1990.showList();

return 0;
}
```

CHAPTER 12

CLASS INHERITANCE

Statement of Purpose

We have now proceeded far enough along to examine one of the primary features of C++: class inheritance. With inheritance the programmer can become far more productive by reusing previously tested code while extending it through a derived class for the task at hand. With power comes responsibility, so the student must understand how inheritance works to use it effectively. With the complete review of classes, the student should have a firm grasp of the concepts of C++ classes.

Objectives

By the end of Chapter 12, the student should understand the following concepts:

- Class inheritance, what it means, and why and how it is used

- Building base classes for use in derived classes

- How functionality is added to a derived class while not taking away from the base class

- Strategies for effective use of base and derived classes

- Public, protected, and private class members and when to use each

- The members that are inherited and those that are not

- Taking full advantage of inheritance by modeling it on an is-a relationship

- What relationships C++ inheritance is not modeled on

- How the compiler decides what methods to use

- How objects are created and destroyed and how to code those functions

- virtual functions: control binding explicitly

- Typical implementation of virtual functions

- Using pure virtual functions to create an abstract base class

Lecture Outline

Class inheritance

This is an introduction to class inheritance so that the student has a good conceptual foundation on which to build.

- Standard C provides libraries that provide limited reusability

- C++ classes allow reuse and ability to modify without changing tested code

  Add functionality

  Add data to the class

  Modify class behavior

Array base class

Here, a simple base class is designed with inheritance in mind. What considerations must the programmer make to use the base class effectively?

Sample programs: bankacct.h—base class declarations

bankacct.cpp—base class methods

usebank.cpp—test function for `bankacct` base class

- Original class is the base class

- Inheriting class is a derived class

- Shortcomings of arrays that can be overcome

  No bounds checking

  Array and pointer to single element frequently indistinguishable

  Called function has no way of knowing size unless passed to it

  Often can't treat array as an entity

- Best strategy: build simple base class and add functionality to derived classes

Protected class members

The base class can open its data to modification by derived classes or keep it private. The risks and benefits of protected class members are

- Private to world at large but public to derived classes

- Private members cannot be accessed by derived classes directly

- Data less secure than with private—derived classes can modify

Inheritance as an `Is-a` relationship

Inheritance models the real world. There are appropriate relationship that base and derived classes can model, such as an apple is a type of fruit.

Sample program: overdrft.h—overdraft derived class declarations

- C++ provides three varieties of inheritance

  Public

    Most common

    Models `is-a` relationship

    Object of derived class is an object of base class

  Protected

  Private

- Other relationship models that aren't C++ inheritance

  `Has-a` relationship: include object as data member of class

  `Is-like-a` relationship: doesn't do similes

  `Is-implemented-as-a` relationship

- C++ inheritance adds properties to base class, but can't take them away

- Declaring derived form: `class Overdraft:public BankAccount`

  Colon indicates `Overdraft` is based on `BankAccount` class

  Public derivation

  Base public members become derived public members

  Base protected members become derived protected members

  Base private members become part of derived class but can't be accessed directly

  Protected and private derivations covered in Chapter 13

- Must add new constructors to derived class

  Constructor name matches class name

  Program first calls base constructor, and then derived constructor

  Don't need to duplicate work of base constructor

- Derived class generally inherits member functions of base class

  Assignment operator function not inherited

  `friend` functions not inherited

- Don't need source code of base class to create derived class

Implementing derived class

With the base class fully implemented, now it can be used in a derived class.

Sample programs: overdrft.cpp—overdrft derived class methods

                                     Useover.cpp—test function for derived class

- When creating object, base constructor called first to create that object—derived object is then created

  Derived constructor called

  Base constructor called and executes

  Derived constructor executes

- Derived class can assume that base objects data members are already set

- If omit derived class constructor, base constructor not called

- Calling base constructors that aren't default

  Form: `Overdraft::Overdraft(const BankAccount & ba, double ml, double r):BankAccount(ba)`

  Passes `ba` to base constructor

  Initialization list, similar to initializing `const` arguments and references

- Reference or pointer to derived class converted to base object when used as an argument declared as base class

  Converting to reference or pointer to base class is upcasting

     No explicit type case needed

     Anything can do with base object can be done with derived object

  Converting base class reference or pointer to derived class is downcasting

     Not allowed without explicit type cast

     `Is-a` relationship is not normally reversible

Virtual functions

Through the use of virtual functions, the base class can communicate information about class members that should and shouldn't be modified in derived classes.

Sample programs: bankacct.h—BankAccount class with virtual functions

                                  useover1.cpp—Test Overdraft class with bankacct.h

- Derived class that adds data and modifies methods

  Problem with redefining base class methods

  Program must determine which version to use

  C++ default is to use version of type of object referenced or pointed to

  At compile time, doesn't know what type of object will be referenced

  Strategy is called early or static binding

  C++ adds another strategy option

  Late or dynamic binding

  Program makes run-time decision

- Activating dynamic binding

  Available only for member functions

  Precede function prototype with `virtual` keyword

  Use `virtual` only once in base class for given member

  Type of object pointed to then determines binding

- Why two kinds of binding?

  Program has overhead to keep track of objects referred to or pointed at

  Flags functions that should and shouldn't be redefined

- Typical implementation of `virtual` functions

  Compiler adds hidden member to each object

  Points to an array of function addresses: table

  Table holds addresses of virtual functions of the class

  Separate table for base and derived classes

  If function not redefined, derived table points to base class function

  If function redefined, derived table points to new function

  Costs of `virtual` functions

  >   Object size increased by size of pointer

  >   Table created for each class level

  >   Looking up address to call function

- `virtual` functions makes function `virtual` for all levels of derived classes
- Constructors can't be `virtual`—not inherited anyway
- Destructors should be `virtual` unless class won't be a base class
- `friend` functions can't be `virtual` because not member functions
- If function not redefined in derived class, base class function is used
- Redefinition of function hides all base class functions of same name

  Function signature doesn't matter

  If redefine, duplicate signature exactly

  If base class function is overloaded, redefine all base class versions in derived class

- Pure `virtual` functions

  `virtual` function with a prototype but no definition

  Form: `virtual void draw() const = 0;`

  Can't create object of that class

  Exist solely to serve as a base class

  Called an abstract base class (ABC)

Inheritance and assignment

Here we investigate the implications of inheritance with respect to destructors, constructors, and the assignment operator. In addition, we learn that common functionality can be captured in an abstract base class, and then implemented in an inherited class.

Sample programs: bankdyn.h—`BankAccountD` class with DMA

bankdyn.cpp—Methods for `BankAccountD` class

overdyn2.h—`OverdraftD` class with DMA

overdyn2.cpp—Methods for `OverdraftD` class

usedyn2.cpp—test `OverdraftD` class

- Assignment operator is not inherited

  `darf` is a bank account object

  `temp1` is a bank account object

  `temp1 = darf` is equivalent to `temp1.operator = (darf)`

  based upon default prototype

  `BankAccount & BankAccount::operator = (const BankAccount &);`

- Mixed assignment

  Default assignment operator for base class will accept derived class object but only base class portion of derived object is copied (`upcast`)

  Assignment of base class object to derived class object (`downcast`) not allowed unless there is a constructor that defines a base class to derived class conversion

- Assignment and Dynamic Memory Allocation (DMA)

  Derived class that doesn't use `new`

  Assignment operator, destructor and copy constructor automatically used from base class

  Derived class that does use `new`

  Assignment operator, explicit destructor, and copy constructor must be defined for derived class

- Abstract Base Class (ABC)

  ABC describes a base class interface using at least one pure `virtual` function

  Any class containing a pure `virtual` function cannot be used to create an object

  ABC contains common functionality

  Derived class uses regular `virtual` functions to implement the interface

  Derived class will then have no pure `virtual` functions

  Derived can be used to create an object

  Derived class will have specific functionality

Class design review

To crystallize the students' knowledge of C++ classes, this is a complete review of the concepts presented in this and the last few chapters.

- Program automatically generates some member functions

  Default destructor

  > No arguments or all arguments have defaults

  > If don't invoke base class constructor in derived constructor, base default constructor is called

  Copy constructor

  > Takes constant reference to the class type as single argument

  > If don't need copy constructor, program provides prototype but no definition

  > Memberwise initialization is default

Assignment operator

    Default handles assigning one object to another

    Not the same as initialization

    Compiler doesn't generate assignment operators for one type to another

- Other considerations for class methods

Constructors create new objects.

    Methods are invoked to access existing objects

    Destructors are defined to remove existing objects and release dynamic memory

Constructor with one argument defines conversion from argument type to class type

    To convert from class type to another type, define conversion function

    No arguments, no return type, and having same name as type converted to

    Don't get carried away!

Passing by value versus by reference

    In general, pass objects by reference for efficiency and use of dynamic binding

    Use `const` if function doesn't modify object

    Function defined with base class argument can be passed derived class object

Returning object versus reference

    Use reference whenever possible

    Only difference is in function prototype and header

    Returning object generates copy of object

    Don't return reference to temporary object

    Return by reference an object passed to the function by reference or a pointer

Use `const` wherever possible

    When method doesn't modify argument

    To ensure that method doesn't modify object that invoked it

    To ensure that reference or pointer returned can't be used to modify object

- Public inheritance considerations

Be guided by the `is-a` relationship

Base class can point and reference derived object without explicit type cast

Derived class cannot point or reference derived object without explicit type cast

- Not inherited by derived class

Constructors

Destructors

Assignment operator

- Assignment operator

    Automatically supplied for assigning class type to another of same type using memberwise assignment

    Uses base class assignment operator for base class data members

    Must use explicit assignment operator if use `new` to initialize pointers

    Can explicitly invoke base class assignment to copy those members

    When assign a derived object to a base object, only base members are involved

    To assign base class object to derived object, provide conversion constructor

- Private and protected members

    Derived class can access protected and public members directly

    Derived class cannot access base class private members directly

- Virtual methods

    If derived should be able to redefine function, define as `virtual` in base class

    Inappropriate code can circumvent protection

    Base destructor should be virtual so that both derived and base destructors are called

Class function summary

Table 12.1 in the text is a recap of class functions, giving the student a concise guide to the use of class members.

Additional Questions

True or False

1. The best strategy to use in designing a base class is to include most, if not all, of the data and function members that are likely to be needed by the derived classes.

2. If `Seasons` is a base class with protected member `avgTemp()` and private member `tempupdate()`, the derived `Summer` class can only directly call `avgTemp()`.

3. Making a base class data member private gives it the best protection against data corruption, and making it protected gives it less protection.

4. In the `ArrayDB` base class designed in this chapter, dynamic memory was used for the array values so those values would not need to be stored contiguously in memory.

5. The copy constructor of the `Seasons` class will be called when the `fall` object is returned from the `tempupdate()` function:

    ```
    class Seasons {
        ...
        Season & tempupdate(Season & fall);
    ...}
    ```

6. In order for the following statement to work as expected, a reference to type `ArrayDB` must be returned from the `operator[]` method.

    ```
    arr[i] = 250.0;
    ```

7. If `arr` is a member of class `ArrayDB`, and `enrollment` is an object of that type, the statement in question 6 is equivalent to

   ```
   enrollment.arr[i];
   ```

8. The following is equivalent to the statement in question 6:

   ```
   *(arr = i) = 250.0;
   ```

9. In the following statement, the `const` refers to object `a`:

   ```
   ArrayDB & ArrayDB::operator=(ArrayDB & a) const {}
   ```

10. When a class contains a pointer, the overloaded assignment operator must have an object argument passed by reference, must return a reference to a new object, must use `delete` to free memory pointed to, and uses `new` to assign new memory.

11. C++ models an `is-a` relationship between the base and derived classes, and is the most common form of protected inheritance.

12. Saying that class inheritance in C++ models an `is-a` relationship is the same as saying that an object of the derived class should also be an object of the base class.

13. In a class `Watch` derived from the class `Time`, `Watch` has direct access to `duration`, `elapsed`, `seconds()`, and `adjust()`.

    ```
    class Time {
        private:
            double duration;
            char * name;
        protected:
            double elapsed;
        public:
            long seconds(double duration);
            friend double adjust(Time &);
    }
    ```

14. When defining a new derived class, the programmer must provide new constructors in all cases.

15. A class derived from the class `Time` in question 13 above will be able to call `adjust()` directly.

16. A major advantage that C++ has over C is that you can expand the functionality of standard classes even if you don't have the source code for the base class available. Modifying standard C libraries requires that you have the source code.

17. If the default constructor for the class `arithArr` were not declared and defined, the default constructor in `ArrayDB` would be the only constructor called.

18. If arguments are not explicitly passed to a base class constructor through the use of an initialization list on the derived class constructor, the default base class constructor is automatically called.

19. An initialization list may be used with either constructors or destructors.

20. A reference or pointer to a derived class object is converted to a reference or pointer to a base class object when used as an argument to a function defined as accepting a reference or a pointer to a base-class object.

21. Upcasting refers to converting a derived class reference or pointer to a base class reference or pointer, and does not require an explicit type cast. Downcasting, on the other hand, requires an explicit type cast.

22. In order for a derived class to redefine any methods of the base class, the function must be declared in the base class as `virtual`.

23. A base class overloads the protected method `sumitup()` with four different signatures. A derived class redefines the `sumitup(int b)` version. The derived class can then use the `sumitup(long a, double b)` version defined in the base class automatically.

24. Early binding means that all function calls are linked by the compiler to the actual function address, whereas late binding means that the program resolves some of the function calls based on the return type defined in the base class.

25. One of the guiding principles in the design of C++ is that you shouldn't need to sacrifice speed or memory for features that are unused in a particular program. This is why static binding is the default behavior.

26. A typical implementation of dynamic binding is for the program to set up tables in memory, one for each base and derived class, which contain the locations of functions. During run time, the program then calls the proper function, depending on whether it is `virtual` and whether it has been redefined.

27. Because a constructor is not inherited anyway, it cannot be `virtual`. `friend` functions, however, can be `virtual`.

28. In order for a function to be redefined by the derived class, it must be declared `virtual`.

29. Either of the following is a valid default constructor declaration:
```
Sheba() {};
Sheba(int a = 5, double star = 130500);
```

30. When a `StarBase` class is defined with the following public member, the compile will provide a default constructor.
```
StarBase(ArrayDb starry);
```

31. The following are all valid copy constructors:
```
StarBase(const StarBase &);
Star(const Star);
Building(const Residence &);
```

32. It is considered good programming practice to use `const` wherever possible.

33. When a derived class object is assigned to its base class object, only the base class portion is copied.

34. When a derived class object is assigned to its base class object, this is known as an `upcast`.

35. An abstract base class cannot instantiate an object.

36. ABC pure virtual functions are redefined in a derived class, thus providing specific functionality to the base class.

Short Answers

1. Describe the following terms, and explain their use in a C++ program.

   a. class inheritance

   b. base class

   c. derived class

   d. public member

   e. protected member

   f. private member

   g. `is-a` relationship

   h. `has-a` relationship

   i. `is-like-a` relationship

   j. `is-implemented-as-a` relationship

k. `uses-a` relationship

l. public derivation

m. protected derivation

n. private derivation

o. upcasting

p. downcasting

q. early binding

r. static binding

s. late binding

t. dynamic binding

u. `virtual` method

v. pure `virtual` function

w. abstract base class

2. What type of relationship does the first item of each of the following pairs have with the second item?

a. Baseball, sport

b. Airplane, wing

c. Dorm, hotel

d. Array, linked list

e. Farmer, combine

f. House, building

g. Programmer, compiler

h. Province, state

i. Car, paint job

j. Woman, human being

k. Woman, man

l. Wolf, carnivore

3. When these statements in `use_lim.cpp` are executed as shown after Listing 12.10, arraydb.h, what functions will be called and in what order?

```
LimitArr copy;
copy = vintages;
```

4. Say that you have a class `Pets`, which is a derived class of `Domestic`, which is a derived class of `Animals`. What must be done to call the constructor in the `Animals` class with arguments of `Guppie` and `25` when creating a new `Pets` object? (A file animal.dat is included on the disk included with the text.)

5. Which of the following assignments are valid, if `Tree` is a class derived from `Forest`?

```
long alpha = 132000;
Forest sierra = alpha;
Tree pine = sierra;
```

   a. `int * beta = &alpha;`

   b. `Forest & haber = pine;`

   c. `Tree & dasher = sierra;`

   d. `double & allo = alpha;`

   e. `Tree * shery = &sierra;`

   f. `Forest * hods = &pine;`

6. Suppose you create something like the following:

```
class Building
{
public:
    Building() {};
    Building(double x, double y);
    virtual void archstyle(int a) const;
    virtual void archstyle(double x) const;
    virtual void archstyle() const;
    ...
};
class Residence: public Building
{
public:
    Residence() {};
    Residence(int size);
    void archstyle(int a) const;
    void archstyle() const;
    ...
};
double index = 5.0;
int nxt = 13;
Building jones;
Residence smith = 4500;
```

   a. What function is executed by a program that calls `smith.archstyle(index)`? Why?

   b. How about `smith.archstyle(nxt)`? Why?

   c. If there are any problems with these declarations, how can they be fixed?

7. What does the following declare? What happens when `ArrayExt highways;` is executed?

```
#include <iostream>
using namespace std;
class ArrayExt
{
private:
    unsigned int size;
protected:
    double * arr;
public:
    ArrayExt();
    ArrayExt(unsigned int n, double val = 0.0);
    ArrayExt(const double * pn, unsigned int n);
    ArrayExt(const ArrayExt & a);
```

```
        virtual ~ArrayExt();
        unsigned int arsize() const {return size;}
        virtual double & operator[](int i) = 0;
        virtual const double & operator[](int i) const = 0;
        ArrayExt & operator=(const ArrayExt & a);
        friend ostream & operator<<(ostream & os, const ArrayExt & a);};
    #endif
```

8. Which of the following are initialization and which are assignment?

    a. `int beagle = 130;`

    b. `double whammy = 125.25;`

    c. `double ventana = {14.25, 100.20, 49.72, 130.0};`

    d. `ArrayDB twirl = ventana;`

    e. `ventana[2] = 163.45;`

    f. `ArrayDB saturn;`

    g. `saturn = twirl;`

    h. `saturn = ventana;`

9. What distinguishes a constructor from other class member methods?

10. What distinguishes a conversion function? What kinds of conversion functions are there?

11. What class members are not inherited by a derived class?

12. Fill in the empty grids of this table:

Function	Inherited	Member or friend	Generated by default	Can be virtual	Can have a return type
constructor					
destructor			yes		
copy constructor					
&	yes		yes	yes	
conversion	yes			yes	
()					yes
[]					yes
->	yes			yes	yes
op=				yes	yes
new	yes		no		
delete	yes		no		
other operators	yes		no	yes	yes
other members	yes		no	yes	yes
friends			no		yes

Programming Projects

1. Here is an equal opportunity for both cat and dog lovers. You are being given the chance to create life from electronics. Say you are given the following partial declaration of an `Animal` class:

```
class Animal
{
private:
    int age;
    char * name;
    char * sound;
protected:
    int weight;
public:
    Animal();
    Animal(int a, char * name, char * s, int w);
    Animal (const Animal & m);     //copy constructor
    ~Animal();
...
}
```

Include the following public methods in `Animal`.

```
speak(): Causes a member of Animal to speak
getage(): Retrieves the age of the Animal
getname(): Retrieves the Animal's name
getsound(): Retrieves the sound that the Animal makes
getweight(): Retrieves the animal's weight
setage(int a = 0): Sets Animal's age
setname(char * n): Sets Animal's name
setsound(char * n): Set the sound of the Animal
setweight(int w): Sets the Animal's weight
operator=(): Assignment of one Animal to another
operator<<(): Print the name and sound
```

Derive a `Dog` class from `Animal`, adding the following members:

```
private:
    int AKCno: American Kennel Club registration number
    bool fixed: true or false, if "fixed"
    Dog();
    Dog(int, char *, char *, int, int, bool)
    ~Dog()
    Dog (const Dog & d);
    speak(): Redefine what a dog says
    setAKC(): Set the AKC number
    setfixed(): Set to true or false
    getAKC(): Retrieve the AKC number
    getfixed(): Retrieve whether dog is "fixed"
    operator<<(): Print Animal info, AKC number, and whether fixed
```

Derive a `Cat` class from `Animal`, adding the following members:

```
    bool mouser;
    bool lucky;
    Cat();
    Cat(int, char *, char *, int, int, bool)
    ~Cat()
    Cat (const Cat & d);
    speak(): Redefine what a cat says
    setmouser(): Set whether the cat is hard on mice
    setlucky(): Set to whether cat is a good luck charm
    getmouser(): Retrieve whether cat eats mice
    getfixed(): Retrieve whether cat is lucky
    operator<<(): Print Animal info, and mouser and luck status
```

Use good programming practices regarding protection of data in the classes, and allocate memory for the names and sounds dynamically. Use this test program:

```cpp
int main(void)
{
    Animal mammoth(1000, "Toothy", "Uuuungh", 10000);
    Dog cockersp(5, "Torrey", "Woof woof!", 35, 0, true);
    Dog collie = cockersp;
    collie.setname("Pug");
    collie.setsound("Ruff ruff!");
    Cat persian(3, "Spot", "Purrrrrr!", 8, true, true);
    Cat manx = persian;
    manx.setname("Pinky");
    manx.setsound("Meooooww!");
    manx.setmouser(false);
    manx.setlucky(false);

    cout << mammoth;
    mammoth.speak();
    cout << cockersp;
    cockersp.speak();
    cout << collie;
    cout << persian;
    cout << manx;
    manx.speak();

    return 0;
}
```

which should produce this output:

```
Toothy says Uuuungh I weigh 10000 pounds, and I'm 1000 years old!
Toothy speaks: Uuuungh

Torrey says Woof woof! I weigh 35 pounds, and I'm 5 years old!
    I have no AKC number, and I've been fixed!
Torrey speaks: I'm a dog! Woof woof!

Pug says Ruff ruff! I weigh 35 pounds, and I'm 5 years old!
    I have no AKC number, and I've been fixed!

Spot says Purrrrrr! I weigh 8 pounds, and I'm 3 years old!
    I'm a champion mouser! And I'm not a black cat, so I'm lucky!

Pinky says Meooooww! I weigh 8 pounds, and I'm 3 years old!
    I live in peace with mice! My black fur shows it--I'm not lucky!
Pinky speaks: I'm a cat! Meooooww!
```

For Further Discussion

1. How do C++ classes and object oriented programming enable better modeling of the world?

2. How do you draw the line between features that are included in a base class and those best left to derived classes? What affect does the particular type of data and its manipulation have on the decision?

3. When might you use C++'s class inheritance to model has-a, is-implemented-as-a, and uses-a relationships, if ever?

4. Abstract base classes are often used as a design tool. Discuss why this is appropriate.

Activities for Learning

1. Run the example programs in this chapter. If your compiler has a debugger that allows you to step through the execution of a C++ program, step through the programs to see what functions are called when. Experiment with changes to get a feel for how the different C++ constructs are used. Modify them to make them more general and more useful to you.

Answers to Text Programming Exercises

1. Start with the following class declaration:

```
// base class
class Cd {      // represents a CD disk
protected:
    char * performers;
    char * label;
    int selections;     // number of selections
    double playtime;     // playing time in minutes
public:
    Cd(char * s1, char * s2, int n, double x);
    Cd(const Cd & d);
    Cd();
    ~Cd();
    void report() const;     // reports all CD data
    Cd & operator=(const Cd & d);
};
```

Derive a **Classic** class that adds a **char *** member that will point to a string identifying the primary work on the CD disc. If the base class requires that any functions be virtual, modify the base class declaration to make it so. Test your product with the following program:

```
#include <iostream>
using namespace std;
#include "Cd.h"

void bravo(Cd & disk);
int main(void)
{
    Cd c1("Beatles", "Capitol", 14, 35.5);
    Classic c2 = classic("Piano Sonata in B flat, Fantasia in C",
                "Alfred Brendel", "Philips", 2, 57.17);
    Cd *pcd = &c1;

    cout << "Using object directly:\n";
    c1.report();     // use Cd method
    c2.report();     // use Classic method

    cout << "Using type cd * pointer to objects:\n";
    pcd->report();  // use Cd method for cd object
    pcd = &c2;
    pcd->report();  // use Classic method for classic object

    bravo(c1);
    bravo(c2);

    return 0;
}
```

```cpp
void bravo(Cd & disk)
{
    disk.report();
}


// pe12cd.h
class Cd {       // represents a CD disk
private:
    char * performers;
    char * label;
    int selections;
    double playtime;
public:
    Cd(char * s1, char * s2, int n, double x);
    Cd(const Cd & d);
    Cd();
    ~Cd();
    virtual void report();     // reports CD data
    Cd & operator=(const Cd & d);
};

class Classic : public Cd {
private:
    char * works;
public:
    Classic();
    Classic(char * w, char * s1, char * s2, int n, double x);
    Classic(const Classic & cl);
    ~Classic();
    Classic & operator=(const Classic & cl);
    void report();
};

// pe12cd.cpp

#include <iostream>
#include <string>
using namespace std;

#include "pe12cd.h"

Cd::Cd (char * s1, char * s2, int n, double x)
{
    performers = new char [ strlen(s1) + 1];
    strcpy(performers, s1);
    label = new char [ strlen(s2) + 1];
    strcpy(label, s2);
    selections = n;
    playtime = x;
}
Cd::Cd(const Cd & d)
{
    performers = new char [ strlen(d.performers) + 1];
    strcpy(performers, d.performers);
    label = new char [ strlen(d.label) + 1];
    strcpy(label, d.label);
    selections = d.selections;
    playtime = d.playtime;
}
Cd::Cd ()
{
    performers = new char [8];
    strcpy(performers, "Unknown");
    label = performers;
    selections = 0;
```

```cpp
        playtime = 0.0;
    }
    Cd::~Cd()
    {
        delete [] performers;
        delete [] label;
    }
    void Cd::report()
    {
        cout << "Performance by " << performers << ": Label = "
                << label << '\n' << selections
                << " selections, playing time = " << playtime << '\n';
    }

    Cd & Cd::operator=(const Cd & d)
    {
        if (this == &d)
            return *this;
        delete [] performers;
        performers = new char [ strlen(d.performers) + 1];
        strcpy(performers, d.performers);
        delete [] label;
        label = new char [ strlen(d.label) + 1];
        strcpy(label, d.label);
        selections = d.selections;
        playtime = d.playtime;
        return *this;
    }

    Classic::Classic(char * w, char * s1, char * s2, int n, double x) :
            Cd(s1, s2, n, x)
    {
        works = new char [ strlen(w) + 1];
        strcpy(works, w);
    }
    Classic::Classic() : Cd()
    {
        works = new char [5];
        strcpy(works, "None");
    }
    Classic::Classic(const Classic & cl) : Cd(cl)
    {
        works = new char [strlen(cl.works) + 1];
        strcpy(works, cl.works);
    }

    Classic::~Classic()
    {
        delete [] works;
    }

    Classic & Classic::operator=(const Classic & cl)
    {
        if (this == &cl)
            return *this;
        Cd::operator=(cl);     // base-portion assignment
        delete [] works;
        works = new char [strlen(cl.works) + 1];
        strcpy(works, cl.works);
        return *this;
    }

    void Classic::report()
    {
        Cd::report();
        cout << "Works:\n" << works << '\n';
    }
```

Answers to Additional Questions

True or False

1.	F	13.	F	25.	T
2.	T	14.	T	26.	T
3.	T	15.	F—friend function	27.	F—not `friend` functions
4.	F—contiguous	16.	T	28.	F
5.	F—returned by reference	17.	F—none called	29.	T
6.	T	18.	T	30.	F
7.	T	19.	F—constructors only	31.	F
8.	F	20.	T	32.	T
9.	F—applies to `this`	21.	T	33.	T
10.	T	22.	F	34.	T
11.	F—public inheritance	23.	F	35.	T
12.	T	24.	F	36.	F

Short Answers

1.

   a. Class inheritance lets you derive new classes from old ones. The properties of the old class are passed on to the new class.

   b. The original class is called the base class.

   c. The new class that inherits the properties of the base class is called the derived class.

   d. A public member is available from the outside world and when inherited is still available to the outside world.

   e. A protected member cannot be accessed from outside the class (it is effectively private); however, it can be inherited by a derived class and hence overridden.

   f. A private member cannot be accessed from outside the class nor can it be overridden by a derived class.

   g. A description of the `is-a` relationship is given on page 545.

   h. A description of the `has-a` relationship is given on page 546 and in Figure 12.1.

   i. A description of the `is-like` relationship is given on page 547.

   j. A description of the `is-implemented-as` relationship is given on page 547.

   k. A description of the `uses-a` relationship is given on page 547.

   l. With public derivation, the public members of the base class become public members of the derived class.

   m. With protected derivation, the protected members can be accessed directly by members of the derived class.

   n. With private derivation, the private portion of the base class becomes part of the derived class but can only be accessed through public and protected members of the base class.

    o. Converting a derived class reference or pointer to a base class reference or pointer is called upcasting.

    p. Converting a base class reference or pointer to a derived class reference or pointer is called downcasting.

    q. The term *binding* refers to attaching a function call to a particular function. If this is done at compile time, it is *early binding*.

    r. The term *static binding* is another term for early binding.

    s. The term *binding* refers to attaching a function call to a particular function. This can be done at runtime with the use of virtual functions and is known as *late binding*.

    t. The term *dynamic binding* is another term for late binding.

    u. Preceding the function prototype with the word *virtual* in the base class creates a virtual method (alternatively known as virtual member function). This turns on the late binding mechanism.

    v. A pure virtual function has `=0` at the end of its declaration.

    w. When a class declaration contains a pure virtual function, it is known as an abstract base class.

2.   a. `Is-a`

    b. `Has-a`

    c. `Is-like-a`

    d. `Is-implemented-as-a`

    e. `Uses-a`

    f. `Is-a`

    g. `Uses-a`

    h. `Is-like-a`

    i. `Has-a`

    j. `Is-a`

    k. `Is-like-a`

    l. `Is-a`

3. `LimitArr` default constructor

    `ArrayDB` default constructor

4. The `Pets` constructor must be called with an initialization list that calls the `Domestic` constructor, which in turn takes a pointer to a string and an integer as arguments. The `Domestic` constructor must then be called with an initialization list that calls the `Animals` class constructor, which takes a pointer to a string and an integer as arguments.

5.   a. Invalid—`beta` is a pointer to `int`

    b. Valid

    c. Invalid without explicit type cast

    d. Invalid—`allo` is a reference to `double`

    e. Invalid without explicit type cast

    f. Valid

6. a. Program executes `Residence::archstyle(double x)` by demoting the `double` to an `int`.

    b. The `Residence` class `archstyle(int a)` will be executed.

    c. The declaration can be fixed by making sure that all of the `archstyle()` signatures of the base class are matched in the derived class.

7. The declaration is for an abstract base class using pure virtual functions, and as such can only be used as a base class. When the statement is executed, an error should result because `ArrayExt` objects cannot be directly created.

8. a. Initialization

    b. Initialization

    c. Initialization

    d. Initialization

    e. Assignment

    f. Initialization

    g. Assignment

    h. Assignment

9. A constructor creates new objects while other member methods are invoked by existing methods.

10. One form of conversion function takes exactly one argument to convert from the argument type to the class type. The second conversion takes no arguments and has no declared return type, and converts a class member to the type of the function name.

11. Constructors, destructors, and assignment operators.

12.

Function	Inherited	Member or friend	Generated by default	Can be virtual	Can have a return type
constructor	no	member	yes	no	no
destructor	no	member	yes	yes	no
copy constructor	no	member	yes	yes	yes
&	yes	either	yes	yes	yes
conversion	yes	member	no	yes	no
( )	yes	member	no	yes	yes
[ ]	yes	member	no	yes	yes
->	yes	member	no	yes	yes
op=	yes	either	no	yes	yes
new	yes	static member	no	no	`void *`
delete	yes	static member	no	no	`void`
other operators	yes	either	no	yes	yes
other members	yes	member	no	yes	yes
`friends`	no	friend	no	no	yes

Programming Projects

1.

```
//animal.h--class declarations
#ifndef _ANIMAL_H_
#define _ANIMAL_H_


#include <iostream>
using namespace std;

class Animal
{
private:
    int age;
      char * name;
      char * sound;
protected:
      int weight;
public:
    Animal();
    Animal(int a, char * name, char * s, int w);
    Animal (const Animal & m);
    ~Animal();

    virtual void speak() const;
    int getage() const;
    char * getname() const;
    char * getsound() const;
    int getweight() const;
    void setage(int a = 0);
    void setname(char * n);
    void setsound(char * n);
    void setweight(int w);
    Animal & operator=(const Animal & m);
    friend ostream & operator<<(ostream & os, const Animal & m);
};

class Dog : public Animal
{
private:
    int AKCno;
    bool fixed;
public:
    Dog();
    Dog(int a, char * name, char * s, int w, int akc, bool b);
    ~Dog();
    Dog (const Dog & d);
    void speak() const;
    void setAKC(int a);
    void setfixed(bool tf);
    int getAKC() const;
    bool getfixed() const;
    friend ostream & operator<<(ostream & os, const Dog & m);
};

class Cat : public Animal
{
private:
    bool mouser;
    bool lucky;
public:
```

```cpp
    Cat();
    Cat(int a, char * name, char * s, int w, bool m = true, bool l = false);
    ~Cat();
    Cat (const Cat & d);
    void speak() const;
    void setmouser(bool m);
    void setlucky(bool l);
    bool getmouser() const;
    bool getlucky() const;
    friend ostream & operator<<(ostream & os, const Cat & m);
};
#endif

// animal.cpp--implementation of Animal methods

#include <iostream>
#include <cstring>
using namespace std;
#include "animal.h"

Animal::Animal()
{
    age = 0;
    name = NULL;
    sound = NULL;
    weight = 0;
}
Animal::Animal(int a, char * n, char * s, int w)
{                                   //this
    age = a;
    weight = w;
    name = new char[strlen(n)+1];
    strcpy(name, n);
    sound = new char[strlen(s)+1];
    strcpy(sound, s);
}
Animal::Animal(const Animal & a)
{
    age = a.age;
    weight = a.weight;
    //delete [] name;
    //delete [] sound;
    int l = strlen(a.name)+1;
    int m = strlen(a.sound)+1;
    name = new char[strlen(a.name)+1];
    strcpy(name, a.name);

    sound = new char[strlen(a.sound)+1];
    strcpy(sound, a.sound);
}
Animal::~Animal()
{
    delete [] name;
    delete [] sound;
}
void Animal::speak() const
{
    cout << name << " speaks:  " << sound << "\n";
}
int Animal::getage() const
{
    return age;
}
char * Animal::getname() const
{
```

```cpp
        return name;
}
char * Animal::getsound() const
{
    return sound;
}
int Animal::getweight() const
{
    return weight;
}
void Animal::setage(int a)
{
    age = a;
}
void Animal::setname(char * n)
{
    name = n;
}
void Animal::setsound(char * s)
{
    sound = s;
}
void Animal::setweight(int w)
{
    weight = w;
}
Animal & Animal::operator=(const Animal & m)
{
    if (this == &m)
        return *this;
    delete [] name;
    name = new char[strlen(m.name)+1];
    strcpy(name, m.name);
    delete [] sound;
    sound = new char[strlen(m.sound)+1];
    strcpy(sound, m.sound);
    age = m.age;
    weight = m.weight;
    return *this;
}
ostream & operator<<(ostream & os, const Animal & a)
{
    cout << "\n";
    cout << a.name << " says " << a.sound << " I weigh " << a.weight
        << " pounds, and I'm " << a.age << " years old!\n";
    return os;
}

Dog::Dog() : Animal()
{
    AKCno = 0;
    fixed = false;
}
Dog::Dog(int a, char * name, char * s, int w, int akc, bool b)
    : Animal(a, name, s, w)
{
    AKCno = akc;
    fixed = b;
}
Dog::~Dog()
{
}
Dog::Dog(const Dog & d) :  Animal(d)
{
```

```
        AKCno = d.AKCno;
        fixed = d.fixed;
}
void Dog::speak() const
{
    cout << getname() << " speaks: I'm a dog! " << getsound() << "\n";
}
void Dog::setAKC(int a)
{
    AKCno = a;
}
void Dog::setfixed(bool tf)
{
    fixed = tf;
}
int Dog::getAKC() const
{
    return AKCno;
}
bool Dog::getfixed() const
{
    return fixed;
}
ostream & operator<<(ostream & os, const Dog & d)
{
    cout << Animal(d);
    if (d.AKCno != 0)
        cout << "     My AKC number is " << d.AKCno << ", ";
    else
        cout << "     I have no AKC number, ";
    if (d.fixed)
        cout << "and I've been fixed!\n";
    else
        cout << "and I've not been fixed!\n";
    return os;
}

Cat::Cat() : Animal()
{
    mouser = false;
    lucky = false;
}
Cat::Cat(int a, char * name, char * s, int w, bool m, bool l)
    : Animal(a, name, s, w)
{
    mouser = m;
    lucky = l;
}
Cat::Cat(const Cat & c) : Animal(c)
{
    mouser = c.mouser;
    lucky = c.lucky;
}
Cat::~Cat()
{
}
void Cat::speak() const
{
    cout << getname() << " speaks: I'm a cat! " << getsound() << "\n";
}
void Cat::setmouser(bool m)
{
    mouser = m;
}
```

```
void Cat::setlucky(bool l)
{
    lucky = l;
}
bool Cat::getmouser() const
{
    return mouser;
}
bool Cat::getlucky() const
{
    return lucky;
}
ostream & operator<<(ostream & os, const Cat & d)
{
    cout << Animal(d);
    if (d.mouser)
        cout << "     I'm a champion mouser! ";
    else
        cout << "     I live in peace with mice! ";
    if (d.lucky)
        cout << "And I'm not a black cat, so I'm lucky!\n";
    else
        cout << "My black fur shows it--I'm not lucky!\n";
    return os;
}
```

REUSING CODE IN C++

Statement of Purpose

Reusing code is one of the central goals of C++ and object-oriented programming, and the class is the primary means to that end. The language provides several methods of inheritance and the means to adapt these methods to the problem at hand. Classes and inheritance make it critical that the programmer understand the implications of choices made so the problem is solved effectively.

Objectives

By the end of Chapter 13, the student should understand the following concepts:

- Public, protected, and private inheritance and when to use each

- Single and multiple inheritance

- Programming changes when using multiple inheritance

- Containment classes and the differences from inheritance

- Deciding when to use inheritance and when to use containment classes

- Different ways in C++ to model the has-a and is-a relationships

- Initialization syntax to control class constructors

- Class interfaces and implementations, and how they work together with inheritance

- Class templates: their structure and how to make them work

- Using pointers and families of classes with class templates

- Template specializations to customize data types needing special algorithms

- Virtual base classes and controlling what code is executed

Lecture Outline

Classes containing object members

One of the best ways to reuse code in C++ is to include tested and proven objects in new classes.

Sample programs:

arraydb.h—array class used by **Student** class

arraydb.cpp—array methods used by **Student** class

studentc.h—containment **Student** class

studentc.cpp—**Student** class methods

use_stuc.cpp—using composite class to record scores

- Composition or containment

  Including object is way of representing components of more extensive class

  Models a **has-a** relationship

  Containment object acquires implementation but not the interface of member objects

  Can explicitly refer to interface of contained objects

- Declaration

  Initialization-list syntax for member objects

  Invokes a specific base class constructor

  If none specified, default constructor used

  Use member names, not class names

  Base class interface

  Isn't public, but class methods can use

  Reduces amount of new code needed

Private Inheritance

Refining the concepts of inheritance from last chapter, private inheritance is another way to keep data protected while making use of it.

Sample programs:

studenti.h—redefined using private inheritance

studenti.cpp—redefined class methods

use_stui.cpp—using private inheritance for student scores

- Base class public and protected members become private members of derived class

  Doesn't inherit base class interface

  Inherits the implementation

  Subobject: unnamed inherited object

  Similar to containment

- Declaration

Use **private** keyword when defining class

private is the default

Multiple inheritance: use multiple base classes

Initialization syntax uses class name for constructors

- Using base class methods

  Limited to use within derived class methods

  Can make public by calling base class methods from derived class method

  Use class name and scope resolution operator

  Use explicit type cast to call from **friend** functions

- Reference or pointer to base class can't be assigned to derived class

  Unless use explicit type cast

  Avoid ambiguity and unwanted recursion

- Containment or private inheritance?

  Most C++ programmers prefer containment

  > Easier to read and follow code

  > Potential problems with inheriting common ancestor or same name

  Private inheritance has features beyond containment

  > Access to protected members

  > Can redefine virtual functions

- Protected inheritance

  Use **protected** when listing base class

  Public and protected members of base class become protected derived class members

  Main difference is when a class is derived from from a derived class

  > Third level can still access second level protected members

- Redefining access

  Use to make public base class methods public in derived class

  Use access declaration in public section of derived class

  Form: `ArithArr::operator[];`

  Data or function member

  Don't use function parentheses or return types

Summary of public, private, and protected inheritance

See Table 13.1 in text: Varieties of Inheritance

Class templates

Class templates simplify coding of classes for different data types, saving time and reducing programming errors.

Sample programs:

stacktp.h—using template to create stack

stacktem.cpp—test template stack class

stcktp1.h—using array of pointers for stack

stkoptr1.cpp—test stack using people's files

arraytp.h—array template

worker.h—working classes for family of classes

worker.cpp—working class methods

workarr.cpp—Cafe Lola's first employees

pairs.cpp—Pair template using more than one type parameter

- Generate generic class declarations
- Parameterized types to allow passing a type name as an argument to algorithm

  Form: `template <class Type>`

  Preface both template classes and member functions

  Can omit for inline functions

  `Type` acts as a generic type specifier for which real type will be substituted

- Instructions to compiler how to generate class
- Particular actualization of a template is an instantiation
- Put template, declaration, and definition information in header file
- Asking for instantiation

  Declare object of template class type

  Form: `Stack<int> kernels;`

  Type parameters act like a variable

  Must explicitly provide data type

- Using pointers with template classes

  Compiler creates a class, but must make sure it works sensibly

  Calling program provides array of pointers to different strings

- Templates most used for container classes

  Apply common storage plan to variety of types

- Expression arguments for array stack

  Apply particular type to template class

  Uses stack rather than free store for faster execution

- Family of classes

  Multiple class levels

Can use array of pointers to base class members to store derived objects

Each level can pass initialization data to immediate lower level

Use `protected` access for implementations that need to be inherited by derived classes

Conversions not allowed in matching expression arguments in a template

Standard function `strchr()`

- Apply same techniques to template classes as to regular classes

    Can be base or component classes

    Can be type arguments to other templates

    Can use recursively

    Use with more than one parameter of different types

- Template specializations

When need different implementation for a data type

Compiler will use specialization over general template when match

Form: `class Classname<specialized-type-name> {...};`

Multiple inheritance

Multiple inheritance makes it possible to take full advantage of existing object classes, allowing multiple base classes to be combined to simplify the creation of new objects.

Sample programs: workermi.h—new working classes using multiple inheritance

                                workermi.cpp—new working class methods

                                workmi.cpp—multiple inheritance

- A class that has more than one immediate base class
- Form: `class SingingWaiter : public Waiter, public Singer {...};`
- New programming problems

    Inheriting different methods of same name from different base classes

    Inheriting multiple instances of a class via related immediate base classes

- Solution: `virtual` base class

    Allow inheritance of just one object of shared base class

    Use keyword `virtual` in class declaration

    Form: `class Singer : virtual public Worker {...};`

- Keyword `virtual` is keyword overloading
- Why not make `virtual` behavior default?

    May want multiple copies of a base object

    Program using `virtual` has extra overhead

    Forces coding changes to accommodate use

- New approach to programming

  Passing initialization data from level to level is disabled to avoid conflict in shared base class

  > Data might pass along different paths

  > Default constructor used instead

  > Invoke other constructors explicitly

  Must redefine some methods to avoid duplication and ambiguity

  > Could use scope resolution operator

  > Better to redefine functions

  > Define methods that display or affect data of one level only

- Dominance ·

  Multiple copies of base object without `virtual` causes ambiguity

  With multiple `virtual` base classes may or may not have ambiguity

  If one name dominates others it can be used unambiguously

  Name in derived class dominates same name in any ancestor

Additional Questions

True or False

1. Public inheritance means that a class inherits an interface and possibly an implementation, while pure `virtual` functions in a base class provides an interface without an implementation.

2. When providing an initialization list, use the objects' names for container classes and the class name for inheritance classes.

3. Omitting an initialization list in a derived class means that the base class will not be created but the data members will be available to the derived class.

4. The following table accurately shows the status of base class members when used in a derived class.

	Private Inheritance	Protected Inheritance	Public Inheritance
Private	Access only through base class	Access only through base class	Access only through base class
Protected	Private	Protected	Protected
Public	Private	Protected	Public

5. The primary difference between containment and private inheritance is that containment adds an object to a class as a named member object and private inheritance adds an object as an unnamed inherited object.

6. When faced with a new class that can utilize an existing class either by inheritance or containment, general programming practice is to use inheritance because the compiler can do a better job of optimizing code.

7. An access declaration allows initialization information to be passed from an object to its ancestors.

8. Function templates differ from class templates in that function templates require that you specifically must ask for a particular function implementation.

9. When more than one level of inheritance is used (an object has two or more ancestors), the lowest base class level must use the default constructors.

10. Class templates can be used recursively and have multiple types of parameters.

Short Answers

1. Describe the following terms, and explain their use in a C++ program.

    a. containment

    b. composition

    c. layering

    d. has-a relationships

    e. multiple inheritance

    f. class implementation

    g. class interface

    h. subobject

    i. private inheritance

    j. protected inheritance

    k. public inheritance

    l. implicit upcasting

    m. access declaration

    n. container class

    o. parameterized types

    p. template

    q. instantiation

    r. type parameters

    s. expression arguments

    t. homogeneous collection

    u. heterogeneous collection

    v. template specialization

    w. virtual

    x. virtual base class

    y. panache

    z. dominations

2. Convert the following to a class template that can use an array of any type in addition to int:

    ```
    //templat1.cpp

    #include <iostream>
    using namespace std;
    const int mSize = 10;
    ```

continues

```
class MachineTool
{
public:
 MachineTool(int);
    MachineTool();
    ~MachineTool() {}
    int GetWeight() const { return mweight; }
    void Display() const { cout << mweight; }
private:
    int mweight;
};

MachineTool::MachineTool(int weight):mweight(weight){}
MachineTool::MachineTool(): mweight(0) {}

class Array
{
public:
    Array(int itsSize = mSize);
    Array(const Array &arr);
    ~Array() { delete [] ptr; }
    Array& operator=(const Array&);
    int& operator[](int offSet) { return ptr[offSet]; }
    const int& operator[](int offSet) const { return ptr[offSet]; }
    int GetSize() const { return itsSize; }
private:
    int *ptr;
    int  itsSize;
};

Array::Array(int lsize):
itsSize(lsize)
{
    ptr = new int[lsize];
    for (int i = 0; i<lsize; i++)
        ptr[i] = 0;
}

Array::Array(const Array &arr)
{
    itsSize = arr.GetSize();
    ptr = new int[itsSize];
    for (int i = 0; i<itsSize; i++)
        ptr[i] = arr[i];
}

Array& Array::operator=(const Array &arr)
{
    if (this == &arr)
        return *this;
    delete [] ptr;
    itsSize = arr.GetSize();
    ptr = new int[itsSize];
    for (int i = 0; i<itsSize; i++)
        ptr[i] = arr[i];
    return *this;
}
```

3. Are the following examples of inheritance or containment? If inheritance, is it single or multiple inheritance?

```
class Tool {...};
class Component {...};
class Saws {
    ...
    Tool Bladesaw;
    Component motor;
    ...};
```

```
class Handtools {
    ...
    Tool utility;
    ...};
a)  class Powered : public Tool, protected Saws {...};
b)  class Builder : {
        Component toolbox;
        Handtools utilitybelt;
        ...};
c)  class Powered : public Tool {...};
```

4. What modifications might you make to the classes in the last question to use `virtual` base classes where it is appropriate?

5. In general, what types of changes do you need to make to code when changing from single inheritance or containment to multiple inheritance using `virtual` functions?

6. If ancestor classes have methods or data with the same names and are being used as `virtual` functions, how does the compiler decide which to use? How does it resolve ambiguities?

7. In the following code, which version of each of the member functions will each of the derived classes inherit?

```
class City {
public:
    short diplomacy();
    long economy();
    ...};
class State : virtual public City {
public:
    int military()
    long diplomacy();
    ...};
class Region : public State {
    ...};
class Country : virtual public City {
private:
    int military();
    long diplomacy();
    ...};
class Continent:  public Region, public Country {
    long economy()
    ...};
```

Programming Projects

1. The following is the class declaration for a linked list of integers.

```
//lists.h - non-template list class
class listItem
{
public:
    int val;
    listItem * next;
    listItem(int value, listItem * cell = 0):val(value), next(cell){}
};

class List
{
private:
    listItem *front;
    listItem *rear;
    int counter;
public:
    List() : front(0), rear(0), counter(0) {}
```

continues

```
        virtual ~List();
        void insert(int value);
        void append(int value);
      void show() const;
        int is_present(int value) const;
        int is_empty() const;
        int count() const {return counter;}
    };
```

a) Write the implementation of the member functions. Use the following test function:

```
// listuse.cpp
#include <iostream.h>
#include "lists.h" - use non-template form
void checkit(const List * listobj, const int value);
int main(void)
{
    List intList;
    intList.show();
    checkit(&intList, 81);
    for (int i = 65; i < 74; i++)
        intList.append(i);
    for (int j = i+5; j <= i+16; j++)
        intList.insert(j);
    intList.show();
    checkit(& intList, 81);

    return 0;
}

void checkit(const List * listobj, const int value)
{
    if (listobj->is_present(value))
        cout << value << " is present in the list.\n";
    else
        cout << value << " is absent from the list.\n";
}
```

Here is the output that the program should produce:

```
List is empty.
81 is absent from the list.

89 88 87 86 85
84 83 82 81 80
79 65 66 67 68
69 70 71 72 73
81 is present in the list.
```

b) Convert the class to a template that will work with arrays of any numerical data types. Modify the test program as necessary to test with integers and **char** arrays. How does the output change in the new versions?

The above code is included in the file **list.dat** on the disk that accompanies the text.

2. Write an account management program for the Bank of the New Age. Include classes for a basic, checking, savings, and master accounts, as shown below. The basic account is a no frills, no interest minor account (use this as the base class). The master account is a special account for large depositors that combines a checking and savings account all in one. Include data members in each of the classes at the lowest common level. Include a **show()** method in each class so that, when used together, they produce the data below. Utilize multiple inheritance as appropriate. Use an array, from ArrayTP if your compiler supports templates, of objects in the test program to input and output the data. Use the String and the **ArrayTP** classes as appropriate, and any other classes as appropriate. Input the account data, and print the following report:

```
BofNA Current Accounts:

Type: Basic account
Account name: Small Fish
Account number: 4099086
Balance: $12.00

Type: Checking
Account name: No Frills
Account number: 5099092
Balance: $1000.00
Monthly fee: $14.50, includes 25 checks.

Type: Savings
Account name: Thrifty Christmas
Account number: 6099026
Balance: $250.00
Savings type: Christmas Club
Current rate is an amazing 3.25%!!

Type: Master account
Account name: VIP Account
Account number: 5
Balance: $125000.00
Monthly fee: $0.00, includes unlimited checks.
Savings type: Other
Current rate is an amazing 4.60%!!

Type: Checking
Account name: Executive
Account number: 5099012
Balance: $12250.00
Monthly fee: $6.00, includes unlimited checks.

Type: Checking
Account name: Golden Age
Account number: 5099008
Balance: $75000.00
Monthly fee: $6.25, includes unlimited checks.

Type: Master account
Account name: Big Spender
Account number: 8
Balance: $250000.00
Monthly fee: $0.00, includes unlimited checks.
Savings type: Other
Current rate is an amazing 5.30%!!

Type: Savings
Account name: Children's Starter
Account number: 4099086
Balance: $27.23
Savings type: Regular
Current rate is an amazing 1.75%!!
```

For Further Discussion

1. When might you want to have multiple copies of a base class in a derived class?

Activities for Learning

1. Will your compiler allow you to place the declarations of a class in a header file and the implementation in a different file?

2. Run the example programs in this chapter. Experiment with changes to get a feel for how the different C++ constructs are used. Modify them to make them more general and more useful to you.

Answers to Text Programming Exercises

1. The `Wine` class has a `String` class object (Chapter 11) holding the name of a wine and a `LimitArr` class object (Chapter 12) holding the number of available bottles for each of several years. Implement the `Wine` class using containment and test it with a simple program. The program should prompt you to enter a wine name, the size of the array, the first year for the array, and the number of bottles for each year. The program should use this data to construct a `Wine` object, and then display the information stored in the object.

```cpp
// winecon.h  -- using containment

#include <iostream>
using namespace std;

#include "limarr.h"
#include "strng2.h"

class Wine
{
private:
    String name;
    LimitArr bottles;
public:
    Wine() : name("No name"), bottles() {}
    Wine (const String & st, const LimitArr & la) : name(st),
        bottles(la) { }
    Wine (const char * s, int size, int lb) : name(s),
        bottles (size, lb) { }
    ~Wine() { }
    double & operator[](int i) { return bottles[i]; }
    const double & operator[](int i) const {return bottles[i];}
    friend ostream & operator<<(ostream & os, const Wine &w);
};
// since there is just one non-inline function, let's
// save files space and put definition here
ostream & operator<<(ostream & os, const Wine &w)
{
    os << w.name << "\n";
    int start = w.bottles.lbound();
    int stop = w.bottles.ubound();
    for (int i = start; i <= stop; i++)
        cout << i << ": " << w[i] << "\n";
    return os;
}

// pe13-1.cpp

#include <iostream>
using namespace std;
#include "winecon.h"
const int Lim = 40;
```

```
int main(void)
{
    cout << "Enter name of wine: ";
    char name[Lim];
    cin.getline(name,Lim);
    cout << "Enter the number of years: ";
    int years;
    cin >> years;
    cout << "Enter the first year: ";
    int firstyear;
    cin >> firstyear;
    Wine cache(name, years, firstyear);
    for (int i = firstyear; i < firstyear + years; i++)
    {
        cout << "Enter number of bottles for " << i << ": ";
        cin >> cache[i];
    }
    cout << cache;
    return 0;
}
```

2. The `Wine` class has a **String** class object (Chapter 11) holding the name of a wine and a **LimitArr** class object (Chapter 12) holding the number of available bottles for each of several years. Implement the **Wine** class using private inheritance and test it with a simple program. The program should prompt you to enter a wine name, the size of the array, the first year for the array, and the number of bottles for each year. The program should use this data to construct a **Wine** object, and then display the information stored in the object.

```
// wineinh.h -- using private inheritance

#include <iostream>
using namespace std;
#include "limarr.h"
#include "strng2.h"

class Wine : private String, private LimitArr
{
public:
    Wine() : String("No name"), LimitArr() {}
    Wine (const String & st, const LimitArr & la) :
        String(st), LimitArr(la) { }
    Wine (const char * s, int size, int lb) : String(s),
        LimitArr (size, lb) { }
    ~Wine() { }
    double & operator[](int i)
        { return LimitArr::operator[](i); }
    const double & operator[](int i) const
        { return LimitArr::operator[](i); }
    friend ostream & operator<<(ostream & os, const Wine &w);
};
// since there is just one none-in-line function, let's
// save files space and put definition here
ostream & operator<<(ostream & os, const Wine &w)
{
    os << (const String &) w << "\n";
    int start = w.lbound();
    int stop = w.ubound();
    for (int i = start; i <= stop; i++)
        cout << i << ": " << w[i] << "\n";
    return os;
}

// pe13-1.cpp

#include <iostream>
using namespace std;
```

continues

```
#include "wineinh.h"
const int Lim = 40;
int main(void)
{
    cout << "Enter name of wine: ";
    char name[Lim];
    cin.getline(name,Lim);
    cout << "Enter the number of years: ";
    int years;
    cin >> years;
    cout << "Enter the first year: ";
    int firstyear;
    cin >> firstyear;
    Wine cache(name, years, firstyear);
    for (int i = firstyear; i < firstyear + years; i++)
    {
        cout << "Enter number of bottles for " << i << ": ";
        cin >> cache[i];
    }
    cout << cache;
    return 0;
}
```

3. Define a `QueueTp` template. Test it by creating a queue of pointers-to-`Worker` (as defined in Listing 13.16) and using the queue in a program similar to that of Listing 13.18.

   The following solution also uses strng2.h, strng2.cpp, workermi.h, and workermi.cpp from the text.

```
// queuetp.h -- interface for a queue template
#ifndef _QUEUETP_H_
#define _QUEUETP_H_


template <class Item, int n>
class QueueTP
{
// class scope definitions
    // Node is a nested structure definition local to this class
    struct Node { Item item; struct Node * next;};
private:
    Node * front;        // pointer to front of Queue
    Node * rear;         // pointer to rear of Queue
    int items;           // current number of items in Queue
    const int qsize;     // maximum number of items in Queue
    QueueTP(const QueueTP & q) : qsize(0) { }    // preemptive definition
    QueueTP & operator=(const QueueTP & q) { return *this;}
public:
    QueueTP();
    ~QueueTP();
    bool isempty() const;
    bool isfull() const;
    int queuecount() const;
    bool enqueue(const Item &item);     // add item to end
    bool dequeue(Item &item);           // remove item from front
};

// QueueTP methods
template <class Item, int n>
QueueTP<Item,n>::QueueTP() : qsize(n)
{
    front = rear = NULL;
    items = 0;
}

template <class Item, int n>
QueueTP<Item,n>::~QueueTP()
```

```
{
    Node * temp;
    while (front != NULL)      // while queue is not yet empty
    {
        temp = front;          // save address of front item
        front = front->next;// reset pointer to next item
        delete temp;           // delete former front
    }
}

template <class Item, int n>
bool QueueTP<Item,n>::isempty() const
{
    return items == 0 ? true : false;
}

template <class Item, int n>
bool QueueTP<Item,n>::isfull() const
{
    return items == qsize ? true : false;
}

template <class Item, int n>
int QueueTP<Item,n>::queuecount() const
{
    return items;
}

// Add item to queue
template <class Item, int n>
bool QueueTP<Item,n>::enqueue(const Item & item)
{
    if (isfull())
        return false;
    Node * add = new Node;     // create node
    if (add == NULL)
        return false;          // quit if none available
    add->item = item;          // set node pointers
    add->next = NULL;
    items++;
    if (front == NULL)         // if queue is empty,
        front = add;           // place item at front
    else
        rear->next = add;      // else place at rear
    rear = add;                // have rear point to new node
    return true;
}

// Place front item into item variable and remove from queue
template <class Item, int n>
bool QueueTP<Item,n>::dequeue(Item & item)
{
    if (front == NULL)
        return false;
    item = front->item;        // set item to first item in queue
    items--;
    Node * temp = front;       // save location of first item
    front = front->next;       // reset front to next item
    delete temp;               // delete former first item
    if (items == 0)
        rear = NULL;
    return true;
}
#endif
```

continues

```
// pe13-3.cpp -- multiple inheritance
// compile with workermi.cpp, strng2.cpp

#include <iostream>
#include <cstring>
using namespace std;
#include "workermi.h"
#include "queuetp.h"
const int SIZE = 5;
int main(void)
{
    QueueTP<Worker *, (int) SIZE> lolas;
    Worker * ptemp;

    while (!lolas.isfull() )
    {
        char choice;
        cout << "Enter the employee category:\n"
            << "e: worker  w: waiter  s: singer   "
            << "t: singing waiter  q: quit\n";
        cin >> choice;
        while (strchr("ewstq", choice) == NULL)
        {
            cout << "Please enter an e, w, s, t, or q: ";
            cin >> choice;
        }
        if (choice == 'q')
            break;
        switch(choice)
        {
            case 'e': ptemp = new Worker;
                        break;
            case 'w': ptemp = new Waiter;
                        break;
            case 's': ptemp = new Singer;
                        break;
            case 't': ptemp = new SingingWaiter;
                        break;
        }
        cin.get();
        ptemp->set();
        lolas.enqueue(ptemp);
    }

    cout << "\nHere is your staff:\n";
    while (!lolas.isempty())
    {
        lolas.dequeue(ptemp);
        cout << '\n';
        ptemp->show();
        delete ptemp;
    }

    return 0;
}
```

4. A `Person` class holds the first name and the last name of a person. In addition to its constructors, it has a `show()` method that displays both names. A `Gunslinger` class derives virtually from the `Person` class. It has a `draw()` member that returns a type `double` value representing a gunslinger's draw time. The class also has an `int` member representing the number of notches on a gunslinger's gun. Finally, it has a `show()` function that displays all this information. A `PokerPlayer` class derives virtually from the `Person` class. It has a `draw()` member that returns a random number in the range 1–52, representing a card value. (Optionally, you could define a `Card` class with suite and face value members and use a `Card` return value for `draw()`). The `PokerPlayer` class uses the `Person` `show()` function. The `BadDude` class derives publicly from the `Gunslinger` and `PokerPlayer`

classes. It has a `gdraw()` member that returns a bad dude's draw time and a `cdraw()` member that returns the next card drawn. It has an appropriate `show()` function. Define all these classes and methods, along with any other necessary methods (such as methods for setting object values), and test them in a simple program similar to that of Listing 13.18.

To conserve space, the following solution places all the class declarations and method definitions in one file.

```cpp
// pe13-4.h

#include <iostream>
#include <cstring>
using namespace std;
#include <stdlib.h>

const int Len = 20;
class Person
{
private:
    char fname[Len];
    char lname[Len];
public:
    Person() { fname[0] = lname[0] = '\0'; }
    Person (const char *fn, const char * ln);
    ~Person() {}
    virtual void show() { cout << fname << " " << lname; }
    virtual void set();
};
Person::    Person (const char *fn, const char * ln)
{
    strncpy(fname,fn, Len - 1);
    fname[Len - 1] = '\0';
    strncpy(lname,ln, Len - 1);
    lname[Len - 1] = '\0';
};
void Person::set()
{
    cout << "Enter first name: ";
    cin.getline(fname, Len);
    cout << "Enter last name: ";
    cin.getline(lname, Len);
}

class Gunslinger : virtual public Person
{
private:
    double drawtime;
    int notches;
public:
    Gunslinger() : Person("Joe", "Doe"), drawtime(0.0),
                        notches(0) { }
    Gunslinger(const char *fn, const char *ln,
                double d = 1.0, int n = 0) : Person (fn, ln),
                drawtime(d), notches(n) { }
    Gunslinger(const Person & p, double d = 1.0, int n = 0) :
                Person(p), drawtime(d), notches(n) { }
// Person(p) is the default copy constructor
    double draw() { return drawtime; }
    void show ();
    void set();
};

void Gunslinger::set()
{
    Person::set();
    cout << "Enter draw time: ";
```

continues

```
        cin >> drawtime;
        cout << "Enter number of notches: ";
        cin >> notches;
}

void Gunslinger::show()
{
        Person::show();
        cout << ": " << drawtime << " drawtime, " << notches
             << " notches\n";
}

class PokerPlayer : virtual public Person
{
public:
        PokerPlayer() : Person("Busted", "Strait") {}
        PokerPlayer(const char *fn, const char *ln) : Person(fn, ln) {}
        PokerPlayer(const Person & p) : Person(p) {}
        int draw() { return rand() % 52 + 1; }
};

class BadDude : public Gunslinger, public PokerPlayer
{
public:
        BadDude() : Person("Bad", "Dude"), Gunslinger() {}
        BadDude(const char *fn, const char *ln,
                     double d = 1.0, int n = 0) : Person (fn, ln),
                     Gunslinger(fn, ln, d, n) { }
        BadDude(const Person & p, double d = 1.0, int n = 0) :
                     Person(p), Gunslinger(p, d, n) { }
        double gdraw() { return Gunslinger::draw(); }
        int cdraw() { return PokerPlayer::draw(); }
        void show() { Gunslinger::show(); }
        void set() { Gunslinger::set(); }
};

// pe13-4.cpp
// workmi.cpp -- multiple inheritance
// compile with workermi.cpp, strng2.cpp
#include <iostream.h>
#include <string.h>
#include "pe13-4.h"
const int SIZE = 5;
int main(void)
{
        Person * gang[SIZE];
        for (int ct = 0; ct < SIZE; ct++)
        {
                char choice;
                cout << "Enter the gang category:\n"
                     << "o: ordinary person  g: gunslinger  "
                     << "p: pokerplayer  b: bad dude  q: quit\n";
                cin >> choice;
                while (strchr("ogpbq", choice) == NULL)
                {
                        cout << "Please enter an o, g, p, b, or q: ";
                        cin >> choice;
                }
                if (choice == 'q')
                        break;
                switch(choice)
                {
                        case 'o':    gang[ct] = new Person;
                                     break;
                        case 'g':    gang[ct] = new Gunslinger;
                                     break;
```

```
                   case 'p':    gang[ct] = new PokerPlayer;
                                break;
                   case 'b':    gang[ct] = new BadDude;
                                break;
            }
            cin.get();
            gang[ct]->set();
        }

    cout << "\nHere is your gang:\n";
    for (int i = 0; i < ct; i++)
    {
        cout << '\n';
        gang[i]->show();
    }
    for (i = 0; i < ct; i++)
        delete gang[i];
    return 0;
}
```

5. Here are some class declarations:

```
// emp.h -- header file for employee class and children

#include <iostream>
#include <cstring>
using namespace std;


const int SLEN = 20;
class employee
{
protected:
    char fname[SLEN];    // employee's first name
    char lname[SLEN];    // employee's last name
    char job[SLEN];
public:
    employee();
    employee(char * fn, char * ln, char * j);
    employee(const employee & e);
    virtual void showall() const;    // labels and shows all data
    virtual void setall();          // prompts user for values
    friend ostream & operator<<(ostream & os, const employee & e);
    // just displays first and last name
};

class manager:  virtual public employee
{
protected:
    int inchargeof;         // number of employees managed
public:
    manager();
    manager(char * fn, char * ln, char * j, int ico = 0);
    manager(const employee & e, int ico);
    manager(const manager & m);
    void showall() const;
    void setall();
};

class fink: virtual public employee
{
protected:
    char reportsto[SLEN];          // to whom fink reports
```

continues

```
public:
    fink();
    fink(char * fn, char * ln, char * j, char * rpo);
    fink(const employee & e, char * rpo);
    fink(const fink & e);
    void showall() const;
    void setall();
};

class highfink: public manager, public fink // management fink
{
public:
    highfink();
    highfink(char * fn, char * ln, char * j, char * rpo, int ico);
    highfink(const employee & e, char * rpo, int ico);
    highfink(const fink & f, int ico);
    highfink(const manager & m, char * rpo);
    highfink(const highfink & h);
    void showall() const;
    void setall();
};
```

Provide the class method implementations and test the classes in a program. Here is a minimal test program. You should add at least one test of a `setall()` member function.

```
// useemp1.cpp -- use employee classes

#include <iostream>
using namespace std;
#include "emp.h"

int main(void)
{
    employee th("Trip", "Harris", "Thumper");
    cout << th << '\n';
    th.showall();

    manager db("Deb", "Bates", "Twigger", 5);
    cout << db << '\n';
    db.showall();

    cout << "Press a key for next batch of output:\n";
    cin.get();

    fink mo("Matt", "Oggs", "Oiler", "Juno Barr");
    cout << mo << '\n';
    mo.showall();
    highfink hf(db, "Curly Kew");
    hf.showall();

    cout << "Using an employee * pointer:\n";
    employee  * tri[4] = {&th, &db, &mo, &hf};
    for (int i = 0; i < 4; i++)
        tri[i]->showall();

    return 0;
}
```

Compatibility note: Symantec C++ requires that the elements of the `tri` array be assigned object addresses individually rather than through an initialization statement.

Why is no assignment operator defined?

The classes use arrays rather than pointers and **new** to hold string data.

Why are `showall()` and `setall()` virtual?

These functions are redefined in derived classes.

Why is `employee` a virtual base class?

The `highfink` class inherits from employee via two paths.

Why does the `highfink` class have no data section?

All the data it uses already is held by its parent classes.

Why is only one version of `operator<<()` needed?

It's used just to print data from the `employee` baseclass, so it also works with all derived classes.

What would happen if the end of the program were replaced with this code?

```
employee  tri[4] = {th, db, mo, hf};
for (int i = 0; i < 4; i++)
    tri[i].showall();
```

The `employee::showall()` function would be used for all cases.

Here is code for the class methods:

```
// emp.cpp -- employee class and children
#include "emp.h"


employee::employee()
{
    fname[0] = '\0';
    lname[0] = '\0';
    job[0] = '\0';
}

employee::employee(char * fn, char * ln, char * j)
{
    strcpy(fname, fn);
    strcpy(lname, ln);
    strcpy(job, j);
}

employee::employee(const employee & e)
{
    strcpy(fname, e.fname);
    strcpy(lname, e.lname);
    strcpy(job, e.job);
}

void employee::showall() const
{
    cout << "Name: " << fname << " " << lname << '\n';
    cout << "Job:  " << job << '\n';
}

void employee::setall()
{
    cout << "First name: ";
    cin.getline(fname, SLEN);
    cout << "Last name: ";
    cin.getline(lname, SLEN);
    cout << "Job: ";
    cin.getline(job, SLEN);
}

ostream & operator<<(ostream & os, const employee & e)
{
    os << e.fname << " " << e.lname;
```

continues

```
        return os;
}

manager::manager()
{
    inchargeof = 0;
}

manager::manager(char * fn, char * ln, char * j, int ico)
    : employee(fn, ln, j)
{
    inchargeof = ico;
}

manager::manager(const employee & e, int ico)
    : employee(e)
{
    inchargeof = ico;
}

manager::manager(const manager & m) : employee(m)
{
    inchargeof = m.inchargeof;
}

void manager::showall() const
{
    employee::showall();
    cout << "In charge of " << inchargeof << '\n';
}

void manager::setall()
{
    employee::setall();
    cout << "Number in charge of: ";
    cin >> inchargeof;
    while (cin.get() != '\n') continue;
}

fink::fink()
{
    reportsto[0] = '\0';
}

fink::fink(char * fn, char * ln, char * j, char * rpo)
    : employee(fn, ln, j)
{
    strcpy(reportsto, rpo);
}

fink::fink(const employee & e, char * rpo)
    : employee(e)
{
    strcpy(reportsto, rpo);
}

fink::fink(const fink & m) : employee(m)
{
    strcpy(reportsto, m.reportsto);
}

void fink::showall() const
{
    employee::showall();
    cout << "Reports to: " << reportsto << '\n';
```

```
}

void fink::setall()
{
    employee::setall();
    cout << "Reports to: ";
    cin.getline(reportsto, SLEN);
}

highfink::highfink()
{
}

highfink::highfink(char * fn, char * ln, char * j, char * rpo, int ico)
    : employee(fn, ln, j), manager(fn, ln, j, ico), fink(fn, ln, j, rpo)
{
}

highfink::highfink(const employee & e, char * rpo, int ico)
    : employee(e), manager(e, ico), fink(e, rpo)
{
}

highfink::highfink(const fink & f, int ico)
    : employee(f), fink(f), manager(f, ico)
{
}

highfink::highfink(const manager & m, char * rpo)
    : employee(m), manager(m), fink(m, rpo)
{
}


highfink::highfink(const highfink & h)
    : employee(h), manager(h), fink(h)
{
}


void highfink::showall() const
{
    manager::showall();
    cout << "Reports to: " << reportsto << '\n';
}

void highfink::setall()
{
    manager::setall();
    cout << "Reports to: ";
    cin.getline(reportsto, SLEN);
}
```

Answers to Additional Questions

True or False

1. T	4. T	7. F	10. T
2. T	5. T	8. F	
3. F	6. F	9. F	

Short Answers

1.

a. Containment is when class members are themselves objects of another class.

b. Composition is an alternative name for containment.

c. Layering is an alternative name for containment and composition.

d. The `has-a` relationship was introduced in Chapter 12 and is described on page 546 of *The Waite Group's C++ Primer Plus, Third Edition.*

e. Multiple inheritance lets you inherit from two or more base classes, combining their functionality.

f. A class implementation is the code that provides the functionality of the class.

g. A class interface is the calling protocol of the class members.

h. A subobject is an object contained within another object.

i. With private inheritance, `public` and `protected` members of the base class become `private` members of the derived class. See Table 13.1 on page 619.

j. With protected inheritance, `public` and `protected` members of the base class become `protected` members of the derived class. See Table 13.1 on page 619.

k. With public inheritance, `public` and `protected` members of the base class become `public` and `protected` members of the derived class respectively. See Table 13.1 on page 619.

l. The term implicit upcasting means that you can have a base class pointer or reference to a derived class object without using an explicit type cast. See Table 13.1 on page 619.

m. An access declaration is the statement of how a class is inherited. That is, `private`, `public`, or `protected`.

n. A container class is designed to hold other objects or data types.

o. A parameterized class is a template that accepts a type name as a parameter for building the actual class instance.

p. A template is a container of a generic data type, which can be customized to a specific data type.

q. The actualization of a template is called an instantiation.

r. Generic type identifiers are called type parameters.

s. An expression argument specifies a particular type such as `int` or `double` rather than a generic type.

t. A homogeneous collection consists of several items of the same data type. For example, an array.

u. A heterogeneous collection consists of several items of different data types. For example, a structure.

v. Template specialization is described on page 644.

w. `virtual` is a keyword in C++ that creates a reference to an object rather than copying that object. See Figures 13.4 and 13.5 on pages 649 and 650.

x. A `virtual` base class means that a reference to the base class is inherited by the derived class rather than an actual copy of the base class.

y. See program listing 13.20.

z. A name in a derived class has a higher precedence than the same name in the base class. This is known as dominance.

2.

```
//template.cpp

#include <iostream>
using namespace std;
const int mSize = 10;

class MachineTool
{
public:
 MachineTool(int);
    MachineTool();
    ~MachineTool() {}
    int GetWeight() const { return mweight; }
    void Display() const { cout << mweight; }
private:
    int mweight;
};

MachineTool::MachineTool(int weight):mweight(weight){}
MachineTool::MachineTool(): mweight(0) {}

template <class Type>
class Array
{
public:
    Array(int itsSize = mSize);
    Array(const Array &arr);
    ~Array() { delete [] ptr; }
    Array& operator=(const Array&);
    Type& operator[](int offSet)  { return ptr[offSet]; }
    const Type& operator[](int offSet) const { return ptr[offSet]; }
    int GetSize() const { return itsSize; }
private:
    Type *ptr;
    int  itsSize;
};

template <class Type>
Array<Type>::Array(int size = mSize):itsSize(size)
{
    ptr = new Type[size];
    for (int i = 0; i<size; i++)
        ptr[i] = 0;
}
template <class Type>
Array<Type>::Array(const Array &arr)
{
    itsSize = arr.GetSize();
    ptr = new Type[itsSize];
    for (int i = 0; i<itsSize; i++)
        ptr[i] = arr[i];
}
template <class Type>
Array<Type>& Array<Type>::operator=(const Array &arr)
{
    if (this == &arr)
        return *this;
    delete [] ptr;
    itsSize = arr.GetSize();
    ptr = new Type[itsSize];
    for (int i = 0; i<itsSize; i++)
        ptr[i] = arr[i];
    return *this;
}
```

3. a) Multiple inheritance

   b) Containment

   c) Single inheritance

4. a) Change to `virtual public Tool`, `virtual protected Saws`

   b) None

   c) None

5. Because automatic passing of initialization data is not allowed, you need to explicitly call base class constructors with appropriate arguments, unless the default constructor is acceptable.

6. If a base class member is dominant, the compiler will use that member. A name in a derived class dominates any in an ancestor class. If the name is ambiguous, the compile will give an error.

7. `City` is a base class. `State` will use its own `military()` and `diplomacy()`, and the `City` version of `economy()`. `Region` will use the same members as `State`. `Country` will use its own `military()` and `diplomacy()` and `economy()` from `City`. `Continent` will use its own `economy()` and the compiler should tag ambiguous uses of `military()` and `diplomacy()`.

Programming Projects

1.

a) Here is the implementation of the non-template version.

```cpp
// lists.cpp - lists implementation

#include <iostream>
using namespace std;
#include "lists.h"
List::~List()
{
    listItem *ptr = front;
    while (ptr)
    {
        listItem *tmp = ptr;
        ptr = ptr->next;
        delete tmp;
    }
    front = rear = 0;
}
void List::insert(int value)
{
    listItem * ptr = new listItem(value, front);
    if (front == 0)
        rear = ptr;
    front = ptr;
    counter++;
}
int List::is_empty() const
{
    return front == 0;
}
void List::append(int value)
{
    listItem *ptr = new listItem(value);
    if (is_empty())
        front = ptr;
    else
        rear->next = ptr;
    rear = ptr;
```

```
        counter++;
    }
    void List::show() const
    {
        if (is_empty())
            cout << "List is empty.\n";
        else
        {
            listItem *ptr = front->next;
            int i = 0;
            do {
                if (i % 5 == 0)
                    cout << "\n";
                cout << ptr->val << " ";
                ptr = ptr->next;
                i++;
            }
            while (ptr != NULL);
            cout << "\n";
        }
    }
    int List::is_present(int value) const
    {
        if (is_empty())
            return 0;
        if (front->val == value || rear->val == value)
            return 1;
        listItem *ptr = front->next;
        for (; ptr != rear; ptr = ptr->next)
            if (ptr->val == value)
                return 1;
        return 0;
    }
```

b) Here is a modified version of the template and implementation. The compiler probably will require that this be in one file.

```
//lists_t.h - template list class
template <class Type>
class listItem
{
public:
    Type val;
    listItem * next;
    listItem(Type value, listItem * cell = 0):val(value), next(cell){}
};

template <class Type>
class List
{
private:
    listItem<Type> * front;
    listItem<Type> * rear;
    int counter;
public:
    List() : front(0), rear(0), counter(0) {}
    virtual ~List();
    void insert(Type value);
    void append(Type value);
    void show() const;
    int is_present(Type value) const;
    int is_empty() const;
    int count() const {return counter;}
```

continues

```
};


template <class Type>
List<Type>::~List()
{
    listItem<Type> *ptr = front;
    while (ptr)
    {
        listItem<Type> *tmp = ptr;
        ptr = ptr->next;
        delete tmp;
    }
    front = rear = 0;
}
template <class Type>
void List<Type>::insert(Type value)
{
    listItem<Type> * ptr = new listItem<Type>(value, front);
    if (front == 0)
        rear = ptr;
    front = ptr;
    counter++;
}
template <class Type>
int List<Type>::is_empty() const
{
    return front == 0;
}
template <class Type>
void List<Type>::append(Type value)
{
    listItem<Type> *ptr = new listItem<Type>(value);
    if (is_empty())
        front = ptr;
    else
        rear->next = ptr;
    rear = ptr;
    counter++;
}
template <class Type>
void List<Type>::show() const
{
    if (is_empty())
        cout << "List is empty.\n";
    else
    {
        listItem<Type> *ptr = front->next;
        int i = 0;
        do {
            if (i % 5 == 0)
                cout << "\n";
            cout << ptr->val << " ";
            ptr = ptr->next;
            i++;
        }
        while (ptr != NULL);
        cout << "\n";
    }
}
template <class Type>
int List<Type>::is_present(Type value) const
{
    if (is_empty())
        return 0;
    if (front->val == value || rear->val == value)
```

```
            return 1;
        listItem<Type> *ptr = front->next;
        for (; ptr != rear; ptr = ptr->next)
            if (ptr->val == value)
                return 1;
        return 0;
    }
```

And this is the modified test program for integers. The output should not change at all.

```
// listuset.cpp - test program for integers

#include <iostream>
using namespace std;
#include "lists_t.h" - use template form
void checkit(const List<int> * listobj, const int value);
int main(void)
{
    List<int> tempList;
    tempList.show();
    checkit(&tempList, 81);
    for (int i = 65; i < 74; i++)
        tempList.append(i);
    for (int j = i+5; j <= i+16; j++)
        tempList.insert(j);
    tempList.show();
    checkit(& tempList, 81);

    return 0;
}

void checkit(const List<int> * listobj, const int value)
{
    if (listobj->is_present(value))
        cout << value << " is present in the list.\n";
    else
        cout << value << " is absent from the list.\n";
}
```

Here is the modified main() test function for the array of char.
Note the cast to char in checkit(), just to make it look nice.

```
// listusec.cpp - char version

#include <iostream>
using namespace std;
#include "lists_t.h"--use template form
void checkit(const List<char> * listobj, const int value);
int main(void)
{
    List<char> tempList;
    tempList.show();
    checkit(&tempList, 81);
    for (int i = 65; i < 74; i++)
        tempList.append(i);
    for (int j = i+5; j <= i+16; j++)
        tempList.insert(j);
    tempList.show();
    checkit(& tempList, 81);

    return 0;
}

void checkit(const List<char> * listobj, const int value)
{
    if (listobj->is_present(value))
        cout << char(value) << " is present in the list.\n";
```

continues

```
        else
            cout << char(value) << " is absent from the list.\n";
    }
```

This is the output for the `char` version. If the cast isn't used in `checkit()`, 81 will be output instead of Q in the `checkit()` lines.

```
List is empty.
Q is absent from the list.

Y X W V U
T S R Q P
O A B C D
E F G H I
Q is present in the list.
```

2.

```
//ckg.h - class declarations for accounts, checking, savings,
//          and special accounts

#include <iostream>
using namespace std;
#include "strng2.h"

class Account
{
private:
    String acctName;
    long acctNo;
    float balance;
protected:
    virtual void data() const;
public:
    Account() : acctName("New Account"), acctNo(0L), balance(0.0f) {}
    Account(const String & an, long anum, float bal)
                : acctName(an), acctNo(anum), balance(bal) {}
    virtual void show() const;
    virtual float getbal() const;
};

class Checking : virtual public Account
{
private:
    float mFee;               //monthly fee on checking
    int fCks;                 //# of free checks per month
protected:
    void data() const;
public:
    Checking() : Account(), mFee(0.0f), fCks(0) {}
    Checking(const String & s, long anum, float bal, float mf, int fc)
                : Account(s, anum, bal), mFee(mf), fCks(fc) {}
    Checking(const Account & acct, float mf = 0.0, int fc = 0)
                : Account(acct), mFee(mf), fCks(fc) {}
    virtual void show() const;
};

class Savings : virtual public Account
{
protected:
    enum {other, xmasClub, retire, regular, pr_deduction, Stypes};
    void data() const;
private:
    static char *ps[20];      //Savings account types available
    int aType;                //Savings account type
    float rate;               //current interest rate on account
```

```cpp
public:
    Savings() : Account(), aType(other), rate(0.0) {}
    Savings(const String & s, long anum, float bal, int at, float r)
            : Account(s, anum, bal), aType(at), rate(r) {}
    Savings(const Account & acct, int at = other, float r = 0.0)
            : Account(acct), aType(at), rate(r) {}
    virtual void show() const;
};

class CkgSvgs : public Checking, public Savings
{
private:
    int yearOpen;              //year the account was open
                               // (for bonus programs)
protected:
    void data() const;
public:
    CkgSvgs() : yearOpen(0) {}
    CkgSvgs(const String & s, long a, float b, float mf, int fc,
            float r, int yo = 0, int at = Savings::other)
                : Account(s, a, b), Checking(s,a,b,mf,fc),
                    Savings(s,a,b,at,r), yearOpen(yo) {}
    CkgSvgs(const Account & a, const Checking & c, const Savings & s, int yo = 0)
                : Account(a), Checking(c), Savings(s), yearOpen(yo) {}
    void show() const;
};

//ckg.cpp - implementation of checking and savings classes

#include <iostream>
using namespace std;
#include "ckg.h"
const int curYear = 1996;
//Account public methods
void Account::show() const
{
    cout << "Type: Basic account\n";
    data();
}
//Account protected methods
void Account::data() const
{
    cout.precision(2);
    cout.setf(ios::showpoint);
    cout.setf(ios::fixed, ios::floatfield);
    cout << "Account name: " << acctName << "\n";
    cout << "Account number: " << acctNo << "\n";
    cout << "Balance: $" << balance << "\n";
}
float Account::getbal() const
{
    return balance;
}

//Checking public methods
void Checking::show() const
{
    cout << "Type: Checking\n";
    Account::data();
    data();
}
//Checking protected methods
void Checking::data() const
{
```

continues

```cpp
        cout << "Monthly fee: $" << mFee << ", includes ";
        if (fCks)
            cout << fCks;
        else
            cout << "unlimited";
        cout << " checks.\n";
}
//Savings public methods
char * Savings::ps[] = {"Other", "Christmas Club", "Retirement",
            "Regular", "P/R Deduction"};
void Savings::show() const
{
    cout << "Type: Savings\n";
    Account::data();
    data();
}
//Savings protected methods
void Savings::data() const
{
    cout.precision(2);
    cout.setf(ios::showpoint);
    cout.setf(ios::fixed, ios::floatfield);
    cout << "Savings type: " << ps[aType] << "\n";
    cout << "Current rate is an amazing " << rate << "%!!\n";
}

// CkgSvgs methods
void CkgSvgs::data() const
{
    Checking::data();
    Savings::data();
}
void CkgSvgs::show() const
{
    cout << "Type: Master account\n";
    Account::data();
    data();
}

//ckguse.cpp - test functions for our bank
#include <iostream>
#include <cstring>
using namespace std;

#include "ckg.h"
#include "arraytp.h"


const int SIZE = 8;
enum {other, xmasClub, retire, regular, pr_deduction};

int main(void)
{
    ArrayTP<Account *, (int) SIZE> BofNA;
    //Account * BofNA[SIZE];        // if don't have templates

    BofNA[0] = new Account("Small Fish",
                    4099086L, 12.00);
    BofNA[1] = new Checking("No Frills",
                    5099092L, 1000.0, 14.5, 25);
    BofNA[2] = new Savings("Thrifty Christmas",
                    6099026L, 250.00, xmasClub, 3.25);
    BofNA[3] = new CkgSvgs("VIP Account",
                    5L, 125000.00, 0.00, 0, 4.6, 1989);
    BofNA[4] = new Checking("Executive",
                    5099012L, 12250.00, 6.00, 0);
```

```
    BofNA[5] = new Checking("Golden Age",
                    5099008L, 75000.00, 6.25, 0);
    BofNA[6] = new CkgSvgs("Big Spender",
                    8L, 250000.00, 0.00, 0, 5.3, 1994);
    BofNA[7] = new Savings("Children's Starter",
                    4099086L, 27.23, regular, 1.75);

    cout << "\nBofNA Current Accounts:\n";
    for (int i = 0; i < SIZE; i++)
    {
        cout << '\n';
        BofNA[i]->show();
    }
    for (i = 0; i < SIZE; i++)
        delete BofNA[i];
    return 0;
}
```

FRIENDS, EXCEPTIONS, AND MORE

Statement of Purpose

Students now have the foundation to expand their knowledge of friends and classes, and to begin using the newest tools of C++. In addition to being able to build software that does the job, they can begin to handle unexpected run-time errors while simplifying the code needed to do the job.

Objectives

By the end of Chapter 14, the student should understand the following concepts:

- Using `friend` functions as class members and as member functions

- How `friend` functions can work with other C++ constructs

- Templates and how `friend`s fit in

- Using nested classes to model relationships, and the new programming issues they cause

- C-style error handling and how it has changed

- Using the three parts of exceptions to handle runtime errors

- Using exception classes to handle run-time errors

- Unwinding the stack to find an error handler

- What RTTI is and how it can be used to write flexible code

- RTTI operators and structure, and when to use each to avoid bloated code

- `dynamic_cast`, `const_cast`, `static_cast`, and `reinterpret_cast` to practice safe coding

Lecture Outline

More About `friends`

Thus far we've only seen a part of what friends can do for C++ programming. This section pulls together a lot of the details of using `friend`s.

Sample programs:
    tv.h—**TV** and **Remote** working together

    tv.cpp—implementation

    use_tv.cpp—test function for **friend** class member

    tvfm.h—**TV** and **Remote** classes using **friend** member functions

    nested.cpp—queue using nested class

- `friend` classes

  Access to private and protected members

  Can restrict friends to be only friends of selected functions

  Friendship can't be imposed from the outside

  Can be declared in private, protected, or public sections

  Most useful when access is needed to the containing class's data

  Doesn't need forward declaration because declaration tells compiler it is a class

- `friend` member functions

  Can make only selected methods friends to another class

  Arrangement of declarations and definitions important

      Compiler needs to know about objects before seeing containing definition

      Forward declaration

- Other friendly relationships

  Classes friends to each other

      Separate declarations from definitions

      Define functions `inline` or in separate file

  Using `friend` to access private data in two classes

      Function can't be a member of both classes

- Templates and friends

  Nontemplate friends

      Single type of `friend` for all objects of class

  Bound template friends

      Type of `friend` determined by type of class

      Can pass template object to `friend` as argument

  Unbound template friends

      All instantiations of `friend` are friends to each instantiation of class

  Specific instantiations of templates can be friends to nontemplate classes

Nested classes

Nesting classes together can be effective to model some relationships, particularly when there is a lot of interaction between the different classes.

- Place class declaration within another class

  Avoids clutter by giving the nested class container class scope

  Member functions of containing class can create and use nested classes

  Not the same as containment

  > `Containment`: class object as member

  > `Nested`: does not create class member

  Assists in creation of other classes

  Helps to avoid name conflicts

  Use scope resolution operator to identify: `Queue::Node::(const Item & i)`

- Access issues

  Location of member class declaration determines scope

  > `private`: known only to container class

  > `protected`: access by container class but not outside world

  > `public`: known by anyone, but need to use class qualifier outside container

- Recap of nested class scope: see Table 14.1 in text

Scope Properties for Nested Classes, Structures, and Enumerations

Usual control through private, protected, and public members

> Once class is in scope, access is the issue

> Nested class has full access to container, but not necessarily vice versa

- Use nested class in template like regular nested classes

Exceptions

C++ has introduced an effective means of handling runtime errors, bringing uniformity rather than the many different ways that compiler vendors have devised to fill the need.

Sample programs:	error1.cpp—using `abort()` with division by 0
	error2.cpp—`return` error code with division by 0
	error3.cpp—same problem with exceptions
	error4.cpp—handling multiple exceptions
	error5.cpp—unwinding the stack
	arraydbe.h—exceptions in classes
	arraydbe.cpp—implementation of exception classes
	exceptar.cpp—test function for exception classes

continues

limarre.h—modified limarr with inherited exceptions

limarre.cpp—inherited exception implementation

excptinh.cpp—implementation of inherited exceptions

newexcep.cpp—the bad_alloc exception

- Provides tools for handling run-time errors
- Newer feature, so not fully implemented
- Response to an exceptional circumstance during runtime
- Consists of three components

  Throwing the exception: `throw`

  > When problem arises

  > Essentially a jump to statements at another location

  > Value thrown to indicate error

  Catching exception with handler: `catch`

  > `catch` an expression from `throw` block

  > Exception handler is a `catch` block

  > Contains code executed when exception occurs

  Using a `try` block

  > Identifies statement block with particular active exceptions

  > Followed by one or more `catch` blocks

- Similar to `return`, except that control isn't passed to calling functions

  Backs up through function calls to find `try` block

- Uncaught exceptions

  When can't find `try` block or matching handler

  Calls `terminate()` standard function

  Modify `terminate()` by providing pointer to custom function

- Gives programmer control over what happens on error

  Qualify function definition to indicate what kinds of exceptions will handle

  > Use `throw(arguments)` in function prototype

  > Comma-separated list for arguments

  `catch` block can handle multiple exception sources

- Multiple `try` blocks possibilities

  Multiple in succession

  Nested `try` blocks

- Unwinding the stack

  Normally return to calling function by using address placed on stack

  Exceptions move up stack freeing memory until an address in a `try` block is found.

Then `catch` block after `try` block is executed

Class destructors called for any automatic class objects on stack

- Handler can catch any type of exception

Form: `catch (...) { //statements }`

- Nested `try` blocks can pass control up to previous blocks

Use `throw` keyword in body of `catch` block

- `try` block can reside in function called by another function in `try` block

- Classes and exceptions

Particularly useful to return a nested exception class

Helps prevent name conflicts

Use different objects to handle different exceptions

Nested class declaration doesn't create objects

Class member creates object if exception occurs

`throw` uses exception class constructor to create and initialize exception object

- Exceptions and inheritance

Derived classes inherit base class exception objects

New exception classes can be derived from others

Base class exception handler can handle derived exception objects

Not vice versa without casting

Order of `catch` blocks becomes important

Arrange so that derived exceptions caught first, and then base class exceptions

- Exceptions incorporated into C++ language as a class using the `exception` header file

RTTI: runtime type information

The use of runtime type information can be used to add flexibility to code, so that the program can respond to different objects in different situations.

Sample programs: rtti1.cpp—using `dynamic_cast` operator

rtti2.cpp—modifies program to use `typeid()` and `name()`

- Provides standard way for program to determine type of object at runtime.

Vendors have provided incompatible versions

Useful for debugging or running uninherited methods

- Three components support RTTI

`dynamic_cast` operator generates pointer to derived type from pointer to base type

Generally most heavily used component

Tells if can safely convert base pointer to derived class pointer

Form: `Superb * pm = dynamic_cast<Superb *>(pg);`

Returns address of object if safe, **NULL** otherwise

Use with references as well

typeid operator returns exact type of object

Returns an object of type **type_info**

Use to determine if two objects are the same type

Argument can be name of class or expression that evaluates to object

Includes **name()** member that returns name of class

type_info object holds information about particular type

- Useable only with class hierarchies having **virtual** functions

- Use **virtual** functions when possible and RTTI only when necessary

- Easy to misuse RTTI

If using long **if else** blocks, try to use **virtual** functions and **dynamic_cast**

Type Cast Operators

- **dynamic_cast**

- **const_cast**

- **static_cast**

- **reinterpret_cast**

Additional Questions

True or False

1. Using a **friend** class is one way to enhance protection of data in a C++ program.

2. Generally the coding required to implement **friend** member functions is simpler and clearer than the code used to implement **friend** classes, but **friend** classes are more effective to protect the container class's data.

3. One **friend** class can be a **friend** to a class, but that second class cannot be a **friend** to the first, much in the same way that a function cannot be defined within another function.

4. **friend** functions are useful when you need to access private data in two different classes.

5. Forward declarations give the compiler the information it needs to know the types of the names used in a program.

6. Using bound template friends means that there will be a number of friends in the final program equal to the number of class instantiations.

7. Nesting classes is not the same as containing classes because the nested class has class scope, whereas the contained class has global scope in all cases.

8. Nesting in a template is one way to model multiple inheritance in C++.

9. The following are examples of exceptions that can be handled with **try**, **throw**, and **catch**.

Attempts to divide by zero

Taking the square root of -345.26

A missing semicolon at the end of a statement

Overflowing a numeric data type

10. C++'s exception handling abilities eliminates the need for `abort()`, `exit()`, and `terminate()`.

11. When a C++ error occurs, the `catch` block catches the error after `throw` tosses it, but only if the execution of the program is within a `try` block in the current function or a previous calling function.

12. When a function does not have a `try` block and an exception occurs, the compiler checks the calling function and finds none, but finds one in the next calling function. Once the exception handling executes, the program can re-execute the called functions with the restored data.

13. The program looks for the first calling function whose address stored on the stack is within a `try` block.

14. For effective use of exceptions, `throw` can throw any type of valid C++ data type, both basic and derived.

15. An exception class is inherited just like any other class.

16. Given the declaration of exception class objects, and that `eMain` is a derived class of `eProper`, the following is a proper order of `catch` blocks.

```
eMain excAlpha;
eProper excTheta;
catch (const eMain & a) {...}
catch (const eProper & b) {...}
```

17. The ability to use RTTI information, when used in conjunction with fully inherited `virtual` functions, is a good way to invoke the proper class method based on the object's type.

18. Assigning the addresses of derived objects to base class pointers in classes not having `virtual` class methods is possible, but is not a recommended practice.

19. If the following is not a safe type cast, `dynamic_cast` will return the null pointer. Otherwise, `pm` is cast to type `TimeCard`.

```
TimeCard * pm = dynamic_cast<TimeCard *>(pl);
```

20. Now that RTTI is becoming part of standard C++, it is recommended to use it rather than `virtual` functions when possible.

Short Answers

1. Describe the following terms, and explain their use in a C++ program.

   a. nested class

   b. `abort()`

   c. `cerr`

   d. throw an exception

   e. catch an exception

   f. exception handler

   g. `catch` block

   h. `try` block

   i. `terminate()`

   j. `set_terminate()`

   k. unwinding the stack

l. exception

m. RTTI

n. `dynamic_cast`

o. `const_cast`

p. `static_cast`

q. `reinterpret_cast`

2. For each of the following, write a **Nesting** class where

   a. A nested class is visible to the nesting class, but not to classes derived from that class

   b. A nested class is visible to derived classes, but also to the outside world

   c. A structure is visible only to the nesting class

   d. An enumeration is visible to everyone in and out of the class

   e. A nested class is only visible to **Nesting**

3. What output does the following produce? For simplicity, the harmonic mean of 10 and 12 is 10.9091, the cube of 2.459 is 14.8688, and the square root of 143567.234 is 378.90267.

```cpp
int main(void)
{       double s = -143567.234;
    double c = 2.459;
    double h = 10;
    double i = 12;
    try
    {
        analysis(s, c, h, i);
    }
    catch (const char * s)
    {
        cout << s << "\n";
        cout << "Sorry, you can't play anymore. ";
    }
    cout << "Bye!\n";
    return 0;
}

double hmean(double a, double b)
{
    if (a == -b)
    {
        cout << "Problem in hmean().\n";
        throw "Bad hmean() arguments: a = -b not allowed.";
    }
    return 2.0 * a * b / (a + b);
}

double squareRoot(double a)
{
    if (a < 0.0)
    {
        cout << "Problem! ";
        throw "Bad squareRoot() operand: -a not allowed.";
    }
    return sqrt(a);
}

void analysis(double s, double c, double h, double i)
{
    try
    {
```

```
        cout << "Harmonic mean of " << h << " and " << i          <<
        " is " << hmean(h,i) << "\n";
        try
        {
            cout << "Cube of " << c << " is " << cubed(c) << "\n";
            cout << "Square root of " << s << " is " << squareRoot(s)
            << ".\n";
        }
        catch (const char * s)
        {
            cout << s << " Sorry!\n";
        }
    }
    catch (const char * s)
    {
        cout << s << " Sorry!\n";
    }
}

double cubed(double a)
{
    if (a > 1.0e50)
    throw "Cubed problem: operand too large.";
    return (a*a*a);
}
```

4. Where must the declaration for a `friend` member function be placed? A `friend` class?

Programming Projects

1. Design a class `Newint` provides "safe" addition, subtraction, multiplication, division, and modulus. Use exceptions to check for underflow and overflow conditions, including division by 0. Include both an `Overflow` and `Underflow` exception class members. Provide overloaded `>>` operators to produce exception notices to the user. Structure the test program so that an error in the addition section aborts that section and moves on to subtraction, rather than quitting the program when an error occurs. Do the same for all sections.

   Hints:

   Use `INT_MIN` and `INT_MAX` in limits.h in the testing for overflow and underflow.

   The tests for addition could be of the form
   ```
   if(op1 > 0 && op2 > 0 && op1 > INT_MAX - op2)
   if(op1 < 0 && op2 < 0 && op1 < INT_MIN - op2)
   ```

   Write a test program that produces the following output:
   ```
   Integer addition:
   10 + 15 = 25
   32767 + -2 = 32765
   Overflow error: Can't do 32767 + 2.

   Integer subtraction:
   1206 - -2890 = 4096
   -17595 - 31789 = 13280
   Underflow error: Can't do -17579 - -31789.

   Integer multiplication:
   14 * 982 = 13748
   542 * 0 = 0
   150 * -150 = -22500
   -150 * 150 = -22500
   Underflow error: Can't do -25000 * 150.
   ```

continues

```
Integer division:
150 / 3 = 50
-22456 / -12 = 1871
Overflow error: Can't do -22456 / 0

Modulus:
150 % 3 = 0
-22456 % -12 = -4
Overflow error: Can't do -22456 % 0.
```

Activities for Learning

1. Has your compiler implemented exceptions? What are the syntax rules that are required?

2. Older implementations of C++ return a null pointer if **new** can't allocate the requested space. Some newer implementations use exceptions. What does your compiler do?

3. Run the example programs in this chapter. Experiment with changes to get a feel for how the different C++ constructs are used. Modify them to make them more general and more useful to you.

Answers to Text Programming Exercises

1. Modify the **Tv** and **Remote** classes as follows:

   • Make them mutual **friend**s.

   • Add a state variable member to the **Remote** class that describes whether the remote control is in Normal or Interactive mode.

   • Add a **Remote** method that displays the mode.

   • Provide the **Tv** class with a method for toggling the new **Remote** member. This method should work only if the **Tv** is in the On state.

   Write a short program testing these new features.

```
// pe14tvh -- Tv and Remote classes

#ifndef _PE14TV_H_
#define _PE14TV_H_


class Tv
{
public:
    friend class Remote;    // Remote can access Tv private parts
    enum State{Off, On};
    enum {MinVal,MaxVal = 20};
    enum {Antenna, Cable};
    enum {TV, VCR};

    Tv(State s = Off, int mc = 100) : state(s), volume(5),
        maxchannel(mc), channel(2), mode(Cable), input(TV) {}
    void onoff() {state = (state == On)? Off : On;}
    bool ison() {return state == On ? true : false;}
    bool volup();
    bool voldown();
    void chanup();
```

```
        void chandown();
        void set_mode() {mode = (mode == Antenna)? Cable : Antenna;}
        void set_input() {input = (input == TV)? VCR : TV;}
        void settings();
        void rmode(Remote & r);
private:
        State state;
        int volume;
        int maxchannel;
        int channel;
        int mode;
        int input;
};

class Remote
{
friend class Tv;

public:
        enum Style {Normal, Interactive};
        Remote(int m = Tv::TV, int s = Normal) :
                    mode(m), style(s) {}
        bool volup(Tv & t) { return t.volup();}
        bool voldown(Tv & t) { return t.voldown();}
        void onoff(Tv & t) { t.onoff(); }
        void chanup(Tv & t) {t.chanup();}
        void chandown(Tv & t) {t.chandown();}
        void set_chan(Tv & t, int c) {t.channel = c;}
        void set_mode(Tv & t) {t.set_mode();}
        void set_input(Tv & t) {t.set_input();}
        void show_style();
private:
        int mode;        // TV or VCR
        int style;   // Normal or Interactive
};

// place definition here where both Tv and Remote
// class declarations are known
inline void Tv::rmode(Remote & r)
{
        if(state == Off)
            return;
        if (r.style == Remote::Normal)
            r.style = Remote::Interactive;
        else r.style = Remote::Normal;
}
#endif

// pe14tv.cpp

#include <iostream>
using namespace std;
#include "pe14tv.h"

bool Tv::volup()
{
        if (volume < MaxVal)
        {
            volume++;
            return true;
        }
        else
            return false;
}
bool Tv::voldown()
```

continues

```
{
    if (volume > MinVal)
    {
        volume--;
        return true;
    }
    else
        return false;
}

void Tv::chanup()
{
    if (channel < maxchannel)
        channel++;
    else
        channel = 1;
}

void Tv::chandown()
{
    if (channel > 1)
        channel--;
    else
        channel = maxchannel;
}

void Tv::settings()
{
    cout << "TV is " << (state == Off? "Off\n" : "On\n");
    if (state == On)
    {
        cout << "Volume setting = " << volume << "\n";
        cout << "Channel setting = " << channel << "\n";
        cout << "Mode = "
            << (mode == Antenna? "antenna\n" : "cable\n");
        cout << "Input = "
            << (input == TV? "TV\n" : "VCR\n");
    }
}

void Remote::show_style()
{
    if (style == Normal)
        cout << "Remote in Normal mode\n";
    else
        cout << "Remote in Interactive mode\n";
}

// pe14-1.cpp
// link with pe14tv.cpp

#include <iostream>
using namespace std;
#include "pe14tv.h"

int main(void)
{
    Tv s20;
    cout << "Initial settings for 20\" TV:\n";
    s20.settings();
    s20.onoff();
    s20.chanup();
    cout << "\nAdjusted settings for 20\" TV:\n";
    s20.settings();

    Remote grey;
```

```
        grey.set_chan(s20, 10);
        grey.volup(s20);
        grey.volup(s20);
        cout << "\n20\" settings after using remote\n";
        s20.settings();

        Tv s27(Tv::On);
        s27.set_mode();
        grey.set_chan(s27,28);
        cout << "\n27\" settings:\n";
        s27.settings();
        grey.show_style();      // check mode
        s27.rmode(grey);          // change mode
        grey.show_style();      // recheck mode
        s27.onoff();             // turn set off
        s27.rmode(grey);          // try changing mode again
        grey.show_style();      // check result

        return 0;
    }
```

2. Modify Listings 14.12, 14.13, and 14.14 to use a template version of the array.

```
    // pe14-2.h -- define array template with exceptions
    #ifndef _ARRAYETP_H_
    #define _ARRAYETP_H_

    #include <iostream>
    using namespace std;

    template <class T>
    class ArrayETP
    {
    private:
        unsigned int size;       // number of array elements
    protected:
        T * arr;                 // address of first element
    public:
        class NoRoom          // exception class for insufficient memory
        {
        public:
            int asked;        // bytes requested
            NoRoom(int i) : asked(i) {}
        };
        class BadIndex         // exception class for indexing problems
        {
        public:
            int badindex;     // problematic index value
            BadIndex(int i) : badindex(i) {}
        };
        ArrayETP();                              // default constructor
        // create an ArrayETP of n elements, set each to val
        ArrayETP(unsigned int n, T val);
        // create an ArrayETP of n elements, initialize to array pn
        ArrayETP(const T * pn, unsigned int n);
        ArrayETP(const ArrayETP & a);          // copy constructor
        virtual ~ArrayETP();                    // destructor
        unsigned int arsize() const;            // returns array size
    // overloaded operators
            // array indexing, allowing assignment
        virtual T & operator[](int i);
            // array indexing (no =)
        virtual const T & operator[](int i) const;
        ArrayETP & operator=(const ArrayETP & a);
```

continues

```
        friend ostream & operator<<(ostream & os, const ArrayETP<T> & a);
};


// default constructor -- no arguments
template <class T>
ArrayETP<T>::ArrayETP()
{
    arr = NULL;
    size = 0;
}

// constructs array of n elements, each set to val
template <class T>
ArrayETP<T>::ArrayETP(unsigned int n, T val)
{
    arr = new T[n];
    if (arr == 0)
        throw NoRoom(n);
    size = n;
    for (int i = 0; i < size; i++)
        arr[i] = val;
}

// initialize ArrayETP object to a non-class array
template <class T>
ArrayETP<T>::ArrayETP(const T *pn, unsigned int n)
{
    arr = new T[n];
    if (arr == 0)
        throw NoRoom(n);
    size = n;
    for (int i = 0; i < size; i++)
        arr[i] = pn[i];
}

// initialize ArrayETP object to another ArrayETP object
template <class T>
ArrayETP<T>::ArrayETP(const ArrayETP & a)
{
    size = a.size;
    arr = new T[size];
    if (arr == 0)
        throw NoRoom(size);
    for (int i = 0; i < size; i++)
        arr[i] = a.arr[i];
}

template <class T>
ArrayETP<T>::~ArrayETP()
{
    delete [] arr;
}

// return array size
template <class T>
unsigned int ArrayETP<T>::arsize() const
{
    return size;
}

// let user access elements by index (assignment allowed)
template <class T>
T & ArrayETP<T>::operator[](int i)
{
    // check index before continuing
```

```
        if (i < 0 || i >= size)
            throw BadIndex(i);
        return arr[i];
}

// let user access elements by index (assignment disallowed)
template <class T>
const T & ArrayETP<T>::operator[](int i) const
{
    // check index before continuing
    if (i < 0 || i >= size)
        throw BadIndex(i);
    return arr[i];
}

// define class assignment
template <class T>
ArrayETP<T> & ArrayETP<T>::operator=(const ArrayETP<T> & a)
{
    if (this == &a)        // if object assigned to self,
        return *this;      // don't change anything
    delete arr;
    size = a.size;
    arr = new T[size];
    if (arr == 0)
        throw NoRoom(size);
    for (int i = 0; i < size; i++)
        arr[i] = a.arr[i];
    return *this;
}

// quick output, 5 values to a line
template <class T>
ostream & operator<<(ostream & os, const ArrayETP<T> & a)
{
    for (int i = 0; i < a.size; i++)
    {
        os << a.arr[i] << " ";
        if (i % 5 == 4)
            os << "\n";
    }
    if (i % 5 != 0)
        os << "\n";
    return os;
}
#endif

// pe14-2.cpp -- use the ArrayETP class

#include <iostream>
using namespace std;
#include "pe14-2.h"

const int Players = 5;
int main(void)
{
    try {
        ArrayETP<double> Team((int)Players,0.0);
        cout << "Enter free-throw percentages for your 5 "
                "top players as a decimal fraction:\n";
        for (int player = 0; player < Players; player++)
        {
            cout << "Player " << (player + 1) << ": % = ";
            cin >> Team[player];
        }
```

continues

```
            cout.precision(1);
            cout.setf(ios::showpoint);
            cout.setf(ios::fixed,ios::floatfield);
            cout << "Recapitulating, here are the percentages:\n";
            for (player = 0; player <= Players; player++)
                cout << "Player #" << (player + 1) << ": "
                        << 100.0 * Team[player] << "%\n";
        }    // end of try block
    catch (const ArrayETP<double>::NoRoom & nr)        // 1st handler
    {
        cout << "ArrayETP<T> exception: "
                << "Insufficient memory for " << nr.asked << "objects\n";
    }
    catch (const ArrayETP<double>::BadIndex & bi)      // 2nd handler
    {
        cout << "ArrayETP<T> exception: "
                << bi.badindex << " is a bad index value\n";
    }
    cout << "Bye!\n";
    return 0;
}
```

Answers to Additional Questions

True or False

1.	T	11.	T
2.	F	12.	F
3.	F	13.	T
4.	T	14.	T
5.	T	15.	T
6.	T	16.	T
7.	F	17.	F
8.	F	18.	T
9.	F	19.	T
10.	F	20.	F

Short Answers

1.

a. A class declared within another class is called a nested class.

b. The `abort()` function is used to terminate a program.

c. The `cerr` ostream object is used to output error messages to the screen. A full description is given on page 382.

d. You throw an exception when a problem occurs at a particular point in a program.

e. The catch exception is used to catch the error that is thrown by an exception.

f. You catch an exception with an exception handler at a point in the program where you want to handle the exception.

g. A `catch` block is another name for exception handler.

h. A `try` block identifies a block of code for which particular exceptions will be activated.

i. An uncaught exception calls the `terminate()` function. By default the `terminate()` function calls `abort()`.

j. The behavior of `terminate()` calling `abort()` can be modified using `set_terminate()` to specify a function call other than `abort()`.

k. Unwinding the stack is a process that occurs when a function terminates via an exception throw rather than via a return call. See page 700 and Figure 14.3.

l. Programs sometimes encounter runtime problems that prevent them from continuing normally. Exceptions provide a tool for dealing with such events.

m. RTTI stands for runtime type information and provides a standard way for a program to determine the type of an object during runtime.

n. The `dynamic_cast` operator answers the question of whether it is safe to assign the address of an object to a pointer of a particular type. It is used for upcasting in a class hierarchy. See page 730.

o. The `const_cast` is for making a type cast with the sole purpose of changing whether a value is `const` or volatile. See page 730.

p. The `static_cast` is only valid if the type name can be converted implicitly to the same type as the expression or vice versa. See page 730.

q. The `reinterpret_cast` requires the programmer to write implementation-dependent code, using the `reinterpret_cast` helps to keep track of such acts. See page 731.

2.
```
a)  class Nesting {
    private:
        class Nested {
            ...
        }
        ...
    }
b)  class Nesting {
    public:
        class Nested {
            ...
        }
        ...
    }
c)  class Nesting {
    private:
        struct Nested {
            ...
        }
        ...
    }
d)  class Nesting {
    public:
        enum Nested { ... }
        ...
    }
e)  class Nesting {
    private:
        class Nested {
            ...
        }
        ...
    }
```

3. The program should produce this:

```
Harmonic mean of 10 and 12 is 10.9091
Cube of 2.459 is 14.8688
Problem! Bad square root operand: -a not allowed. Sorry!
Bye!
```

4. The declaration of a `friend` can be anywhere in the class declaration, in any of the private, protected, or public sections.

Programming Projects

1. There are a lot of ways to do this one:

```cpp
//newint.h - header for ints with exceptions

#include <iostream>
using namespace std;
class Newint
{
private:
    int op;
public:
    Newint(int i) : op(i) {};
    ~Newint() {};
    class Overflow
    {
        public:
            int opA, opB;
            char operate;
            Overflow(int i, int j, char s) : opA(i),
                    opB(j), operate(s) {}
    };
    class Underflow
    {
        public:
            int opA, opB;
            char operate;
            Underflow(int i, int j, char s) : opA(i),
                    opB(j), operate(s) {}
    };
    int operator+(const Newint & a) const;
    int operator-(const Newint & a) const;
    int operator/(const Newint & a) const;
    int operator*(const Newint & a) const;
    int operator%(const Newint & a) const;
    friend ostream & operator<<(ostream & os, const Overflow & of);
    friend ostream & operator<<(ostream & os, const Underflow & of);
    friend ostream & operator<<(ostream & os, const Newint & a);
};

//newint.cpp - ints with exceptions

#include <climits>
using namespace std;
#include "newint.h"
int Newint::operator+(const Newint & a) const
{
    if (op > 0 && a.op > 0 && op > INT_MAX - a.op)
        throw Overflow(op, a.op, '+');
    if (op < 0 && a.op < 0 && op < INT_MIN - a.op)
        throw Underflow(op, a.op, '+');
    return op + a.op;
}
int Newint::operator-(const Newint & a) const
```

```
{
    if (op > 0 && a.op < 0 && op > INT_MAX + a.op)
        throw Overflow(op, a.op, '-');
    if (op < 0 && a.op < 0 && op < INT_MIN + a.op)
        throw Underflow(op, a.op, '-');
    return op + a.op;
}
int Newint::operator*(const Newint & a) const
{
    if (op < 0 && a.op > 0 && op < INT_MIN/a.op)
        throw Underflow(op, a.op, '*');
    if ((op > 0 && a.op < 0) && op > INT_MIN/a.op)
        throw Underflow(op, a.op, '*');
    if (((op < 0 && a.op < 0) || (op > 0 && a.op > 0)) && op >
                    INT_MAX/a.op)
        throw Overflow(op, a.op, '*');
    return op*a.op;
}
int Newint::operator/(const Newint & a) const
{
    if (a.op == 0)
        throw Overflow(op, a.op, '/');
    return op/a.op;
}
int Newint::operator%(const Newint & a) const
{
    if (a.op == 0)
        throw Overflow(op, a.op, '%');
    return op%a.op;
}

ostream & operator<<(ostream & os, const Newint::Overflow & a)
{
    os << "Overflow error: Can't do " << a.opA << " "
        << a.operate << " " << a.opB << ".\n";
    return os;
}
ostream & operator<<(ostream & os, const Newint::Underflow & a)
{
    os << "Underflow error: Can't do " << a.opA << " "
        << a.operate << " " << a.opB << ".\n";
    return os;
}
ostream & operator<<(ostream & os, const Newint & a)
{
    os << a.op;
    return os;
}

//newintu.cpp - test function for Newint

#include <iostream>
#include <climits>
using namespace std;

#include "newint.h"
int main(void)
{
    Newint i = 10;
    Newint j = 15;

    try {                       //Addition try block
        cout << "Integer addition: \n";
        cout << i << " + " << j << " = " << (i+j) << "\n";
```

continues

```
        i = INT_MAX;
        j = -2;
        cout << i << " + " << j << " = " << (i+j) << "\n";
        j = 2;
        cout << i << " + " << j << " = " << (i+j) << "\n";
    }
    catch (Newint::Overflow & a)
    {
        cout << a;
    }
    catch (Newint::Underflow & a)
    {
        cout << a;
    }
    try {                        //Subtraction try block
        cout << "\nInteger subtraction: \n";
        i = 1206;
        j = -2890;
        cout << i << " - " << j << " = " << (i-j) << "\n";
        i = -17579;
        j = -30859;
        cout << i << " - " << j << " = " << (i-j) << "\n";
        j = 31789;
        cout << i << " - " << j << " = " << (i-j) << "\n";
    }
    catch (Newint::Overflow & a)
    {
        cout << a;
    }
    catch (Newint::Underflow & a)
    {
        cout << a;
    }
    try {                        //Multiplication try block
        cout << "\nInteger multiplication: \n";
        i = 14;
        j = 982;
        cout << i << " * " << j << " = " << (i*j) << "\n";
        i = 542;
        j = 0;
        cout << i << " * " << j << " = " << (i*j) << "\n";
        i = 150;
        j = -150;
        cout << i << " * " << j << " = " << (i*j) << "\n";
        i = -150;
        j = 150;
        cout << i << " * " << j << " = " << (i*j) << "\n";
        i = -25000;
        cout << i << " * " << j << " = " << (i*j) << "\n";
    }
    catch (Newint::Overflow & a)
    {
        cout << a;
    }
    catch (Newint::Underflow & a)
    {
        cout << a;
    }
    try {                        //Division try block
        cout << "\nInteger division: \n";
        i = 150;
        j = 3;
        cout << i << " / " << j << " = " << (i/j) << "\n";
        i = -22456;
        j = -12;
        cout << i << " / " << j << " = " << (i/j) << "\n";
```

```
        j = 0;
        cout << i << " / " << j << " = " << (i/j) << "\n";
    }
      catch (Newint::Overflow & a)
    {
        cout << a;
    }
}
catch (Newint::Underflow & a)
{
    cout << a;
}
try {                        //Modulus try block
    cout << "\nModulus: \n";
    i = 150;
    j = 3;
    cout << i << " % " << j << " = " << (i%j) << "\n";
    i = -22456;
    j = -12;
    cout << i << " % " << j << " = " << (i%j) << "\n";
    j = 0;
    cout << i << " % " << j << " = " << (i%j) << "\n";
}
catch (Newint::Overflow & a)
{
    cout << a;
}
catch (Newint::Underflow & a)
{
    cout << a;
}

    return 0;
}
```

CHAPTER 15

THE string CLASS AND THE STANDARD TEMPLATE LIBRARY

Statement of Purpose

In this penultimate chapter, we examine two new powerful features of the new generation of C++ compilers. The first is the **string** class, which moves previous null-terminated array-based C-style strings into the realm of object-oriented programming and provides powerful methods to manipulate **string** objects. The second is the Standard Template Library, which is a collection of useful templates and methods for handling a range of container objects. As a bonus we examine a new feature called **auto_ptr**, which is a smart pointer template class designed to make the management of dynamic memory somewhat easier.

Objectives

By the end of Chapter 15, the student should understand the following concepts:

- The concept of the C++ **string** class library

- How to use the main member functions and operators in the **string** class library

- The management of dynamic memory using **auto_ptr**

- The concept of generic programming and its role in reusable code

- The main features of the Standard Template Library

- The role of the Standard Template Library in handling container objects

Lecture Outline

The C++ `string` class

So far we have used C-style strings through the string.h or the cstring.h header files. However, modern C++ compilers have an extensive string-handling armory within the **string** class.

Sample programs: str1.cpp—introducing the **string** class

                                     str2.cpp—string input

                                     str3.cpp—some string methods

- Constructing a string
- **string** class has six constructors
- The +=, =, <<, and [] operators are overloaded to perform special string operations
- The **string** class input
- Comparison of **string** class objects
- All six relational operators are overloaded to deal with **string** objects
- Each operator is overloaded three times to deal with
- **string** object—**string** object
- **string** object—C-style **string**
- C-style **string**—**string** object
- Contains member functions to return the number of characters in a **string** object
- **size()** and **length()** essentially do the same thing
- There are overloaded member functions to perform searches in a **string** object
- These are given in Table 15.2 on page 742 of *The Waite Group's C++ Primer Plus, Third Edition.*

The `auto_ptr` Class

In the past the use of C++ dynamic memory allocation has relied upon the programmer to specifically allocate memory using the new keyword, and then release that memory using the delete keyword. Failure to release that dynamic memory is known as a memory leak. The shortcomings of this method are now addressed by the **auto_ptr** template class, which invisibly releases dynamic memory back to the heap.

- The inherent problems associated with **new** and **delete**
- How to use **auto_ptr**
- **auto_ptr** is a template class
- Include the memory header file
- No need to use **delete**
- **Auto_ptr** considerations
- Invisibly uses **new** coupled with **delete**
- Does not use **new[]**, therefore cannot directly use dynamic arrays
- Avoid copying one **auto_ptr** to another **auto_ptr**

The Standard Template Library

The Standard Template Library (often referred to as the STL) is a collection of useful frequently used routines. They are consistent with the C++ philosophy of code reuse but differ from previous reuse concepts by introducing generic programming. Here we discuss the vector STL and draw comparisons with ArrayDb from Chapter 13. Recall that ArrayDB program was based upon the ArrayDB class and used to hold the details of students' examination scores. It contained private data members and public member functions to instantiate and manipulate that data.

Sample programs: vect1.cpp—introducing the **vector** template

vect2.cpp—methods and iterators

vect3.cpp—using STL functions

- The **vector** template class
- Things to do to your vectors
- More things to do to your vectors

Generic Programming

In the past a useful function would have to be written many times to be used by every conceivable data type. The STL with generic programming is revolutionary in that it is type-independent and needs only be written once, yet customized by the programmer to fit all data types.

Sample programs: copy.cpp—**copy( )** and iterators

inserts.cpp—**copy( )** and insert iterators

list.cpp—using a list

set.cpp—some set operations

multmap.cpp—use a multimap

- Why iterators?
- Understanding iterators is the key to understanding the STL
- Should be able to dereference an iterator
- Should be able to assign one operator to another
- Should be able to compare one operator to another
- Should be able to move operator through all elements of a container
- Kinds of iterators
- Input iterators
- Output iterators
- Forward iterators
- Bidirectional iterators
- Random access iterators
- Permitted operations on iterators are given in Table 15.3 of *The Waite Group's C++ Primer Plus, Third Edition*
- Iterator Hierarchy—shown in Table 15.4 of *The Waite Group's C++ Primer Plus, Third Edition*
- Concepts, Refinements, and Models

- The word concepts is used to describe a set of requirements
- Uses the term refinement to indicate a conceptual inheritance
- A model is a particular implementation of a concept
- The pointer as iterator
- The STL provides some predefined iterators
- `copy()`
- ostream_iterator
- istream_iterator
- Other useful iterators
- Kinds of containers
- The container concept
- The basic properties are shown in Table 15.5 on page 778 of *The Waite Group's C++ Primer Plus, Third Edition*
- Sequences
- Sequence requirements are shown in Table 15.6 on page 781 of *The Waite Group's C++ Primer Plus, Third Edition*
- Sequence optional requirements are shown in Table 15.7 on page 782 of *The Waite Group's C++ Primer Plus, Third Edition*
- vector—is a form of sequence
- deque—another form of sequence
- list—yet another form of sequence
- Some list member functions are shown in Table 15.8 on page 784 of *The Waite Group's C++ Primer Plus, Third Edition*
- queue—is a restricted deque and hence a sequence
- queue operations are shown in Table 15.9 of *The Waite Group's C++ Primer Plus, Third Edition*
- `priority_queue`
- stack
- stack operations are shown in Table 15.10 of *The Waite Group's C++ Primer Plus, Third Edition*
- Associative Containers—is another refinement of the container concept
- A set example
- A multimap example

Function Objects

Function objects, also known as functors, are any object that can be used with () in the manner of functions. These are normal function names, pointers to functions and class objects with the () operator overloaded.

Sample program: funadap.cpp—using function adaptors

- Functor concepts
- Predefined functors

- Table 15.11 on page 799 of *The Waite Group's C++ Primer Plus, Third Edition* describes operators and function object equivalents
- Adaptable functors and function adapters

Algorithms

The STL contains many non-member functions for working with containers. They use templates to provide generic data typing and they use iterators to provide generic representation for accessing data in a container.

Sample program: usealgo.cpp—displays the contents of three containers

- Algorithm Groups—STL divides the library into four groups

    Nonmodifying sequence operators

    Mutating sequence operators

    Sorting and related operations

    Generalized numeric operations
- General properties
- Using the STL
- Other libraries

Additional Questions

True or False

1. The string class has six overloaded constructors and six overloaded destructors.

2. Two string objects can be concatenated using the overloaded + operator.

3. The auto_ptr class is a template class and is defined in the vector header file.

4. In a computing context a vector corresponds to an array holding a set of like values that can be accessed in a random fashion.

5. All STLs contain basic methods including size(), swap(), begin(), and end().

6. Templates allow you to define a class in terms of a generic type, the actual data type is then always determined by the program at runtime.

7. Elements in sequence have a definite order.

8. Because the stack allows data to be added at the back and leave from the front it is known as First-In, First-Out (FIFO) sequence.

9. After creating a vector object, it is possible to access individual elements using the usual array notation because of the way [] is overloaded.

10. An iterator is a generalization of a pointer and is contained in the STL.

11. The goal of generic programming is to write code that is independent of data types.

12. Functors are generic versions of functions that require the programmer to overload operators such as () before they are used in a program.

Short Answers

1. Briefly describe why any algorithm based upon the input iterator should be a one pass algorithm.

2. Describe the main reason for using a deque object rather than a vector.

3. Why should `auto_ptr` be only directly used for memory allocation related to `new`?

4. Explain what is meant by the term "past-the-end."

5. List the basic properties of a container and briefly state their purpose.

Programming Projects

1. Define an integer list and individually assign the numbers **2**, **1**, **3** into the list. By defining an iterator, output the contents of the list to the screen.

2. Write a program that will allow a store manager to input a list of five prices into an array. These prices should be copied into a list and any duplicate values removed. The full list should then be displayed to the screen.

3. Write a program that will allow a store manager to input a list of five prices into an array. These prices should be copied into a list and full list should then be displayed to the screen. Another five prices should be entered into an array and copied into another list before being displayed to the screen. The lists must then be merged, duplicates removed, and the resulting list displayed to the screen.

Activities for Learning

1. Investigate the other member functions that are available in the `string` class to interrogate and manipulate `string` objects.

2. The section on `auto_ptr` suggests a mechanism for dealing with arrays. Investigate this area by writing a program to deal with this topic.

3. Make a list of the operations available in the containers sequence, deque, list, queue, and stack. From your list, determine the hierarchical structure of inheritance between these containers.

Answers to Text Programming Exercises

1. A possible solution to the palindrome problem is
```
// PE15.1
// Palindrome

#include <string>
#include <iostream>
using namespace std;

bool IsAPalindrome(string  s);

main()
{
    string TheWord;

    cout << "Enter the word : ";
    getline(cin,TheWord);
```

```
    if (IsAPalindrome(TheWord) == true)
        cout << "Palindrome" << endl;
    else
        cout << "Not a palindrome" << endl;
    return (0);
}

bool IsAPalindrome(string  s)
{
    unsigned int x = s.size(); // get size of object
    unsigned int y;
    string t(s);     // create and size t object

    x--;     // set maximum offset

    // reverse s and store in t
    for (y = 0; y <= x; y++)
    {
        t[y] = s[x - y];
    }

    // compare the two strings objects
    // and return boolean result
        return(s == t);
}
```

2. A possible solution to the palindrome that ignores spaces, punctuation, and capitals problems is

```
// PE15.2
// Palindrome with spaces, punctuation and capitals

#include <string>
#include <iostream>
#include <cctype>
using namespace std;

bool IsAPalindrome(string  s);
string Shrink(string s);

main()
{
    string TheWord;

    cout << "Enter the word : ";
    getline(cin,TheWord);
    TheWord = Shrink(TheWord);
    if (IsAPalindrome(TheWord) == true)
    cout << "Palindrome" << endl;
    else
        cout << "Not a palindrome" << endl;
    return (0);
}

string Shrink(string s)
{
    unsigned int x = s.size(); // get size of object
    unsigned int y;
    unsigned int z = 0;
    char r[256];

    x--;     // set maximum offset
    for (y = 0; y <= x; y++)
    {
        if (isalpha(s[y]))
        {
```

```
            r[z] = tolower(s[y]);     //build truncated C type string
            z++;
        }
        r[z] = NULL;     //terminate C type string
    }
    string t(r);
    return(t);
}

bool IsAPalindrome(string  s)
{
    unsigned int x = s.size(); // get size of object
    unsigned int y;
    string t(s);     // create and size t object

    x--;     // set maximum offset

    // reverse s and store in t
    for (y = 0; y <= x; y++)
    {
        t[y] = s[x - y];
    }

    // compare the two strings objects
    // and return boolean result
        return(s == t);
}
```

3. The possible program solution to remove duplicate values in the array is given next. Note how the array is copied into a list container thus giving access to list member functions. First the list is sorted with the **sort()** member function, and then adjacent duplicate values are removed with the unique member function. A running count is kept of the elements in the new reduced array and this value returned to the calling module.

```
// pe3.cpp

#include <iostream>
#include <list>
using namespace std;

#define MAX 10

int reduce(long ar[], int n);

main()
{
    long myarray[MAX] = {12, 12 ,5, 6, 11, 5, 6, 77, 11,12};

    cout << "The are " << reduce(myarray,MAX)
            << " elements in the reduced array" << endl;
    return (0);
}

int reduce(long ar[], int n)
{
    list<long> x;
    list<long>::iterator pd;
    int elements = 0;    // reduced elements

    x.insert(x.begin(),ar, ar+n);
    x.sort();
    x.unique();
    for (pd = x.begin(); pd != x.end(); pd++)
    {
        cout << *pd << endl;
        elements++;
    }
```

```
        cout << endl;
        return(elements);
    }
```

4. Here is one possible solution to the template problem:

```
// pe4.cpp

#include <iostream>
#include <list>
using namespace std;

#define MAX 10
#define MAX2 4

template <class T>
int reduce(T ar[], int n);

main()
{
    long myarray[MAX] = {12, 12 ,5, 6, 11, 5, 6, 77, 11,12};
    int res = 0;

    res =  reduce<long>(myarray,MAX);
    cout << "The are " << res
        << " elements in the reduced long array" << endl;

    return (0);
}

template <class T>
int reduce(T ar[], int n)
{
    list<T> x;
    list<T>::iterator pd;
    int elements = 0;   // reduced elements

    x.insert(x.begin(),ar, ar+n);
    x.sort();
    x.unique();
    for (pd = x.begin(); pd != x.end(); pd++)
    {
        cout << *pd << endl;
        elements++;
    }
    cout << endl;
    return(elements);
}
```

5. A possible solution to PE 5 is as follows:

```
// PE 5
//customer.h


#ifndef _CUSTOMER_H_
#define _CUSTOMER_H_

class Customer
{
private:
    long arrive;
    int processtime;
```

```
public:
    //Customer() {arrive = processtime = 0; }
    void set(long when);
    long when() const {return arrive;}
    int ptime() const {return processtime;}
};

typedef Customer Item;

#endif

// PE 5
// customer.cpp

#include "customer.h"
#include <cstdlib>

void Customer::set(long when)
{
    processtime = rand() % 3 + 1;
    arrive = when;
}

// PE 5
// newbank.cpp

#include <iostream>
#include <queue>
using namespace std;
#include <cstdlib>
#include <ctime>
#include "customer.h"

const MIN_PER_HR = 60;

bool newcustomer(double x);

main()
{
    srand(time(0));
    cout << "Case study" << endl;
    cout << "Enter max size of queue : ";
    int qs;
    cin >> qs;
    queue<int> line;

    cout << "enter number of simulation hours : ";
    int hours;
    cin >> hours;

    long cyclelimit = MIN_PER_HR * hours;

    cout << "Enter number of customers per hour : ";
    double perhour;
    cin >> perhour;
    double min_per_cust;
    min_per_cust = MIN_PER_HR / perhour;

    Item temp;
    long turnaways = 0;
    long customers = 0;
    long served = 0;
    long sum_line = 0;
    int wait_time = 0;
    long line_wait = 0;
```

```
        for (int cycle = 0; cycle < cyclelimit; cycle++)
        {
            if (newcustomer(min_per_cust))
            {
                if (line.size() >= qs)
                    turnaways++;
                else
                {
                    customers++;
                    line.push(cycle);
                }
            }
            if (wait_time <= 0 && !line.empty())
            {
                line.pop();
                wait_time = temp.ptime();
                line_wait += cycle -temp.when();
                served++;
            }
            if (wait_time > 0)
                wait_time--;
            sum_line += line.size();
        }

        if (customers > 0)
        {
            cout << "customers accepted: " << customers << endl;
            cout << "  customers served: " << served << endl;
            cout << "          turnaways: " << turnaways << endl;
            cout << "average queue size: ";
            cout.precision(2);
            cout.setf(ios_base::fixed, ios_base::floatfield);
            cout.setf(ios_base::showpoint);
            cout << (double)sum_line / cyclelimit << endl;
            cout << " average wait time: "
                << (double)line_wait / served << " minutes\n";
        }
        else
            cout << "No customers!\n";
        return(0);
    }

    bool newcustomer(double x)
    {
        return(rand() * x / RAND_MAX < 1);
    }
```

Answers to Additional Questions

True or False

1. F
2. T
3. F
4. T
5. T
6. F

7. T
8. F
9. T
10. T
11. T
12. F

Short Answers

1. If you set an input operator to the first element in a container and increment it until it reaches the end, it will point to every container item on route. However, if you repeat the process, there is no guarantee that the input iterator will move through the values in the same order.

2. Use the deque when most operations take place at the beginning and end of the sequence.

3. Using `auto_ptr` allocates dynamic memory using `new` and automatically invokes `delete` when the object terminates. You cannot use anything associated with `new []` that in turn is associated with `delete []`.

4. Past-the-end is an iterator referring to an element one past the last element in a container.

5. The answers are given in Table 15.5.

Programming Projects

1. One possible solution to project one is as follows:

```
// PP1

#include <list>
#include <iostream>
using namespace std ;
typedef list<int> LISTINT;

void main()
{
        LISTINT listInt;
        LISTINT::iterator i;

    // Insert one at a time
        listInt.insert (listInt.begin(), 2);
    listInt.insert (listInt.end(), 1);
        listInt.insert (listInt.end(), 3);
    // 1 2 3
        for (i = listInt.begin(); i != listInt.end(); ++i)
        cout << *i << " ";
        cout << endl;
}
```

2. A possible solution to project 2 is given next:

```
// PP2

#include <iostream>
#include <list>
#include <iterator>
using namespace std;

main()
{
    const MAX = 5;
    int i;
    list<float> one;
    ostream_iterator<float,char> oot(cout," ");
    float stuff[MAX];

    for (i = 0; i < MAX; i++)
    {
        cout << "enter a number : ";
        cin >> stuff[i];
    }
    one.insert(one.end(),stuff,stuff+5);
```

```
            one.sort();
            one.unique();
            copy(one.begin(),one.end(),oot);
            cout << endl;
            return (0);
        }
```

3. A possible solution to project 3 is given next:

```
    // PP3

    #include <iostream>
    #include <list>
    #include <iterator>
    using namespace std;

    main()
    {
        const MAX = 5;
        int i;
        list<float> one;
        list<float> two;
        ostream_iterator<float,char> oot(cout," ");
        float stuff[MAX];
    // Do first price list
        for (i = 0; i < MAX; i++)
        {
            cout << "enter a number : ";
            cin >> stuff[i];
        }

        one.insert(one.end(),stuff,stuff+5);
        copy(one.begin(),one.end(),oot);
        cout << endl;

    // Do second price list
        for (i = 0; i < MAX; i++)
        {
            cout << "enter a number : ";
            cin >> stuff[i];
        }

        two.insert(two.end(),stuff,stuff+5);
        copy(two.begin(),two.end(),oot);
        cout << endl;

        one.sort();
        two.sort();
        one.merge(two);
        one.unique();
        copy(one.begin(),one.end(),oot);
        cout << endl;
        cout << endl;

        return (0);
    }
```

INPUT, OUTPUT, AND FILES

Statement of Purpose

This final chapter in the book looks outward from C++ to input and output data to the external world. The draft standard is evolving, so the material includes both the traditional and draft standard ways of I/O. The student will now be able to use simple I/O with the standard I/O and file I/O.

Objectives

By the end of Chapter 16, the student should understand the following concepts:

- The principles of C++ input and output using streams
- The `iostream` family of classes: what is available and when to use which tool
- How to association a stream with program and connecting the stream to a file
- Buffered I/O and why it is used
- Using redirection with operating systems that support it
- Formatting output when appearances are important
- Determining and setting stream states to control I/O
- Using file I/O with disk files, both sequentially and simultaneously
- Using the right file mode
- Processing data files using the command line, and using command line arguments
- Random and sequential files
- Text versus binary files and when to use each
- Random file access to update data
- Incore formatting to input and output formatted strings

Lecture Outline

Overview of C++ input and output

C++ takes a whole new approach to input and output, using classes to manage to handle the work.

- Background

  I/O not built into either C or C++

  Most implementations based on UNIX library functions

  C++ uses classes in `iostream.h` and `fstream.h` in standard class libraries

- I/O conceptual framework

  Treats I/O as a stream of bytes

  Input stream can come from any input device

  Output stream can flow to any output device

  Stream acts as intermediary between program and device

  Managing input

    Associate stream with input to program

    Connect stream to file

  Buffer makes stream handling more efficient

    Block of memory for temporary storage for transfer of data

    Allows reading and writing in manner most efficient for device

    Keyboard: one byte at a time

    Disk: chunk of data at a time

    `<ENTER>` flushes keyboard input buffer

- Streams, buffers, and `iostream.h`

  `iostream.h` brings classes for I/O management

    `streambuf`: buffer management

    `ios`: general stream properties

    `ostream`: derives from `ios` for output methods

    `istream`: derives from `ios` for input methods

    `iostream`: based on `istream` and `ostream` inheriting both input and output methods

  Using these objects opens stream, creates buffer, and associates buffer with stream automatically

  `iostream` class library

    `cin`: standard input stream, usually keyboard

    `cout`: standard output stream, usually monitor

    `cerr`: standard error stream, usually monitor, no buffer

    `clog`: standard error stream but buffered

- Redirection

Changes association for standard input and output

Redirecting standard output doesn't affect `cerr` or `clog`

Operating system may allow redirecting `cerr` and `clog`

Output with cout

So far, C++ output has been used in the most simple ways. It is time to discover the many tools available in the language.

Sample programs:

write.cpp—using `write()` to print Utah

defaults.cpp—display `cout` default formats

manip.cpp—using format manipulators

width.cpp—using `width()` function

fill.cpp—change field fill character

precise.cpp—set the precision for output

showpt.cpp—setting precision showing the decimal point

setf.cpp—using `setf()` to control formatting

setf2.cpp—more formatting with `setf()`

iomanip.cpp—using `iomanip.h` manipulators

check_it.cpp—input with `cin`

get_fun.cpp—reading string input

peeker.cpp—using `istream` methods

truncate.cpp—using `peek()` to see if entire line read

- `ostream` class members convert C++ data types to and from a stream of characters representing text
- Class methods

  Overloaded `<<` insertion operator

  Default use is bitwise left-shift operator

  Recognizes all basic C++ data types and string and `void` pointer types

  Returns a reference to `ostream` object to allow chaining

  Matches any pointer with type `void *` to print numerical representation of address

  `put()` method to display characters

  Traditionally returns `ostream` object reference

  Form is evolving: `cout.put('W').put('I');`

  Current standard calls for `int` return, so can't concatenate

  Converts numeric to `char`

  `write()` method to display strings

  First argument for address of string

  Second for number of characters to print

  Returns the `cout` object, so can concatenate

  Doesn't stop printing characters when reaches `null` character

  Doesn't translate numeric data

- Flushing output buffer

  Output isn't sent to destination immediately

  Normally flushes buffer automatically

    When buffer is full

    When newline sent

    Upon pending input

  Force flushing using manipulator

    `flush`: flushes buffer

    `endl`: flushes buffer and inserts newline

    Form: `cout << flush:` or `flush(cout);`

- Formatting with `cout`

  `ostream` insertion operators convert values to text form

    `char`, if printable, displayed as a character one character wide

      Numeric integers displayed as decimal integers in field wide enough for number and sign

    Strings displayed in field width of string

  Floating point

    Old style: six places to right of decimal, no trailing zeros, fixed point or E notation

    New: total of six digits, no trailing zeros, fixed point, or E

    Both: field just wide enough to hold number

  Must provide any spaces between numbers manually

  Changing number base of display

    `ios` class stores information describing format state

    `dec`, `hex`, `oct` manipulators

    Form: `hex(cout);` or `cout << hex;`

    Remains in that state until changed

    Not member functions so not invoked by object

  Adjusting field widths

    `width()` with no arguments returns current setting

    `width(int i)` sets new width and returns old setting

    Affects only next item displayed, and then reverts to default

    C++ doesn't truncate: expands field to fit data if necessary

  Fill characters

    Default: fills unused parts of field with spaces

    `fill()` changes to another character

    Form: `cout.fill('*');`

    Stays in effect until changed

Floating-point display precision

> Traditionally means maximum number of digits to right of decimal

> New standard defines as total number of digits displayed (default is 6)

> New setting stays in effect until changed

Trailing zeros and decimal points

> `set()` allows setting formatting features

> Controls bits of flag member of `ios`

> `fmtflags` is `typedef` holding format flags

> `ios::showpoint` displays trailing decimal points

> `ios::showbase` adds base prefixes on output

> `ios::uppercase` sets uppercase for hex output and E notation

> `ios::showpos` uses + before positive base 10 numbers

> Form: `fmtflags setf(fmtflags)` for settings using one bit

> Form: `fmtflags setf(fmtflags, fmtflags)` for settings requiring more than one bit

> Table 16.2 contains arguments for `setf()` with two arguments

- `iomanip.h` header file

Provides additional manipulators to make setting formatting more convenient

`setprecision()` for setting precision

`setw()` for setting field width

- Input with `cin`

Converts character sequences from input stream to C++ data types

`istream` class overloads `>>` operator to work with all C++ basic types and character pointer types

Returns reference to invoking object, so can concatenate

Skips whitespace until encounter nonwhitespace

If input doesn't meet `cin`'s expectation, leaves input variable unchanged and returns `0`

- Stream states

`eofbit` set when reach end of file

`badbit` set if stream is corrupted

`failbit` set if expected characters are not received

Table 16.4 lists the stream states member functions

Setting any of the bits closes the stream for further input or output

Reset stream to good by calling `clear()` method

- Other `istream` class methods

Single character input

> `get()` methods return next character even if whitespace

> `get(char &)` assigns input character to argument

get(void) returns next input character

Table 16.5 summarizes features of single character input functions

How decide which form to use?

To skip whitespace, use >>

Use a get() form to examine every character

String input

get() and getline() both take 3 arguments: address of string, max bytes, and termination character

get() form leaves newline character in input stream

getline() form discards newline character

Unexpected string input

eofbit, badbit, and failbit as with single character input

No input: null character placed into input string and sets failbit

Exceed length of string: getline() sets failbit, get() doesn't

Table 16.6 summarizes input changes from traditional C to C++

Other istream methods

read() reads given number of bytes and storing without appending null

peek() returns next character from input without extracting from input stream

gcount() returns number of characters read

putback() inserts a character into input stream

File input and output

Much of a program's work involves reading and writing data to and from permanent storage. C++ simplifies a lot, extending the standard I/O classes.

Sample programs:
file.cpp—simple I/O to file

count.cpp—processing multiple files from command line

append.cpp—opening a file for appending

binary.cpp—appending data to binary file

random.cpp—random access to binary file in traditional C++

- File I/O is handled much as standard I/O
- Uses new classes in fstream.h header file
- Derived from iostream, so can use those methods
- Simple file I/O

To write a file

Create an ofstream object to manage output

Associate that object with a file

Form for output: ofstream fout("cookies")

istream is a base class for ofstream class, so use all those methods

`ifstream` and `ofstream` use buffered I\O

Creates new file if doesn't exist

Truncates existing file

To read a file

Create an `ifstream` object to manage input

Associate that object with a file

Form: `ifstream fin("cookies")`

Connections closed automatically when objects expire

Explicitly close I/O with `close()`

Does not eliminate stream

Can reconnect later to same file or another

Closing file flushes the buffer

- Opening multiple files

Create separate streams for each file open simultaneously

To process files sequentially, use one stream and connect to each file in turn

Declare stream object without initializing

Associate stream with each file as needed

`object.open()` to associate file

`object.close()` to terminate association

Command-line processing

Use `int main(int argc, char *argv[])`

`argc` represents number of arguments including command itself

`argv` is pointer to array of command line parameters

- Stream checking

File stream classes inherit stream-state member from `ios` class

If all is okay, state is `0`

Bits set indicate problem

Inherit stream-state methods as well

- File modes

Specify when associating stream with file

Table 16.7 lists constants from `ios` for file modes

`ifstream open()` uses `ios::in` for reading as default

`ofstream open()` uses `ios::out` for writing as default

`fstream` class doesn't provide a default (traditional C++)

Use ¦ operator to combine modes

Best approach is to use all desired open modes explicitly

Table 16.8 lists C++ and C file-opening modes

File storage formats

>Text format converts data types to individual characters

>Binary format stores data using C++ internal representation

>Representation is same for character in text and binary formats

Text versus binary format

>Text is easier to read and access using text editors

>Text files can be transferred between different computer systems

>Binary format is more accurate for numbers—no conversion or rounding

>Binary is faster because no conversion is necessary

>Binary usually takes less space

>Transferring files between systems can be a problem

Random access files

>Can move to any location in file rather than process sequentially

>Simplest if done with fixed length records

Traditional C++ random access

>Differs from the draft standard

>Use `ios::in` to read and `ios::binary` for binary files

>Use `ios::out` to write anywhere in file or `ios::app` to append only

>Use `ios::ate` to avoid truncating the file

>`seekg()` moves input pointer to given file location measured from beginning, end, or current position

>`seekp()` moves output pointer to given file location

>`tellg()` returns current file position for input streams

>`tellp()` returns current file position for output streams

>Using `fstream`, `tellg()`, and `tellp()` move in tandem.

>Using `ifstream` and `ofstream`, move separately

>Use `clear()` to reset the stream state, including turning off `eof`

Random access in draft standard

>No `fstream` class for simultaneous I/O

>No `seekg()` and `seekp()` class methods

>Can simulate simultaneous I/O by setting `ifstream` and `ofstream` to same buffer

>Can simulate `seekg()` with `rdbuf()->pubseekoff(...)`

Incore formatting

C++ further expands I/O by providing special functions to input and output arrays of `char`.

Sample programs: strout.cpp—using incore formatting for output

                                        strin.cpp—using incore formatting for input

- C++ library provides `strstream` family for I/O interface with `char` array

- Reading and writing formatted information to array is incore formatting

- `strstream.h` defines an `ostrstream` class derived from the `ostream` class

    `str()` member function returns address of array

       Freezes object so no longer can write to it

       Must manually free memory when finished with it

    Maintains a `char` array, so doesn't append null character

    Can use a fixed array rather than dynamic memory

- `istrstream` class lets you use `istream` methods to read data from `char` array

Additional Questions

True or False

1. The basic input/output features, such as `read()`, `write()`, `get()`, and `getline()` are built in functions of C++.

2. Essentially, a C++ program treats all input and output as a stream of characters, whether coming from a disk file or keyboard, or going to a monitor or printing device.

3. A big advantage of using the `ostream` and `istream` classes is that the objects will automatically open a stream, create a buffer, associate it with a stream, and give access to the member functions.

4. The insertion operator is one of C++'s most heavily overloaded operators, working as it does with all the basic data and several pointer types.

5. The `cin` object uses the type of variable into which data is being input to determine what method to use to convert the text input to the proper data type.

6. Other input methods skip whitespace characters, but the extraction operator does not. It will, however, stop reading characters into a type `long` input variable when a letter character is entered.

7. The main difference between using `get()` and `getline()` for input is that `get()` reads individual characters, whereas `getline()` reads entire lines.

8. Opening a single input or output stream that is then used with multiple files sequentially conserves system resources.

9. When you are not using the default modes for opening disk files, it is good programming practice to specify *all* the appropriate modes.

Short Answers

1. Describe the following terms, and explain their use in a C++ program.

   a. insertion operator

   b. streams

   c. `istream`

   d. `ostream`

   e. `iostream`

   f. `fstream`

   g. buffer

   h. flushing

   i. `streambuf`

   j. `ios`

   k. `clog`

   l. redirection

m. `void *`

n. `write()`

o. manipulators

p. `flush`

q. `endl`

r. `width`

s. right-justification

t. `fill`

u. left-justified

v. `precision`

w. `setf()`

x. `ios::showpoint`

y. flag bits

z. `hex`

aa. `dec`

ab. `oct`

ac. `fmtflags`

ad. `ios::showbase`

ae. `ios::uppercase`

af. `ios::showpos`

ag. `ios::basefield`

ah. `ios::adjustfield`

ai. `ios::left`

aj. `ios::fixed`

ak. `ios::scientific`

al. `iomanip`

am. `setprecision()`

an. `setw()`

ao. stream state

ap. `eofbit`

aq. `badbit`

ar. `failbit`

as. `good()`

at. `clear()`

au. `fail()`

av. `ignore()`

aw. `peek()`

ax. `read()`

ay. `gcount()`

az. `putback()`

ba. `ifstream`

bb. `close()`

bc. `argc`

bd. `argv`

be. `argv[0]`

bf. `eof()`

bg. file open mode

bh. `ios::trunc`

bi. `ios::app`

bj. `ios::ate`

bk. `ios::binary`

bl. `ios::beg`

bm. `ios::cur`

bn. `ios::end`

bo. `streampos`

bp. `streamoff`

bq. `tellg(), tellp()`

br. `rdbuf()`

bs. `pubseekoff()`

bt. `strstream`

bu. incore formatting

bv. `ostringstream`

2. What are the advantages of buffering input and output? What are the disadvantages?

3. Describe generally what each of the following classes do:

   a) `ios`

   b) `streambuf`

   c) `ostream`

d) `istream`

e) `iostream`

4. What three times does the `ostream` class normally flush the buffer automatically?

5. What is the output from this rather convoluted program?

```
//outp.cpp

#include <iostream>
#include <iomanip>
using namespace std;

int main(void)
{
    long hatch = 564589L;
    float stall = 4.4562385942671e2;
    char * district = "Southern Regional";
    int tamal = 345;
    float * plat = &stall;
    char runout = 74;
    float trib = 6.8093493302e-10;
    int dot = 5;
    cout << hatch << tamal << runout << dot << "\n";
    cout << hatch << "\n";
    cout << stall << "\n";
    cout << district << "\n";
    cout << *district << "\n";
    cout.write(district, dot) << endl;
    cout << ":" << trib << ":" << endl;
    cout << tamal * dot << "\n";
    cout << (++runout + 4) << "\n";
    cout << runout << "\n";
    hex(cout);
    cout << tamal << " " << oct << tamal << " " << tamal << "\n";
    int wi = cout.width(5);
    cout << dec << hatch << " " << dot;
    cout.width(wi);
    cout << plat << " " << *plat << endl;
    wi = cout.width(30);
    cout.fill('~');
    cout << district << endl;
    cout.precision(6);
    cout << "$" << stall << endl;
    cout.setf(ios::showbase);
    cout.setf(ios::showpos);
    cout << hex << (tamal) << "\n";
    cout << setw(6) << hatch
        << "\n" << setw(6) << runout
        << "\n" << setprecision(4) << stall << "\n";
    return 0;
}
```

6. After some `cin` input code runs, `badbit` is found to be set. What does that tell you? What if `failbit` was set? Can you immediately begin reading more input?

7. What could be changed about this code to make it more effective?

```
int i=5;
char response;
cin >> ch;
while ((response != '\n') != 0)
{
    cout << response;
    i++;
```

continues

```
        cin >> response;
    }
    cout << response;
```

8. What is wrong with this code?

```
char ch;
while ((ch = cin.get()) != EOF)
{
    cout << ch;
}
```

9. Which form of input, `>>`, `get(char &)`, or `get(void)`, should you use for each of the following situations?

   a) Reading in a text disk file of the Gettysburg Address for which you want to count the number of words

   b) As part of a business writing analysis, you need to count the number of times that an exclamation point is used in a set of 50 text files.

   c) You are entering names for a customer database. The name is input then added to a disk file.

   d) A children's learning game puts a picture of a shape on the monitor, and the child must type in the name of the shape.

10. When using incore formatting, how do you get access to the array? Is it an array of `char` or a string?

Programming Projects

1. Write a program that prints a grid of 21 rows of 5 columns of numbers like the following. Generate the numbers by adding 15 to the previous number. Make sure that the columns align on the decimal points.

```
  $5.00   $20.00   $35.00   $50.00   $65.00
 $80.00   $95.00  $110.00  $125.00  $140.00
$155.00  $170.00  $185.00  $200.00  $215.00
$230.00  $245.00  $260.00  $275.00  $290.00
```

   and so on to $1565.00.

2. Write a program that takes a line of input and substitutes an exclamation point for each space. For example, turn

```
There once was a beautiful princess named Julia who didn't live
in a castle.
```

   into this

```
There!once!was!a!beautiful!princess!named!Julia!who!didn't!live!
in!a!castle.
```

3. Write a program that reads a disk text file and gives a count of each letter of the alphabet without regard to case (so that 'A' and 'a' count as the same character), total alphabetic characters, and total non-alphabetic characters. Produce this output:

```
In the text.txt file, there are 967 characters.
Of those, 764 are alphabetic, and 203 are non-alphabetic.
Count of each letter:
A    63
B     4
C    33
D    29
E    77
```

   and so on for all the letters of the alphabet. Note the right justification of each letter count. As a challenge, use no more than 12 declared variables and objects, and keep the code to under 55 lines of code, including `#include` lines. Use the file text.dat included on the disk that accompanies the text to test your program.

Activities for Learning

1. Does you operating system provide redirection? How is it used? Can you redirect `cerr` and `clog` output? How?

2. Look at the `iostream.h`, `fstream.h`, and `iomanip.h` files provided with your C++ compiler. What operators are overloaded? What classes are provided? What additional manipulators are available? What prototypes are included in each file? When do you need to use each file?

3. Run the example programs in this chapter. Experiment with changes to get a feel for how the different C++ constructs are used. Modify them to make them more general and more useful to you.

4. Does your compiler allow concatenating `put()`? How do you know?

5. When using `fstream.h`, do you need to also include `iostream.h` with your compiler?

Answers to Text Programming Exercises

Note: The exercise answers were prepared using Borland C++ 4.02. Users of other compilers may need to make some modifications.

1. Write a program that counts the number of characters up to the first `$` in input and that leaves the `$` in the input stream.

```
// pe16-1.cpp

#include <iostream>
using namespace std;

int main(void)
{
    char ch;
    int count = 0;

    while (cin.get(ch) && ch != '$')
        count++;
    if (ch == '$')
        cin.putback(ch);
    else
        cout << "End of file was reached\n";
    cout << count << " characters read\n";
    return 0;
}
```

2. Write a program that copies your keyboard input (up to simulated end-of-file) to a file named on the command line.

```
// pe16-2.cpp
#include <iostream>
#include <fstream>
#include <cstdlib>
using namespace std;

int main(int argc, char * argv[])
{
    if (argc < 2)
    {
        cerr << "Usage: " << argv[0] << " filename\n";
```

continues

```
        exit(EXIT_FAILURE);
    }
    ofstream fout(argv[1]);
    char ch;
    while (cin.get(ch))
        fout << ch;
    return 0;
}
```

3. Write a program that copies one file to another. Have the program take the file names from the command line. Have the program report if it cannot open a file.

```
// pe16-3.cpp
#include <iostream>
#include <fstream>
#include <cstdlib>
using namespace std;


int main(int argc, char * argv[])
{
    if (argc < 3)
    {
        cerr << "Usage: " << argv[0]
            << " source-file target-file\n";
        exit(EXIT_FAILURE);
    }
    ifstream fin(argv[1]);
    if (!fin)
    {
        cerr << "Can't open " << argv[1] << " for input\n";
        exit(EXIT_FAILURE);
    }
    ofstream fout(argv[2]);
    if (!fout)
    {
        cerr << "Can't open " << argv[2] << " for output\n";
        exit(EXIT_FAILURE);
    }
    char ch;
    while (fin.get(ch))
        fout << ch;
    return 0;
}
```

4. Consider the class definitions of Programming Exercise 13.5. If you haven't yet done that exercise, do so now. Then do the following:

Write a program that uses standard C++ I/O and file I/O in conjunction with data of types employee, manager, fink, and highfink, as defined in PE 13.5. The program should be along the general lines of Listing 16.17 in that it should let you add new data to a file. The first time through, the program should solicit data from the user, show all the entries, and then finally save all the information in a file. On subsequent uses, the program should first read and display the file data, let the user add data, and then show the user all the data. One difference is that data should be handled by an array of pointers to type employee. That way, a pointer can point to an employee object or to objects of any of the three derived types. Keep the array small to facilitate checking the program:

```
const int MAX = 10;    // no more than 10 objects
...
employee * pc[MAX];
```

For keyboard entry, the program should use a menu to offer the user the choice of which type of object to create. The menu will use a switch to use `new` to create an object of the desired type and to assign the object's address to pointer in the `pc` array. Next that object can use the virtual `setall()` function to elicit the appropriate data from the user:

```
pc[i]->setall();    // invokes function corresponding to type of object
```

To save the data to a file, devise a virtual `writeall()` function for that purpose:

```
for (i = 0; i < index; i++)
    pc[i]->writeall(fout);// fout ofstream connected to output file
```

Note: use text I/O, not binary I/O, for this exercise. Unfortunately, virtual objects include pointers to tables of pointers to virtual functions, and `write()` copies this information to a file. An object filled by using `read()` from the file gets weird values for the function pointers, which really messes up the behavior of virtual functions. Use a newline to separate each data field from the next; this makes it easier to identify fields on input.

The tricky part is recovering the data from the file. The problem is, how can the program know whether the next item to be recovered is an `employee` object, a `manager` object, a `fink` type, or a `highfink` type? One approach is to precede the data with an integer indicating the type of object to follow when writing the data for an object to a file. Then, on file input, the program can read the integer, and then use a switch to create the appropriate object to receive the data:

```
enum classkind{Employee, Manager, Fink, Highfink}; // in class header
...
while((fin >> classtype).get(ch)){ // newline separates int from data
    switch(classtype) {
        case Employee    : pc[i] = new employee;
                    : break;
```

Then you can use the pointer to invoke a virtual `getall()` function to read the information:

```
pc[i++]->getall();

// pe16empf.h -- header file for employee class and children
#include <string.h>
#include <iostream.h>
#include <fstream.h>

#include <iostream>
#include <fstream>
#include <cstring>
using namespace std;

enum classkind{Employee, Manager, Fink, Highfink};

const int SLEN = 20;
class employee
{
protected:
    char fname[SLEN];
    char lname[SLEN];
    char job[SLEN];
public:
    employee();
    employee(char * fn, char * ln, char * j);
    employee(const employee & e);
    virtual void showall();
    virtual void setall();    // prompts user for values
    friend ostream & operator<<(ostream & os, const employee & e);
    virtual ofstream & writeall(ofstream & of);
    virtual ifstream & readall(ifstream & ifs);
};
```

continues

```
class manager: virtual public employee
{
protected:
    int inchargeof;
public:
    manager();
    manager(char * fn, char * ln, char * j, int ico = 0);
    manager(const employee & e, int ico);
    manager(const manager & m);
    void showall();
    void setall();
    ofstream & writeall(ofstream & of);
    ifstream & readall(ifstream & ifs);
};

class fink: virtual public employee
{
protected:
    char reportsto[SLEN];
public:
    fink();
    fink(char * fn, char * ln, char * j, char * rpo);
    fink(const employee & e, char * rpo);
    fink(const fink & e);
    void showall();
    void setall();
    ofstream & writeall(ofstream & of);
    ifstream & readall(ifstream & ifs);
};


class highfink: public manager, public fink
{
public:
    highfink();
    highfink(char * fn, char * ln, char * j, char * rpo, int ico) ;
    highfink(const employee & e, char * rpo, int ico);
    highfink(const fink & f, int ico);
    highfink(const manager & m, char * rpo);
    highfink(const highfink & h);
    void showall();
    void setall();
    ofstream & writeall(ofstream & of);
    ifstream & readall(ifstream & ifs);
};

// pe16empf.cpp -- employee class and children
#include "pe16empf.h"
char * init = "-----------------";

employee::employee()
{
    fname[0] = '\0';
    lname[0] = '\0';
    job[0] = '\0';
    strcpy(fname+1, init);
    strcpy(lname+1, init);
    strcpy(job+1, init);
    fname[SLEN-1] = lname[SLEN-1] = job[SLEN-1] = '!';
}

employee::employee(char * fn, char * ln, char * j)
{
    strcpy(fname, fn);
    strcpy(lname, ln);
    strcpy(job, j);
```

```
}

employee::employee(const employee & e)
{
    strcpy(fname, e.fname);
    strcpy(lname, e.lname);
    strcpy(job, e.job);
}

void employee::showall()
{
    cout << "Name: " << fname << " " << lname << '\n';
    cout << "Job:  " << job << '\n';
}

void employee::setall()
{
    cout << "First name: ";
    cin.getline(fname, SLEN);
    cout << "Last name: ";
    cin.getline(lname, SLEN);
    cout << "Job: ";
    cin.getline(job, SLEN);
}

ofstream & employee::writeall(ofstream & of)
{
    int kind = Employee;
    of << kind << endl;
    of << fname << endl;
    of << lname << endl;
    of << job << endl;
    return of;
}

ifstream & employee::readall(ifstream & ifs)
{
    ifs.getline(fname, SLEN);
    ifs.getline(lname, SLEN);
    ifs.getline(job, SLEN);
    return ifs;
}

ostream & operator<<(ostream & os, const employee & e)
{
    os << e.fname << " " << e.lname;
    return os;
}

manager::manager()
{
    inchargeof = 0;
}

manager::manager(char * fn, char * ln, char * j, int ico)
    : employee(fn, ln, j)
{
    inchargeof = ico;
}

manager::manager(const employee & e, int ico)
    : employee(e)
{
    inchargeof = ico;
```

continues

```
    }

    manager::manager(const manager & m) : employee(m)
    {
        inchargeof = m.inchargeof;
    }

    void manager::showall()
    {
        employee::showall();
        cout << "In charge of " << inchargeof << '\n';
    }

    void manager::setall()
    {
        employee::setall();
        cout << "Number in charge of: ";
        cin >> inchargeof;
        while (cin.get() != '\n') continue;
    }


    ofstream & manager::writeall(ofstream & of)
    {
        int kind = Manager;
        of << kind << endl;
        of << fname << endl;
        of << lname << endl;
        of << job << endl;
        of << inchargeof << endl;
        return of;
    }

    ifstream & manager::readall(ifstream & ifs)
    {
        employee::readall(ifs);
        ifs >> inchargeof;
        while (ifs.get() != '\n') continue;
        return ifs;
    }

    fink::fink()
    {
        reportsto[0] = '\0';
        strcpy(reportsto+1,init);
        reportsto[SLEN-1] = '!';
    }

    fink::fink(char * fn, char * ln, char * j, char * rpo)
        : employee(fn, ln, j)
    {
        strcpy(reportsto, rpo);
    }

    fink::fink(const employee & e, char * rpo)
        : employee(e)
    {
        strcpy(reportsto, rpo);
    }

    fink::fink(const fink & m) : employee(m)
    {
        strcpy(reportsto, m.reportsto);
    }
```

```cpp
void fink::showall()
{
    employee::showall();
    cout << "Reports to: " << reportsto << '\n';
}

void fink::setall()
{
    employee::setall();
    cout << "Reports to: ";
    cin.getline(reportsto, SLEN);
}

ofstream & fink::writeall(ofstream & of)
{
    int kind = Fink;
    of << kind << endl;
    of << fname << endl;
    of << lname << endl;
    of << job << endl;
    of << reportsto << endl;
    return of;
}


ifstream & fink::readall(ifstream & ifs) {
    employee::readall(ifs);
    ifs.getline(reportsto,SLEN);
    return ifs;
}

highfink::highfink()
{
}


highfink::highfink(char * fn, char * ln, char * j, char * rpo, int ico)
    : employee(fn, ln, j), manager(fn, ln, j, ico), fink(fn, ln, j, rpo)
{
}


highfink::highfink(const employee & e, char * rpo, int ico)
    : employee(e), manager(e, ico), fink(e, rpo)
{
}


highfink::highfink(const fink & f, int ico)
    : employee(f), fink(f), manager(f, ico)
{
}


highfink::highfink(const manager & m, char * rpo)
    : employee(m), manager(m), fink(m, rpo)
{
}


highfink::highfink(const highfink & h)
    : employee(h), manager(h), fink(h)
{
}
```

continues

```
void highfink::showall()
{
    manager::showall();
    cout << "Reports to: " << reportsto << '\n';
}

void highfink::setall()
{
    manager::setall();
    cout << "Reports to: ";
    cin.getline(reportsto, SLEN);
}

ofstream & highfink::writeall(ofstream & of)
{
    int kind = Highfink;
    of << kind << endl;
    of << fname << endl;
    of << lname << endl;
    of << job << endl;
    of << inchargeof << endl;
    of << reportsto << endl;
    return of;
}

ifstream & highfink::readall(ifstream & ifs)
{
    employee::readall(ifs);
    ifs >> inchargeof;
    while (ifs.get() != '\n') continue;
    ifs.getline(reportsto,SLEN);
    return ifs;
}
// pe16-4.cpp -- use employee classes
// link with pe16empf.cpp


#include <iostream>
#include <fstream>
#include <cstdlib>
using namespace std;

#include "pe16empf.h"

const char * myfile = "emp.dat";
const int MAX = 10;
char menu(void);

int main(void)
{
    employee * pc[MAX];
    int index = 0;
    int choice;
    int classtype;
    char ch;

    ifstream fin;
    fin.open(myfile);
    if (fin.good())
    {
        cout << "Here are the current contents of the "
            << myfile << " file:\n";
        while((fin >> classtype).get(ch))
        {
            switch(classtype)
            {
```

```
                case Employee    :
                    pc[index] = new employee;
                    break;
                case Manager     :
                    pc[index] = new manager;
                    break;
                case Fink      :
                    pc[index] = new fink;
                    break;
                case Highfink    :
                    pc[index] = new highfink;
                    break;
                default             :
                    cerr << "Switch problem\n";
                    break;
            }
            pc[index++]->readall(fin);
            if (!fin.good())
                break;
        }
        for (int i = 0; i < index; i++)
            pc[i]->showall();
    }

    while (index < MAX)
    {
        choice = menu();
        if (choice == 'q')
            break;
        switch(choice)
        {
        case 'e'    :    pc[index] = new employee;
                         break;
        case 'm'    :    pc[index] = new manager;
                         break;
        case 'f'    :    pc[index] = new fink;
                         break;
        case 'h'    :    pc[index] = new highfink;
                         break;
        }
        pc[index++]->setall();
    }
    cout << "Finished with data entry.\n";

    if (index == MAX)
        cout << "File is full.\n";
    fin.close();
    cout << "Recapitulating:\n";
    for (int i = 0; i < index; i++)
        pc[i]->showall();
    ofstream fout(myfile, ios::out);
    if(!fout)
    {
        cerr << "Can't open file for writing\n";
        exit(2);
    }
    for (i = 0; i < index; i++)
    {
        pc[i]->writeall(fout);
    }

    return 0;
}
```

continues

```
char menu(void)
{
    cout << "Please make a choice as to what to add:\n";
    cout << "e) employee         m) manager\n";
    cout << "f) fink             h) highfink\n";
    cout << "q) quit\n";
    char ch;
    while (cin >> ch && ch != 'e' && ch != 'm' && ch != 'f'
            && ch != 'h' && ch != 'q')
        cout << "Try again!\n";
    while (cin.get() != '\n') continue;
    return ch;
}
```

Answers to Additional Questions

True or False

1. F

2. T

3. T

4. T

5. T

6. F

7. F—**get** can read lines

8. T

9. T

Short Answers

1.

a. The insertion operator << is used to insert any of the basic C++ data types into the output stream.

b. A C++ program views input and output as a stream of bytes arriving or leaving one after the other from or to a channel such as the keyboard or the monitor.

c. **istream** is the input stream class that carries bytes of data from an external device to the program.

d. **ostream** is the output stream class that carries bytes of data from the program to an external device.

e. **iostream** is a class derived from both **istream** and **ostream** and inherits both of their properties.

f. **fstream** derives from **iostream** and adds functionality to deal with file handling.

g. A buffer is a block of memory used as an intermediate temporary storage facility for the transfer of information.

h. Clearing the data from the buffer is known as flushing the buffer.

i. The **streambuf** class provides memory for a buffer along with class methods for filling, accessing, flushing, and managing the buffer.

j. **ios** is a class based on **ios_base** and includes a pointer member to a **streambuf** object.

k. The `clog` object corresponds to the standard error stream. By default it is associated with the standard output device.

l. Standard input and output is normally the keyboard and monitor respectively. Redirection allows these devices to be changed to an alternative device; thus, a printer could replace the monitor.

m. The void pointer (`void *`) is used to match a pointer of any other type.

n. `write()` is a member function of the `ostream` class used to display strings.

o. Manipulators are used to format the way data is output to the output device.

p. The expression `cout << flush;` is used to clear the `ostream` buffer.

q. The `endl` command is a symbolic constant used to move the cursor to the beginning of the next line.

r. The member function `width` belonging to `ostream` is used to line up numbers in neat columns

s. The right justification manipulator causes the output to line up from the right-hand side of the column.

t. The `fill` member function is used to pad out the leading spaces of a justified output with a chosen character.

u. The left justification manipulator causes the output to line up from the left-hand side of the column.

v. The `precision` member function lets you select the number of digits displayed to right of the decimal place.

w. The `setf()` method is used to control several formatting choices such as number base.

x. `ios::showpoint` is used to display a trailing decimal point.

y. Flag bits are used to switch on or off the various options associated with output.

z. The `hex` manipulator is used to set numeric base 16.

aa. The `dec` manipulator is used to set numeric base 10.

ab. The `oct` manipulator is used to set numeric base 8.

ac. `fmtflags` is a type definition name for `bitmask` type used to hold the format flags.

ad. `ios::showbase` prefixes the numeric output with `0x` for `hex` and `0` for `oct`.

ae. `ios::uppercase` uses uppercase letters for `hex` output.

af. `ios::showpos` prefixes positive numbers with +.

ag. `ios::basefield` is used in conjunction with the `hex`, `dec`, or `oct` manipulators to select the output numeric base.

ah. `ios::adjustfield` is used in conjunction with the left, right, or internal manipulators to select the justification.

ai. `ios::left` specifies left justification.

aj. `ios::fixed` specifies fixed point notation output.

ak. `ios::left` specifies scientific output notation.

al. `iomanip` is a header file used to access a set of manipulators that are easier to use the `ios` collection of operations.

am. The `setprecision` manipulator takes an integer argument specifying the precision.

an. The `setw()` manipulator is used with `cout` to set the width of the output field.

ao. The stream state consists of three elements, `eofbit`, `badbit`, and `failbit`.

ap. When a `cin` operation reaches the end of file it sets the `eofbit`.

aq. The `badbit` is set when an undiagnosed failure corrupts the stream.

ar. When a `cin` operation fails to read the expected character it sets the `failbit`.

as. The member function **good()** returns **true** if the stream can be used.

at. The **clear()** member function is used to set the eof, **badbit**, and **failbit** back to **logic 0** (back to **false**).

au. The **fail()** member function returns **true** if **badbit** or **failbit** is set.

av. The **ignore()** member function is used to read and discard characters from the input stream.

aw. The **peek()** member function is used to look ahead into the input stream before reading the input.

ax. The **read()** function is used to recover data inserted into a file by the **write()** function.

ay. The **gcount()** method returns the number of characters read by the last unformatted extraction method.

az. The **putback()** function inserts a character back into the input stream.

ba. **ifstream** is a class designed for file input.

bb. The **close()** member function is used to close a file.

bc. **argc** represents the number of arguments in the command line.

bd. **argv** is a pointer to a string table array that contains the actual arguments in the command line.

be. **argv[0]** is the first element of the string array and is reserved for the command name entered at the keyboard.

bf. **eof()** returns **true** if the **eofbit** is set.

bg. The file open mode is used to associate a stream with a file and open it with **in**, **out**, **ate**, **app**, **trunc**, or binary mode.

bh. **ios::trunc** trucates a file upon opening, if it exists.

bi. **ios::app** opens a file in append mode, adding data to its end.

bj. **ios::ate** seeks the end of file upon opening.

bk. **ios::binary** opens a file in binary mode.

bl. **ios::beg** is used along with an integer value to move "x" bytes beyond the beginning of the file.

bm. **ios::cur** is used along with an integer value to move "x" bytes from the current position in the file.

bn. **ios::end** is used along with an integer value to move "x" bytes from the end of the file.

bo. A **streampos** value represents the absolute location in a file measured in bytes from the beginning of the file.

bp. The **streamoff** argument represents the file position in bytes measured as an offset from one of three locations.

bq. To check the current position of the file pointer use the **tellg()** method for input streams and the **tellp()** method for output streams.

br. **rdbuf()** returns a pointer to the file buffer that is associated with the stream.

bs. **pubseekoff()** is used to alter the current positions of the stream.

bt. The **strstream** library supports character arrays; it is superseded by **sstream**.

bu. The process of reading and writing formatted information with a **string** object is termed incore formatting.

bv. The **ostringstream** is derived from **ostream** and provides a buffer for formatted text.

2. Advantages:

    a) More efficient, because the stream can use the most effective mode of the device

    b) Easier on the hardware for the same reason

    c) Adds functionality, such as when a user can edit keyboard entry before sending to program

    d) C++ uses a class to manage the system

Disadvantages:

a) Takes memory, although frequently not much

b) Need to be careful to flush the buffer under certain conditions, or risk losing data

3. a) The `ios` class is the base class of I/O, and provides general stream properties

b) The `streambuf` class manages the I/O buffers

c) The `ostream` class is derived from `ios` and provides output methods

d) The `istream` class is derived from `ios` and provides input methods

e) The `iostream` class provides general I/O methods, and inherits from both `ostream` and `istream`

4. The `ostream` class normally flushes the buffer when it is full, when a newline is sent, and when input is pending.

5.
```
564589345J5
564589
445.624
Southern Regional
S
South
:6.80935e-010:
1725
79
K
159 531 531
564589 50x36E8 445.624
~~~~~~~~~~~~~Southern Regional
$445.624
0x159
0x89d6d
~~~~~K
+445.6
```

6. If `badbit` is set, it means that something happened to terminate input. If reading a disk file, it may mean a malfunction or corrupted file. If `failbit` was set, unexpected characters were encountered. Before reading more input, you must reset with `cin.clear()`.

7. The main thing is that since `cin` skips whitespace, the loop will never end. Also, the `while` condition doesn't need to check for inequality to `0` because when the newline is encountered the expression is `0`.

8. `ch` should be an `int`, because `EOF` may not be expressed as a `char` type.

9. a) Either `get(char &)` or `get(void)` will work—need to see whitespace

b) Either `get(char &)` or `get(void)` will work—need to examine individual characters

c) Again, either of the `get()` functions, so that spaces in names stay intact

d) `cin` works, as long as input is only single words

10. You can get access to the array using the `ostrstream` class's `str()` method. Unless you add a null to the end, it is an array of `char`.

Programming Projects

1. The trick is setting the column width for the `$` sign, not the number:
```
// dollars.cpp -- print columns of dollar figures
#include <iostream>
```

continues

```
#include <iomanip>
#include <cmath>
using namespace std;

int main(void)
{
    cout.setf(ios::showpoint);
    cout.setf(ios::fixed, ios::floatfield);
    cout.setf(ios::right, ios::adjustfield);
    float figure = 5.00;
    int w;
    for (int i = 0; i <=20; i ++)
    {
        for (int j = 0; j < 5; j++)
        {
            if (figure < 10.0)
                w = 5;
            else if (figure < 100.0)
                w = 4;
            else if (figure < 1000.0)
                w = 3;
            else
        w = 2;
            cout << setw(w) << "$";
            cout << setprecision(2) << figure;
            figure += 15.00;
        }
        cout << "\n";
    }
    return 0;
}
```

2. Here is one easy way to do it:

```
// putb.cpp -- making '!' the space character
#include <iostream>
using namespace std;

int main(void)
{
    char ch;
    while(cin.get(ch))
    {
        if (ch == ' ')
            cin.putback('!');
        else
            cout << ch;
    }
    return 0;
}
```

3. Part of the challenge here was to figure out to use an array for the count and avoid a long `if else` or `switch` block, and to get the count right and the numbers aligned.

```
// cntalpha.cpp -- count letters in a text file

#include <iostream>
#include <fstream>
#include <cctype>
#include <iomanip>
using namespace std;

int main(void)
{
    ifstream fin;
    long total = 0;
```

```
        char ch;
        int count[26], whtsp = 0, alpha = 0;
        char fname[] = "text.dat";

        for (int i = 0; i < 26; i++)
            count[i] = 0;

        cout.setf(ios::right, ios::adjustfield);
        fin.open(fname);
        while (fin.get(ch))
        {
            if (isalpha(ch))
            {
                alpha++;
                if (isupper(ch))
                    count[ch - 'A']++;
                else
                    count[ch - 'a']++;
            }
            else
                whtsp++;
            total++;
        }
        cout << "In the " << fname << " file, there are ";
        cout << total << " characters.\n";
        cout << "Of those, " << alpha << " are alphabetic, and "
             << whtsp << " are non-alphabetic.\n";
        cout << "Count of each letter:\n";
        for (i = 0; i < 26; i++)
            cout << char(i+'A') << setw(5) << count[i] << endl;
        fin.close();

        return 0;
    }
```

4. Here are the actual results for the first paragraph of the chapter, using `text.dat` on the disk.

```
In the text.dat file, there are 980 characters.
Of those, 764 are alphabetic, and 216 are non-alphabetic.
Count of each letter:
A    63
B     4
C    33
D    29
E    77
F    15
G    21
H    26
I    46
J     3
K     6
L    31
M    15
N    69
O    66
P    24
Q     1
R    36
S    52
T    79
U    41
V     7
W     8
X     1
Y    11
Z     0
```

INDEX

Symbols

Other Related Titles

The Waite Group's C++ How-To
Kalev, Tobler, and Walter, et al.
ISBN: 0-57169-159-6
$39.99 USA/$57.95 CAN

C++ Unleashed
Jesse Liberty, et al.
ISBN: 0-672-31239-5
$39.99 USA/$57.95 CAN

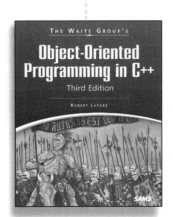

The Waite Group's Object-Oriented Programming in C++, Third Edition
Robert Lafore
ISBN: 0-57169-160-X
$34.99 USA/$50.95 CAN

Using C++
Rob McGregor
ISBN: 0-7897-1667-4
$29.99 USA/$42.95 CAN

NOTES

NOTES

NOTES

NOTES

NOTES

NOTES

NOTES

NOTES

NOTES

NOTES

NOTES

NOTES

NOTES

NOTES

NOTES

NOTES

NOTES

NOTES

NOTES

NOTES